POLAR BRIDGE

For Susan and Brad,

In memory of special shared experiences through the Northwest and Northeast Passages, and with best wishes for fulfilling adventures across many more "Bridges" ahead.

August 20, 2000

Laurie Dexter

POLAR BRIDGE

AN ARCTIC ODYSSEY

RICHARD WEBER

LAURIE DEXTER

CHRISTOPHER HOLLOWAY

MAX BUXTON

KEY PORTER BOOKS

Canadian Cataloguing in Publication Data
Main entry under title:

Polar bridge

ISBN 1-55013-199-0

1. Canadian-Soviet Polar Bridge Expedition.
2. Arctic regions – Discovery and exploration –
Canadian.   3. Arctic regions – Discovery and
exploration – Soviet. 4. Arctic regions – Description
and travel.   I. Weber, Richard.

G630.C3P63 1990   919.804   C89-090767-6

Key Porter Books Limited
70 The Esplanade
Toronto, Ontario
Canada M5E 1R2

Typesetting: MacTrix DTP

Printed and bound in Canada

90 91 92 93 94 6 5 4 3 2 1

This book is dedicated to our wives:
Josée Auclair
Nancy Buxton
Pia Cole
Sheena Dexter

Contents

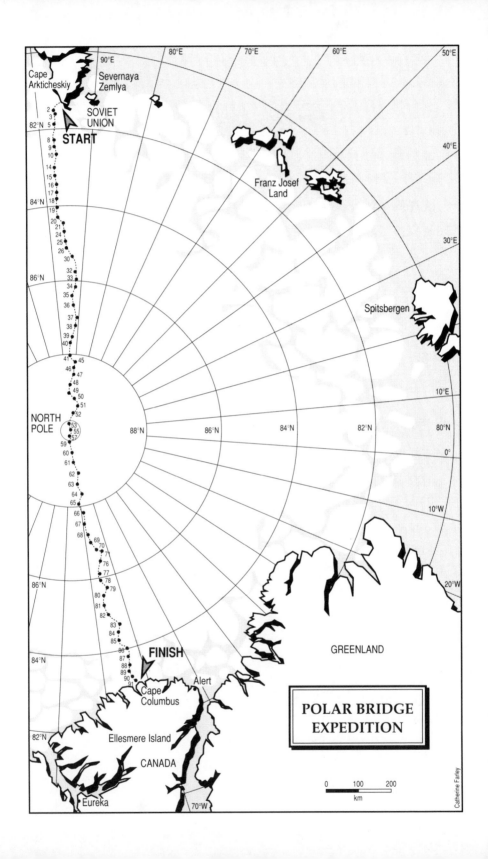

The Team Members

THE CANADIANS

Max Buxton

Max was born in 1957, grew up on a farm near Bethany, Ontario, and went to high school in Lindsay, Ontario. After graduating from grade thirteen he worked in the oilfields of northern Alberta and the high Arctic, spending several months as a seismic technician on the frozen ocean near Resolute Bay.

When he returned south, he bought a motorcycle and travelled, before going to Carleton University, where he earned a BSc in psychology in 1980. He went from Carleton to Queen's University, to graduate with an MD in 1984.

Max was the last member of the Canadian team to be taken on. He went to the Pole, he says, because, as a typical middle-class North American of his generation, he had never experienced suffering or a severe personal test. He has an aptitude for languages and learned to speak passable Russian on the trek. As a result, he got to know the Russians better, perhaps, than the others, and to enjoy their company.

Max lives with his wife, Nancy, in Calabogie, Ontario, where he is a general practitioner. He skis, cycles, rows, and is active in Little Theatre.

Laurie Dexter

Laurie was born in 1945 and spent his boyhood in the Shetland Islands north of Scotland, where his father was a clergyman. He trained as a physical education teacher in Glasgow and as an Anglican minister in Bristol, England.

In 1970, with his new wife, Sheena, Laurie immigrated to Canada and, after spending a year in the Arctic, completed his theological studies at Saskatoon, Saskatchewan. For the next thirteen years he served as a minister in the high Arctic (North Baffin Island) and more recently in Fort Smith, N.W.T. He continued his athletic pursuits: kayaking, running marathons, mountaineering, rock climbing, skiing, mountain bike racing, winter and summer triathlons, and even competitive table tennis. He holds a number of all-time Canadian age-group records for ultra running at distances from 300 kilometres to 640 kilometres [400 miles] and from three days to six days.

He is involved in a wide variety of social and cultural activities, including playing the viola and violin, choir directing, public speaking, and translation work in the Eskimo language [Inuktitut]. His wife is an elementary school teacher and they have two children, Andrew and Alison, both in high school.

Laurie undertook the Polar Bridge expedition because, as he says, "It was a statement of who and what I am." He saw it as a physical challenge, an extension of a boyhood fascination with explorers, particularly polar explorers, and most importantly as an opportunity to expand his ministry. He sought to establish links with the church in the Soviet Union and to increase international understanding overall – and he believes that Polar Bridge was a not-insignificant cog in the wheels of change that have been seen in motion in the last two years of East-West relations.

Christopher Holloway

Christopher Holloway was born in England in 1956 and grew up in Canada, in Ottawa, Ontario. He excelled at cross-country skiing, flat-water paddling, and sailing, winning a total of thirteen national championship medals in these sports.

At the age of nineteen, Christopher gave up serious competition in favour of a career as a cross-country skiing coach. From 1976 to

1981, he worked his way from technical director of the Northwest Territories Ski Association to head coach of the Ontario Ski Team, and was appointed to assist the Canadian national team.

Christopher retired from coaching to attend university, graduating with a BSc in computer science. In 1986, he joined Gandalf Data Ltd., in Ottawa, as a network test specialist and programmer.

During the winter of 1989, Christopher led the ICEWALK International Student Expedition, taking twenty-two students from fifteen countries to Ellesmere Island for environmental studies.

Christopher currently works as a computer consultant. He lives with his wife, Pia Cole, in Old Chelsea, Quebec.

Richard Weber

Richard was born in Edmonton, Alberta, in 1959. He started skiing shortly after he could walk. He completed a BSc in mechanical engineering at the University of Vermont, on a sports scholarship for cross-country skiing. His father, Dr. Hans Weber, was a keen climber and a geophysicist with Geological Survey, Energy, Mines and Resources Canada. Dr. Weber's research has taken him all over the Arctic, even to the North Pole. Richard grew up with Arctic artifacts in his home, and talk of the Arctic was an everyday occurrence.

Richard was a member of the Canadian national cross-country ski team from 1977 to 1985. He won twenty national titles and represented Canada in four world championships. He retired from international competition in order to do polar expeditions.

Richard was a member of the 1986 Steger International Polar Expedition, which was the first confirmed journey to the North Pole without resupply or outside assistance.

Richard joined the Polar Bridge expedition because he was intrigued by the idea of working with the Soviets and by the opportunity to travel in the Soviet Arctic. He finds expeditions intense experiences, where "life is reduced to a primitive equation of survival and travel." Richard enjoys the challenges of travel on the moving surface of the Arctic Ocean. Reaching the North Pole was not the high point of the journey for him. He was excited about the idea of leaving land and returning to land – a tangible achievement. He lives with his wife, Josée, and son, Tessum, in Kingsmere, Quebec.

THE SOVIETS

Alexander (Sasha) Believ

Sasha was a graduate student at the Institute of Metallurgy in Moscow, where Dmitri also worked. Married with one daughter, at the age of twenty-eight, he was the youngest of the Soviet group. He joined the "*Komsomolskaya Pravda* Permanent Expedition" in 1978, and was partly responsible for organizing diet and food resupplies. Generally he was a very pleasant guy to be with.

He did, however, display a knack for infuriating Richard. In particular, he would get away late in the morning and lag for the first few marches near the back of the pack. Richard felt this unduly obstructed progress; usually by midday, Sasha had caught up and was in "synch" with everyone else. He may just not have been a morning person. Though his easygoing side predominated, he did have a boiling point and lashed out on a couple of occasions under the stress of expedition life. Physically, he was capable, though his limbs were thin and his epicentre a little ample. He had steel-blue eyes and short-cropped, sand-coloured hair. After three months without a razor, he had a few patches of adolescent facial fuzz that made him look even younger.

He enjoyed photography and took some very good shots of the expedition. Demographically he might have seemed an odd man out. He was almost a generation younger than most of the Russians; but his role in the group dynamics was well established. In particular, he was a good friend of Dmitri, and probably his closest confidant on the ice.

Anatoli (Toli) Fedjakov

Toli Fedjakov, a specialist in metal-welding engineering at the Electro-Technical Institute in Moscow, was one of the senior trekkers, at age forty-nine. Russian was his only language, but he loved music, and what he lacked in conversational skill, he made up for in song. He had learned several English songs by rote without understanding the lyrics – "Daisy, Daisy, give me your ants or two," for example. He also knew the Russian versions of melodies that the Canadians knew. On the most festive occasions, he led the group in versions of "Chattanooga Choo-Choo" and "Those Were the Days." Of the whole Soviet gang, he showed the most musical talent. In lieu of his usual guitar, he settled for *a capella* music.

Toli was anxious to impart his experience in just about every activity, and though his advice was well-received and very helpful initially, it eventually bordered on being patronizing. He was a very serious fellow; a man who liked routines and rules and who knew how things should be done. This tendency caused conflict on a couple of occasions. He may also have been the most sensitive member of the group. The relationships he established with Canadians he met were of great importance to him.

Yura (Yuri) Khmelevski

Yuri Khmelevski, though a mathematician at the Moscow Academy of Science, hardly resembled a staid academic. Certainly his appearance became ever more striking as the days on the ice passed. At fifty-two, he was the oldest trekker. His short, stocky form supported a balding head adorned with thick-rimmed glasses held on by one intact arm and one piece of string looped around his left ear. The lenses were retained at various times by pieces of tape or putty, and there was concern that the whole apparatus might slide over his mouth as the last vestiges of his nose froze off.

It was Yuri who provided the Canadians with an understanding of the sordid elements of the Russian language. Profanities rolled musically from his lips and occasionally aligned themselves into operettas of slang. But his mastery of language was certainly not restricted to that domain. He had a very good grasp of English, and dialogue with him was entertaining and provided much-needed insight into the dynamics within the Soviet group. He had a proverb or saying for just about every situation. He was most noted for his confusing tendency to say, "Normal, normal" – a word inappropriately translated from the Russian "*Normalna,*" meaning "It's okay" – at the most abnormal times.

In terms of the expedition hierarchy, Yuri was a member of the "inner circle," having been a founding member of the *Komsomolskaya Pravda* Permanent Expedition, the name attached to the Soviet group. He exerted considerable influence in terms of the initial planning.

On the ice, he was slow and steady, perennially cheerful, and oblivious to the severity of the elements – perhaps the reason for his ravaged face. He was certainly the most candid of the Soviets – something that often put him into the centre of any controversy.

Fiodor Konukhov

Fiodor might best have undertaken a trek such as ours on his own and, as fate would have it, he subsequently did. He was a soul apart, in many respects. His home in the Soviet Orient was nearly 9000 kilometres from those of the rest of the gang, who were mostly from Moscow or its environs. Even to us linguistic novices, his dialect came through strongly.

As an artist, he was permitted certain eccentricities, but even his artistic style suggested a character verging on the schizoid. His charcoal drawings depicted chaotic overlapping images of human and animal forms on distorted landscapes that left one feeling inexplicably uneasy.

In his more gregarious moods, he had some wonderful stories of love and adventure. He had spoken with aliens, hidden in the woods from lovers' jealous husbands, been lost at sea . . . . His blue eyes flashed madly as he punctuated his anecdotes with broad gestures and riotous laughter. Unfortunately, he spoke absolutely no English, and the content was obviously so florid that no translation would do it justice.

His scruffy red beard and pageboy hairstyle fittingly created the image of a sixties hippie. His wiry arms sported the tattooed words "Son of a Fisherman." At five foot seven and 67 kg, he was the smallest member of the group. On the trail, he was an indefatigable workhorse and, despite his volatility and isolationism, a solid travelling companion. He was the first to jump to any task, no matter how onerous, and could trudge along merrily with immense weight on his back. His pack was nearly as heavy as he at the beginning of each stage; he carried it like an army ant shouldering a horsefly.

Fiodor's travel experience was extensive. He had sailed vast distances alone in small boats and had trekked through much of Siberia. His intense drive to reach the Pole supposedly arose from the final words of his explorer grandfather as he lay on his deathbed. He was committed to fulfilling that destiny.

Back home in Nahodka (near Japan), Fiodor's wife, son, and daughter awaited his return.

Volodja (Volodi) Ledenov

Volodja Ledenov was a "man's man" – a bit of a rogue, a little volatile, but mostly a good-hearted comrade with a taste for wine, women, and song. In his other life, he was a bio-engineer at the Moscow Institute of Biotechnology. He had a wife and a couple of kids, and was the only member of the Soviet group who owned his own car – a four-year-old Lada.

His English was very good, and he was easily engaged in conversation. He wasn't big on the subjects of politics or religion, but loved to compare Soviet and North American sexual norms, drinking patterns, and personal finances – all the juicy stuff. He was a practical joker and wasn't beyond having a good laugh at someone else's expense, which the trip provided ample opportunity for.

Though he belonged to a sports club, he bore the physical hallmarks of an armchair athlete – short, with a little "cumulus" around the waist – a man of no great apparent strength. But with a hundred pounds of ballast and planks on his feet, he became a machine. It was inspiring, though tiring, to watch him. He and Vasili generally alternated the job of trail-blazer on the ice.

Volodja was another of the original members of the Permanent Expedition. His avocation as an amateur filmmaker and cameraman had been put to good use on previous expeditions, but was never more appreciated than on the Polar Bridge. Under extreme temperatures and using the most basic equipment imaginable, he provided footage and expertise for a feature-length Soviet film, later modified for North American audiences.

Mikhail (Misha) Malakhov

Misha Malakhov was everybody's pal. Good-looking, athletic, the most fluent of the Russians in English, he soon gained the confidence of the Canadians. It was obvious that he was a kingpin within the Soviet ranks, too. By trade, Misha was an academic physician. His research interest had been tuberculosis, but over the last few years the glamour of Arctic exploration had stolen his interest.

He had served as the physician at a Soviet Antarctic base for several months and had been with the present group for the "Polar

Night" trip of 1986. His academic talents accommodated nicely the physiological studies conducted en route. From a therapeutic perspective he seemed knowledgeable and exercised reasonable judgment. Moreover, he was gifted with an ideal physician's quality that enabled him to use those resources optimally – he was very serious and could impress upon the sufferer of even the most minor condition its potential gravity. With Mish there were no jokes about finding one's toes thawing in the teapot.

More than the other Soviets, Misha had an air of worldliness, a cosmopolitan openness that was endearing to the outnumbered Canucks. He was not a Communist Party member, and though no doubt happy enough to be Russian, wanted a taste of what the rest of the world had to offer. He was eager to try Western equipment and techniques and seemed to be able to involve himself in some special way with each of the Canadians on a personal level. Max was his colleague, Richard and Christopher were his athletic peers and fellow snow house dwellers, Laurie's concept of God intrigued him. He was also the most likely person to relate to us the arcane issues brewing within the Soviet ranks.

Misha's wife, a particularly charming and attractive woman, works as an ophthalmologist in Ryazan, 200 kilometres southeast of Moscow. They have two young sons, completing an idyllic home picture.

Anatoli (Toli) Melnikov

Toli Melnikov was the grandfather of our group. He was slightly younger than Yuri, but he had a grandchild, and his face and manner conjured images of a Soviet Santa Claus. He had sand-colored hair and soft blue eyes, and always looked either jovial or relaxed. He had been with the Permanent Expedition from the beginning, and had been on all their treks.

Ironically, for a number of reasons, he was unsuited to Arctic travel. He was big; at well over six feet and 100 kg, he occupied more than his share of tent space. And he sweated. He always needed an extra cup of tea if there was one to be had, and his clothes were usually drenched by the end of the travelling day. It might have been that curse that resulted in the loss of two of his toes in the "Polar Night" trip of 1986. It is hard to keep wet feet warm in the Arctic.

In spite of his limitations, he was a true veteran of the floes. His professional expertise as an electronics engineer made him a natural to oversee communications. The radio (as with much of our equipment) always looked like a rat's nest of wires and mismatched components, but through sheer perseverance, Melnikov always managed to keep the expedition in touch with the outside world.

Through the days when conversation lapsed into silence, it was he who maintained morale, probably without realizing it, by relaying details of progress, news briefs, and so on.

He seemed to be a real family man. He spoke often of his wife and two daughters, and the musical greetings they sent on cassette kept the trekkers entertained.

Vasili (Vasa) Shishkarov

Vasili personified perfectly the ideals Lenin had prescribed for Soviet society. He had originally moved to Moscow in order to be part of Dmitri's 1979 North Pole expedition. He was the prototypical socialist worker; a foreman in an automotive assembly plant, with strong grass-roots affiliations and membership in the Communist Party. In the political arena, his convictions were unswerving and formed the basis for a more general day-to-day code of ethics. One day while discussing religion with Laurie, he produced a picture of Lenin, and said, "This is my God."

He was never vulgar, though he was very blunt in both his words and his actions. Though profanities abounded throughout the trip in both languages, his most extreme expression of displeasure was "yolgi palki" – literally "to pull out Christmas trees," but roughly equivalent in vehemence to "darn."

Despite his insistence that he was just one voice in the group, he wielded much more leadership power than Dmitri during our days on the ice. His natural ability to do anything mechanical or physical commanded considerable respect, though it was often disconcerting to have him snatch some half-completed project from one's hands to do it better himself.

He always skied at the front of the pack, his dark Kazakhstani features exposed in even the harshest weather. If anyone could be said to look good in fur and green canvas, he could. He had a powerful stride, stood six feet tall, and was an impressive presence on the ice.

He spoke no English, but had acquired skills in conversational French from his wife, who was a professor of languages. He spoke of

her often, and it was obvious that he loved her with an intensity characteristic of their newlywed status, despite the fact that they were in
their late thirties. They had no children.

Dmitri Shparo

Dmitri, our leader, was well known. That is, his accomplishments and
appearance were familiar to the average Soviet citizen. Moreover, he
fostered an informal familiarity in all his relationships, and was a confidant to many. He always seemed sincere, and his gift for easy rapport
served his ambitions very well also. He was a "networker" and a diplo-
mat, always striving to achieve goals through dialogue and to expand
his personal horizons whenever possible, as all explorers do.

He spoke well to crowds – and enjoyed doing so. His comfortable
posture at the podium, warm gestures, and skill at impromptu presen-
tation won the hearts of audiences from Calabogie to Vladivostok.
When everyone, including Dmitri, had had a turn at the microphone,
he would reliably return to have the last word. With all his gregarious-
ness, however, he could also go through silent melancholy stages.
Apparently, on a previous expedition, he had sustained a silent funk
for most of the trip.

On the ice, he was more of an arbiter than a leader; others mapped the
route, led the group, and made most of the significant decisions. His principal role was to defuse tension, usually after conflict arose.

Dmitri was tall, lanky, dark, and well proportioned, although not,
strictly speaking, of "athletic" build. His endearing smile was accented
by a mischievous gleam in his very black eyes. He had a habit of non-
chalantly draping himself over pieces of furniture at the focal point of
formal events. While ambassadors stood stiffly at attention, Dmitri
assumed the configuration of an ill-pruned philodendron.

Dmitri's wife, Tatyana, was a jolly redhead with whom he had two
sons. She was among the best-dressed women in the eastern bloc as
was no doubt expected of the wife of a world traveller.

Introduction

ON WEDNESDAY, JUNE 1, 1988, THIRTEEN JUBILANT SKIERS lined up and stepped simultaneously onto Canadian land at Ward Hunt Island, marking a triumphant end to the Soviet-Canadian trans-polar ski expedition.

The "Polar Bridge" was an unqualified success: all thirteen members completed the trek without serious injury, reaching their goal within the set time. Sharing their sense of triumph were the millions of people world-wide who had followed their progress as they struggled across ice floes through howling winds. The Polar Bridge was also, as the name implies, a symbolic journey, a "bridging" not just of an ocean but of two peoples, neighbours.

The skiers were then flown by Twin Otter to Eureka, on Ellesmere Island, to be greeted by wives and supporters. The first man off the plane was Soviet team leader Dmitri Shparo. He emerged carrying giant Soviet and Canadian flags. A dynamic forty-six-year-old mathematician who had been to the North Pole once before, Shparo had first brought the idea of a joint expedition to the Canadian government ten years earlier.

On his heels came the four Canadians: Richard Weber, Christopher Holloway, Max Buxton, and Laurie Dexter. They looked in remarkably good health after ninety-one days of polar trekking, though their faces were blackened and blistered from the sun. That day their comments were cryptic.

"It's one of those things you have to do once in a lifetime," said the Reverend Laurie Dexter of Fort Smith, Northwest Territories. "It was successful, but not every moment was fun."

"It was a pilgrimage," said Max Buxton, a doctor from Calabogie, Ontario. "Very much an inward thing. Like anaesthesia – ninety-five per cent boredom and five per cent panic."

"Physically it was no problem, it was a psychological test," said Richard Weber, who also termed it "a complete success." Christopher Holloway said simply, "We made it. We didn't lose anybody. We didn't lose any toes."

This expedition is fascinating – the intimacy of a passage on skis over this unmapped terrain, and the idea of Canadians and Soviets walking together over this shared northern border that is so little in our minds. It is a curious thing that the public has been most inclined to remember the Arctic expeditions that ended in starvation and death – Sir John Franklin's 1845 journey of the *Terror* and the *Erebus* – for example, and to forget those explorations by men who came to terms with the Arctic and survived it – men like William Parry, who explored Lancaster Sound in 1819–20. The very success of the Polar Bridge led to its achievement being underestimated, especially in Canada. It was, however, a truly remarkable feat for such a large team to trek safely across the Polar Sea; in the unsparing Arctic environment, the greater the number of men, the greater the chance of failure. In this case, too, hardships associated with any Arctic expedition were combined with the tensions of having two cultures, two ideologies, and two languages under one tent.

That night celebratory fire crackers flared in the midnight sun over the rolling purple tundra usually inhabited only by browsing musk-ox and prowling wolves. The welcoming group of sponsors, diplomats, wives, and reporters then headed back to Eureka, popu-lation eleven – Canada's second-most northerly weather station. Frank, the weather station chef, had cooked up spareribs, Cornish hens, and homemade pies, which the men fell upon with awesome appetite – three months of muesli, pemmican, and limited rations had left them hungry.

There were the obvious questions. What were the worst moments? What have you learned? about the polar sea? about the Soviets? yourselves? Though the answers differed, a consensus did emerge: the primary achievement of the expedition was that nine

Soviets and four Canadians, with the most rudimentary grasp of one another's language, had managed to finish the expedition without, as Dmitri Shparo put it, "cutting the throats of each other." Obviously, there was a story here that had not been told in the newspapers. That story unfolds here in the diary entries the Canadian team members recorded along the route and in the photographs they took.

Canada's Arctic frontier, glittering in the upper reaches of our imagination, has represented the ultimate earthly test for individuals and nations. The drama of the slow, single-file trudge across windswept ice comes through in the photographs by Weber and Holloway. The ice formations and horizons of the Arctic are less colourful and varied than rain forests or rocky mountain peaks, but equally beautiful in their own way.

Photographs help us imagine the persistent subzero temperatures and treacherous terrain, but the skiers' daily accounts bring home their effects. The cold they experienced – downwards of minus 40°C – bears on every waking action from tying shoelaces and drinking tea to sleeping. Nature reserves for the polar explorer some of its more excruciating small indignities – the threat of losing fingers, toes, and bits of nose, of snow blindness, intestinal problems, and broken teeth.

Arctic travel is mentally daunting as well: there are no visible milestones, no maps, and no point in making a map, because everything moves and changes on the frozen sea. Skiers might walk in one direction for nine hours while hidden currents under the ice carry them away from their goal at the same rate. Even more difficult to measure is that other journey, of thirteen men divided by language, in physical discomfort and constant danger, learning to co-exist – because staying alive depends on it.

BACKGROUND TO THE EXPEDITION

Dmitri Shparo raised the concept of a joint polar ski trek with Canadian government officials in 1979, but before the idea could take shape the Soviet invasion of Afghanistan and the subsequent Canadian boycott of the Moscow Olympics in 1980 killed the plan. Shparo, however, persisted with his ambition and in March 1987 came to

Canada along with Mikhail (Misha) Malakhov. With the backing of Dr. Alexander Yakolev, the former Soviet ambassador to Canada, Ottawa accepted the idea in principle, through the office of External Affairs Minister Joe Clark.

Dmitri Shparo was the leader of the *Komsomolskaya Pravda* Permanent Expedition. The core of his group of skiers had been together since their first expedition in 1969, and did expeditions regularly. In 1979 they had gone to the North Pole from the Soviet side. It was the first time the Pole had been reached without dogs or machines. The next obvious step was to keep skiing across the ocean to Canada. Although their numbers had grown, the group knew each other well; their equipment and travelling systems were established and they preferred not to change them, which proved problematic in the joint expedition that was eventually organized. The Canadian team had yet to be chosen.

Canadian government participation was to be limited to ensuring that some safety conditions were met. The skiers were to gather snow samples for chemical analysis and make measurements of the earth's magnetic field to investigate the Soviet theory of the second magnetic North Pole. They were also to participate in joint medical tests aimed at discovering the effects on human beings of prolonged cold and exertion. Both nations agreed to a network of short-wave radio operators. The skiers were to carry a SARSAT (Search and Rescue Satellite-aided Tracking System) beacon, This 1-kg instrument would be turned on once a day at a predetermined time. The ground stations for SARSAT in Trenton, Ottawa and Moscow would receive the latitude and longitude co-ordinates which were then relayed back to the team on the ice by radio.

During the day, the skiers would navigate using the sun or a compass if it was cloudy.

The expedition was to be resupplied by air every two weeks. There were to be three resupplies by parachute drop on the Soviet side, a joint resupply at the North Pole, and two resupplies on the Canadian side in which the planes would land on the ice. Even so, they would each have to carry a minimum of forty kilograms of food and equipment on their backs.

When Canadian officials agreed to participate it was with the guarantee that there would be seven Soviet skiers and four Canadians, the latter to be approved by Shparo. Shparo contacted Laurie Dexter with whom he had communicated in 1980. Shparo also telephoned Richard Weber, who, he had discovered, had been to the North Pole with Will Steger. Weber was ambivalent about joining. Memories of the Steger expedition, during which he had suffered minus 60°C temperatures, were still fresh. Weber was also concerned about the Soviets' equipment and their ideas about nutrition. However, after meeting the Soviets in March 1987 he said he wanted to join.

Eventually, Shparo advertised to find other Canadian skiers, and chose four possible team members from three hundred applicants. In August 1987, six Canadians and eleven Soviet skiers flew to the Tien Shan mountains, near the Soviet-Chinese border, for a month-long training session. The Soviets arrived with support crew and radio operators, making a total of twenty-four people, and introducing the Canadians to their habit of paying back favours with a free trip. The Canadians were uncomfortable, partly because they were outnumbered, partly because they were alarmed by some procedures. The training took the group through high mountains and over dangerous territory. The Canadians were left with the impression that the Soviets were somewhat reckless. This was later attributed to the Soviets' lack of experience in the mountains. The Canadian members had also been having difficulties with the original management group for the expedition. These problems now became insurmountable, and Conexus Research Group in Ottawa were retained as expedition managers. Weber and Conexus took on the task of raising nearly $600,000 from private and government sponsors in cash, services, and goods to get the trip going from the Canadian side. The Canadian skiers were responsible for the financial success or failure of the expedition; the Soviets were not. As a consequence, Richard had a great deal more to argue for than the other Canadians later on during the trek. For this he was sometimes accused of being undiplomatic.

From mid-November to mid-December the Soviets and the Canadians had another month-long training session near Iqaluit on Baffin Island. The Soviets arrived in Canada with sixteen people (for an intended number of seven skiers). There are forty-foot tides in the water around Iqaluit, which leave piles of broken ice much like those to be found in the Arctic Ocean. Here the Canadians adopted the Soviet system of travel – skiing for fifty minutes and resting for ten, for eight to ten hours a day.

The skiers had very different strengths. Weber observed that the

Soviets, while physically strong, were less adept technically and, when carrying their heavy backpacks, were not able to kick and glide, but basically hiked on skis. However they had more Arctic experience. The Soviet-designed tents, which were held up with skis (see photographs), were not large enough for the numbers using them and became drenched with condensation. A spell of unusually warm weather in Iqaluit at the time (minus 25°C) prevented the skiers from testing themselves and their equipment at the low temperatures (minus 50°C) expected on the expedition. Again, in debates over these matters, the Canadians were overwhelmed by Soviet numbers. Richard Weber realized that the Canadians would have to be very determined if they were to make this expedition truly a joint one.

In Iqaluit a *modus operandi* was agreed upon for the trip. The skiers would travel for twelve to fourteen days and then be resupplied. The resupply would be followed by two days of rest. The day would consist of eight to ten fifty-minute marches. After the fourth march there would be a coffee break. Diet would contain both Soviet and Canadian food. They agreed to eat the following: for breakfast, a porridge of Shaklee muesli, Soviet dehydrated meat, Soviet dehydrated butter, and Soviet dry milk, with dry biscuits and instant decaffeinated coffee. During the day they would have Soviet sausage, a Soviet "surprise pack" containing dried apricots, chocolate truffle, halva, and hazel nuts, plus dry biscuits, Shaklee bars, peanut butter, and instant decaffeinated coffee. For supper their porridge would contain Canadian pemmican, Soviet buckwheat groats, dehydrated butter, and dry milk; they would eat this with Soviet dry bread, garlic, assorted spices, white sugar, and Canadian herb tea or Soviet black tea.

Both Soviets and Canadians preferred their own food; but as it was to be a joint exercise, each agreed they would have to give a little. Diet was to prove a contentious issue.

At this time also, the Canadians undertook to get custom-made outfits from their clothing sponsor, Chlorophylle Haute Technologie. According to the Soviet team leader, all the Soviet skiers had said they would like to wear the clothing. It was explained to them that if the sponsor contributed eleven custom-made outfits, all team members would have to wear the clothing. To this the Soviet team leader agreed. This commitment, too, proved to be a problem later on.

After Iqaluit many problems remained for the expedition. Four Canadian skiers backed out, concerned not just about their ability to cope in the Arctic, but also about safety, leadership, and the language barrier, which was even more difficult for two who were Francophones.

In December 1987, with only six weeks remaining before departure for Moscow, Richard Weber undertook to find two more Canadian skiers. His first choice was a friend, Christopher Holloway, who agreed to join. Max Buxton, a medical doctor, had been one of the original applicants for Shparo's team, but had been out of the country when Shparo was interviewing. When he heard that new members were needed, he called Weber and, after one ski trip in Gatineau Park, was accepted for the team.

In early February 1988, the Canadians flew to Moscow, where they underwent medical and psychological tests at the Moscow Institute of Biophysics. After one week in Moscow they flew to Dikson, in Soviet Siberia. Here began the only training trips that the two new Canadian members ever had, one four days in length and the other two. For two weeks the skiers were kept busy doing interviews and public appearances, sewing on patches and clips, and doing the countless small tasks that are necessary before departure. One night, in an attempt to acclimatize themselves to the cold, three of the Canadian skiers slept outside in the public square in Dikson, only to be wakened in the middle of the night by journalists with huge lights and cameras!

Dimitri Shparo had originally said he would choose Soviet members in August, but he delayed doing so in order to have additional manpower working for him, while candidates were competing for positions on the team. It was only on the last night in Dikson, with the departure scheduled for the next day, that Dmitri made his final decision about which of the Soviet skiers would make the trip. Unwilling to eliminate candidates (and friends) who had worked for years to be included, he added first one then another skier to the Soviet team. The Canadians were very unhappy to be outnumbered nine to four. The imbalance in numbers affected daily decisions and made for overcrowding in the tent; as a result Richard and Christopher chose to sleep outside every night. On March 3, with all these tensions in the air, thirteen skiers flew by helicopter from Dikson to Cape Arkticheskiy, the most northerly point in Soviet Siberia, and the Polar Bridge expedition began.

The rhetoric surrounding the expedition was considerable. "We are joining East and West through North," Shparo had announced. "Joining the old world to the new." Then Energy Minister Marcel Masse spoke of greater sharing of scientific information with his Soviet counterpart. But within the group, "international co-operation" acquired very specific dimensions. Points of contention were immediately evident.

Food was an emotional issue: the Canadian skiers did not want to eat as much salt and sugar as the Soviets did. The Soviets were sceptical about the nutritional value of the Canadian food. Daily routines posed another problem – generally, the Soviets were less concerned than the Canadians with keeping to a set schedule. Even relaxed conversation at the end of the day's skiing was trying for the Canadians, who might listen to ten minutes' talk in Russian and be given a one-sentence translation. And the decision-making process itself revealed a great cultural gap. "If you want to change something, you have to give them lots of warning. You ask them three days in a row. They say no at first and then finally you get around to yes," said Richard Weber.

Different cultural attitudes resulted in opposed approaches to the expedition itself. These became evident early on. For the Canadians probably the most upsetting moment occurred on the night before they set out, when a Russian skier would not accept that he had been cut from the team. He became violently angry and broke a costly Canadian theodolite (an instrument for taking measurements concerning the possible existence of a second magnetic north pole). Though the Canadians were against the skier's inclusion, he was allowed to join the group, which was already larger than planned for. Shparo's decision left the Canadians feeling manipulated.

Because of their larger numbers, cultural differences affected the Soviets less. Their greatest sources of tension were in their own interactions. As Dmitri Shparo summed it up: "I had more problems with Soviets versus Soviets, than Canadians versus Soviets."

Of course, underlying the tensions were different attitudes to property, to achievement, and to other people. Even the very thing that bound the two groups together – dazzling, shared land of ice and sky – sometimes divided the skiers. Before the trip began, some Soviets alarmed the Canadian skiers with talk about "conquering" the Arctic Ocean. Canadians looked at it differently: "We haven't changed the Arctic Ocean," Richard Weber said. "It's still the same. Any change is within us."

The Canadians preferred fibreglass skis and synthetic fabrics in their gear, while the Soviets, who had not had access to any synthetic fibres before their contact with the Canadians, displayed great loyalty to their old-fashioned wooden skis and their heavy clothing of natural fibres. They were accustomed to and familiar with not only the good but also the bad qualities of their equipment. This made them reluctant to change or even try something new.

It is far too easy to say that all the Russians behaved one way and all the Canadians another. There were undeniable cultural gaps between the Soviets and the Canadians; there were also great differences within the Canadian contingent. The Canadians were a collection of four individuals, each with his own reason for going to the North Pole, rather than a team.

Richard Weber, the Canadian leader, at twenty-eight was the youngest of all the skiers. He was outgoing and competitive. After the successful unsupported 1986 Steger International North Pole Expedition, he was the most experienced of the Canadians. He undertook the trip because he enjoyed Arctic travel and all the challenges it offers. The joint aspect of the expedition was of great importance to Richard.

Laurie Dexter, at forty-three the oldest of the Canadians and an Anglican minister, sought spiritual lessons from the land and from the Russians. It was of great importance to Laurie that this expedition set an example of international co-operation. It was Laurie who said, "We have to learn to sit lightly on our possessions . . . . [The fact] that other nations don't have our advantages doesn't mean their people are less hard-working, or less intelligent . . . . I come away with a great awareness of the lack of owner-ship of the world."

Max Buxton, thirty, the physician, was affable and outgoing. He learned to speak passable Russian and was inclined to see the Soviets' side as well as the Canadians' in any dispute. Early on he was cast as the romantic because he proposed to his girlfriend en route. In fact, he was on a personal odyssey, seeking to bring some perspective on hardship and suffering into his life.

Christopher Holloway, thirty-one, a computer programmer and close friend of Weber, had a long involvement in competitive cross-country skiing. He joined the expedition because he thought that co-existing with the Soviets and skiing to the Pole would be an interesting and rewarding challenge. He was physically the strongest of the Canadians. His sense of humour and normally positive attitude, even when morale was low, were assets.

With such diverse motives for undertaking the venture, the stage was set for conflict among the Canadians. The fact that these four managed to keep their emotions in control, at least outwardly, testifies to their commitment to their respective goals.

Diaries are intimate and revealing. The entries that follow were composed mostly at "night,"* in sleeping bags, at rest breaks, or even on the trail itself, by the men speaking into their "little black boxes" – their personal recorders. In the lonely days when conversation was impossible on the trek, and in the evenings when privacy could only be got by going out in the cold alone, the skiers' confessions to the recorder became a means of safely venting frustrations and expressing moods.

By definition, diaries lack perspective – they deal with the here and now. Like the ski trek itself, they seem to be constant close-up with no overview. Both the physical hardship – day-to-day routine, grinding exhaustion, cold and hunger – and the roller-coaster ride of constantly changing feelings – the frustrations, the pain and the immediate joys of the expedition – are all there. Four voices tell the story, which is as it should be, because the four men were first of all themselves, and only secondly representatives of a country.

Many of the issues the skiers faced en route to and from the Pole are as old as Arctic exploration – hunger and cold, emotional upheaval caused by isolation and the personal animosities that loom large among people living in close quarters. In the pioneer period of exploration, decisions such as whether the strong or the weak set the pace sometimes had fatal consequences. It was not unknown for men who stole food to be shot. Arctic exploration was a great test of leadership.

Here these issues appeared again, but were resolved democratically. Today's technology and commerce facilitated the trip immensely, but also added new pressures to the traditional polar dramas. The military, under whose governance many early Arctic trips were carried out, was no longer a factor. Instead, the sponsoring corporations made demands, but did not keep discipline. The skiers kept up daily radio contact with the rest of the world – a safety measure that removed the sense of wilderness for some skiers and made extra work, particularly for Laurie Dexter.

Today's Arctic landscape is no longer pristine. Airborne pollutants bring traces of industry from other parts of the globe. The silence has

---

* During the second half of the journey the sun did not set, and the skiers actually slept by day to avoid the glare, and skied by night.

been broken, and isolation is illusory – as the skiers found when they were buzzed by planes. Apparently you can't take a sauna even on the polar ice-cap without someone coming to your door. What, then, do we call wilderness? Contemporary life, with all its contrivances of commerce and communication, is inescapable. For all its vastness, the wilderness of the Polar Sea is no longer absolute.

No visible, physical feature marks the North Pole; yet, as a "place" on the surface of the globe that marks the axis of the earth's rotation, it has carried extraordinary significance through the centuries. It is impossible to read this story without being struck equally by the symbolic significance of the Polar Bridge journey: four and nine men divided by language and personality, by individual frailties and strengths, but joined almost despite themselves by mutual need, not just on the ski trail, but in that unreal-seeming world of national power and politics.

The following pages tell the story of how they reached their goal, and what happened on the ice. The impact of this venture was felt by the millions of people in all countries of the world who followed their progress. That impact is still being felt, though the journey is over. Expedition sponsors such as McDonald's Restaurants of Canada, Olympia and York and Gowling and Henderson gained valuable exposure in the U.S.S.R. Studies continue on airborne pollutants using snow samples the skiers collected. The skin damage that most of the skiers suffered has given credence to concern about the thinning ozone layer. The skiers have all travelled and spoken to audiences about what they learned in the high Arctic. A year after their triumphant arrival on Canadian land, the four Canadian skiers were flown to the Kremlin and presented with the Order of Friendship of Nations, the highest honour the Soviet Union can bestow on a foreigner. In September 1989 the thirteen again were acknowledged internationally, receiving the Pierre de Coubertin International Fair Play trophy from the International Committee of UNESCO. The trophy is awarded annually to those who promote world brotherhood through sports. This was the first time in its twenty-five-year history that the trophy has been won by non-competitive athletes. Canada has yet to offer official honours to its skiers, though the unofficial response has been gratifying. All four Canadians regularly receive – and accept – invitations to speak to interested groups about their experiences.

In the end Polar Bridge was many things: an athletic and psychological endurance test; an exercise in international co-operation; an ongoing, tent-bound cultural exchange. And a fascinating story.

Stage One

MARCH 3. DAY 1

Max

We awoke at 8:15, and began our final preparations. After breakfast I claimed my share of the group equipment and food and loaded my pack. The complete bundle weighed in at 42.7 kg. This was the first time I actually confronted my new friend head on. With considerable effort, I managed to navigate it out the doors of the dilapidated hotel and onto the airstrip, where a massive helicopter awaited us.

The deafening hiss of the helicopter turbines made conversation difficult, and I was both hoarse and deaf halfway through the journey. From my tiny window, I was able to discern a few interesting land-forms, in particular, "hoodoo" rock formations; but most of what I saw was endless white ocean blending with endless white sky. I rethought what heaven must be like, having always perceived it as an immaculate expanse of celestial vapour. Faced now with that picture, it didn't strike me as heavenly.

Christopher

This is it. The trek has begun. We started at 2:30 this afternoon from Cape Arkticheskiy. It was about minus 40°C with a slight wind when we landed on the Cape. And I've never seen so many reporters. There were three helicopters. We came on the biggest, which has a payload of 8000 kg. Our start time was supposed to be 10:00 a.m., but . . . I was assigned one box of bacon fat to carry which came to 15 kg. So my pack is nice and small. Richard has been given three bulky boxes, containing muesli, crackers, and, I think, meat. He also has to carry a boat and a thermos. These items fill his knapsack up entirely, and he has no extra room. In all it came to three large boxes, that were the same size as his pack, with no room for clothing, or group equipment. So I traded half my weight of fat for the same weight of crackers.

The main part of our packs is filled with group equipment. Your sleeping bag is attached to the bottom of the pack. There are two side pockets for your personal stuff. On the very top, underneath the top flap, you try and jam your parka and any wind gear you might have. We look like we belong in a flea market more than an expedition. Once we were packed up, we went off to be weighed. I was very pleased that my pack weighed 39.5 kg, – under the magic number of 40 kg. Most people are around 41 to 42 kg. Vasa ensures each of us carries the same weight of group equipment and food, so differences in pack weight come from the clothing and personal items. The most important thing is weight, because weight determines your speed, and your speed determines whether you make it or not.

We started skiing, and things went pretty well. It's very hard to tell here what's land. We went over to a ridge which was ice that had been piled up against the shore. When I look over this, I see mounds and mounds of ice, and I think, "Holy cow, are we going to make it through that?" It just looks awesome from a distance, because your vision of the ice is compressed. We all lined up for pictures. Vladimir Snegirev (deputy head of the expedition staff, and deputy editor-in-chief of *Komsomolskaya Pravda*, the sponsoring Soviet newspaper) said a few words about how hard everyone had worked and co-operated to get us to this point. Vladimir asked Laurie Dexter to say a few words, and he was as eloquent as usual, although we knew him to be in bad spirits from the discussions of the night before. Then we jumped on our skis, and off we went.

We had gone maybe 0.5 km, when we came across our first pressure ridge. It was about twelve feet high. There was a vertical drop on the far side of it, but you just had to be careful getting down. Dmitri was the first one to fall over with his pack. He just caught the edge of his ski, and over he went . . . There are a lot of flat pans of ice here, with crumpled bits at the edges, which are the pressure ridges. These are only four feet high. We have seen a few monoliths of blue-green ice about fifteen feet high which stand on their ends.

We've seen no open water at all, not even thin ice. We did see polar bear tracks, which were about eight to ten inches across. They were old, because there hasn't been wind for a couple of days, and these were definitely wind-blown tracks. It was sunny, no wind, about minus 30°C, and it's still quite light this late. The sun is down and the moon is about ten degrees above the horizon. You can see a wonderful sunset, with a few stars out.

We stopped and put up the tent at about 5:30 p.m. on a big, flat pan of ice. We put up a radio antenna made out of ski poles. It is very cold. I have my big parka, my fur hat, and my big mitts, and I'm walking around just to keep my feet warm.

Misha saw me dictating as I was skiing along, and he said, "Oh, you're talking on a walkie-talkie are you?" and I said, "Yes, I'm talking to my wife." He said, "Oh, that's very nice. Can I talk to her too?" I said, "Well, you can, but I'm afraid she won't reply."

As I stand out here looking at the tent, there are only one or two people left wandering around outside. Most people are inside with their sleeping bags rolled out. The whole tent steams quite viciously from the door and vent, and actually right through the material itself, i.e., the whole roof steams.

This whole trip is concerned about water. A few feet below us is water, we ski on frozen water, there's the problem of keeping enough water to drink, the problem of sweating too much, and getting too wet, and then getting too cold because of the water in your clothing. And then there's the matter of "water" we going to do tomorrow?

Laurie

Tuesday I phoned home to Scotland. I spoke to both my Mum and Dad, and my Dad is very seriously ill indeed. The cancerous growth in the area of the wound left after his operation had, in fact, spread further, although the cancer was originally in the pancreas. He is in a great deal of pain, hardly eating, and vomiting any time he does eat. I wonder if, in fact, he can last another month.

I know that at this time I should be available as a son and should go back to take care of things in the latter stages, but while the phone call was brief, both my Mum and Dad understood my feelings and insisted that I should go on with the expedition. It is a fearful thing to consider that this was perhaps the last time I would hear my Dad's voice.

Also, I feel bad about what happened last evening. Dmitri had announced that there would be twelve members and Fiodor would be the next one to be cut. We realized that the Soviet members were having a meeting by themselves in one of the upstairs rooms of the clubhouse. We decided to go and join them to support the choice of Fiodor over Toli F. As we observed the debate move backwards and forwards, suddenly Fiodor jumped up in an absolute fury, dashed out of the room, grabbed the tripod with the Canadian theodolite on it, and began to swing it repeatedly against the doors of the room in which we were meeting. The theodolite is worth thousands of dollars and is very strongly constructed, but it couldn't withstand this treatment, being as it was, on the end of the tripod system which he was swinging with full force against the doors. It is greatly sobering to contemplate what the consequences could be if somebody lost control like that out on the sea ice. He is demanding that we take him to Cape Arkticheskiy and leave him there to undertake his own expedition to the North Pole. Of course, it would not be possible for somebody to travel on his own without supplies.

Later Richard came into our hotel room to say that Fiodor was threatening to destroy the expedition. We all felt that if he was allowed to blackmail us at this time then he could use similar tactics at any stage of the game to get his own way during the trip. For this reason we no longer wanted him on the team. He threatened to phone Moscow and have the expedition cancelled. Seeing what he did already, we know that he is capable of destroying the expedition.

After lunch, Dmitri called yet another meeting. Basically, they would like the expedition to go ahead with twelve members, Fiodor to go as a reserve but not as part of the expedition, and yet travelling close by and eating with us, of course, but not sleeping, and only as far as the North Pole. From there he would return to the Soviet Union. Again we see this is just semantics, because if he is there he is there. I can understand their position in that Fiodor and they have been on expeditions many times together already, and they had all been good friends. They would prefer not to leave him behind where he would be able to work against us. Further, as Fiodor has pointed out, he has given six years of preparation for this moment, considers himself totally ready and committed, and sees it as a terrible injustice to be denied.

Personally, I am willing to go with thirteen even though it is inconvenient in the tent. The problem must be reconciled more on philosophical grounds than physical. The rest of the Canadians were all fairly adamant against any sort of compromise. Max seemed to understand my attitude, but the other two seemed to despise my reasoning, despise me for trying to be reasonable. What I perceive as a reasoned attempt to bridge cultural and human division, they see as weakness.

After a long and convoluted debate, which I fear has opened division among the Canadian members greater than any fissure in the Arctic ice, the others agreed that if the Soviets are willing to pay for the two extra members, then they would be willing to accept them.

Late at night, Dmitri held a press conference, and most of the first half hour was taken up with questions hammering the same point — the number of participants, how and why this decision was made. I was very, very unhappy with Dmitri's answers, because he evaded the truth and deliberately deceived them. He said things like there was no argument, just discussion; that it would make the team stronger to have two more members; that the tent was designed for thirteen members and was larger than the previous one; that the tent would be comfortable with thirteen in it, and so on.

Having made such an emotion-draining effort to persuade the other Canadian members to come to a compromise, I felt betrayed. Dmitri had the chance to say something significant, to reveal the process and show how we had negotiated and come to an agreement in spite of apparently insurmountable difficulties. This would have been a dramatic way of highlighting the contribution that this expedition can make. Instead, he covered up.

Later I told Dmitri quite openly that I was disillusioned. I feel we have been forced into a position in which we were outnumbered, in a strange country and an unusual environment.

We did a total of three hours. The ice is never good. It's thick enough to be quite safe, but it's a maze of small ridges and breaks and cracks frozen over. I found that I was handling it very badly, and was at the tail of the group most of the time.

Making camp was cold and uncomfortable, although most people seemed to be all right. Until the last three days, I have felt so positive about this expedition, but it seems as if the excitement and even the purpose has been seriously undermined. I know I am physically dog-tired and therefore seem to feel the cold more, but also, unlike previous times, I have not even enjoyed settling into the tent. Part of the problem is the strained state of our relationships. I thought we were a cohesive group, but instead we are starting out with splintered emotions and shattered ideals.

Richard

Before we left from Sredny, Dmitri said, "Okay, okay, everyone from the expedition into this room, into this room, everyone, everyone, it will only take a couple of minutes." So we all went into the room, he sat us all down, and he said, "Okay, this is Russian tradition – ten seconds of silence." So we all sat there for ten seconds – "Okay let's go," and we all jumped up and off we went. This gives you ten seconds to think, "Okay, here we go, good luck, and try to do my best," or whatever. When we set off, the camera crews were filming at the beginning. Vasa and I were up front. He said, "Go on, Richard, get up there," so Vasa and I tramped along side by side. After a while I let him go ahead, as I wasn't sure which direction to take. I knew our longitude, but I had not calculated what direction we had to take, and so Vasa led. As we set out, we yelled: "*Demoy, demoy.*" "*Demoy*" means "towards home" in Russian, and that is where we are going, home! We are heading home now!

It's a lovely evening, minus 34.5°C on Vasa's thermometer. Chris and I decided that, in order to avoid the snoring and the moisture in the tent, we would sleep outside. We simply placed our sleeping bags side by side, down on the ice, and crawled in. This is our new home for the next three months, kind of a strange home, but this is it – like it or not. We have a full moon, to boot.

MARCH 4. DAY 2

Christopher

The worst thing about sleeping outside is getting up in the morning.

The sun comes up around 9:00 a.m., but from 6:00 a.m. you can feel your way around. I was in my long underwear, and the bags are not really wide enough that you can get dressed inside them. So what you have to do is open the bag (at minus 30°C to minus 40°C, when you haven't been getting much circulation in your body), and get dressed really quickly. The first thing you want to do is put on your polar suit, but your socks have to go on first, and the plastic bag vapour barriers. (As we can't dry things out it is important not to get things wet. Richard and I are using plastic bags inside our socks to keep them dry.) So then you have to jump back into bed after putting socks on, to warm up before continuing.

We saw some Arctic fox tracks. We have just gotten out the thermoses for the midday stop, and have made the momentous decision that everyone will carry their own cup with them. Formerly, one person would carry all the pots and pans. We are carrying thermoses so that at midday we all get some liquid.

There was a brief discussion at the previous rest stop about how long we should ski today. Richard said we should ski a maximum of seven hours, because a lot of people haven't done any sort of exercise for a month. I feel that we are risking a bit of injury if we push at the beginning, but it is pretty easy going, and the terrain is flat. The only problem is that if we get an offshore wind we could get a lot of open water around here, because of the sudden drop in the ocean floor and the shore currents. I feel it is important to push on in good weather; sit and rest in bad weather.

We stopped at 3:00. We played frisbee with an empty film canister for a while. First we were playing football with Max's sleeping bag, and then he realized that his tape recorder was rolled up inside it, so we went to the film canister. That worked pretty well, until Max took a running dive after it and landed on top of the antenna. The whole situation was kind of comical. Here were these people with mittens three inches thick, hats covering our faces, enormous parkas and warm-up pants, and overboots on our feet, playing Frisbee. We have to get a buzz somehow.

Richard

A friend went to see a psychic about the expedition. I don't believe in psychics. They are always rather vague. You can't do anything with the information they provide, but it's kind of interesting.

Their statement was as follows: "This expedition is likely to succeed."

Is there anything that he, Richard, should be aware of?

"There will be much difficulty. It can succeed if all individuals work together in a group, if they work as a team and not individuals working independently from each other. We do indeed see difficulties here, strong winds, temperature dropping, the individuals will have to pace themselves and not try to do much beyond their capabilities. There is no reason to prove yourself at this time."

"You mean because it is a great adventure there is a tendency for him to compete?"

"Indeed, to compete with the others, to show their own endurance and power to the other individuals. Work as a team, and only in this way will they meet success."

The sun today was beautiful, like a big red explosion. Perhaps it went as high as 5 degrees above the horizon, or less, but nice for pictures. It will be a long time before we will be able to feel its warmth. It comes up around 9:30, it starts to come up and stays up til 4:00 or 5:00 – that is getting quite long already.

We skied about seven marches, but one was kind of short, I know this is supposed to be a team effort, so I could not say anything, but I had a good chuckle to myself, anyway. I could have said, "Hey, I told you so." Dmitri broke a ski in two and a little while later de-laminated another one. Now they are talking, "Oh, maybe the Canadian skis aren't so bad after all."

This evening Toli Fedjakov, who looks after the gun, asked me if I wanted to try it. He and Vasa took me out past the end of the camp. Once they got it out, I was very surprised: the gun itself was empty, and the bullets were in a separate bag, which took Toli five minutes to open. He had a lot of problems getting them out, and eventually I said, "The polar bear has eaten you!" I started counting: "One man, two men, three men." That is how many people the bear had eaten while he was trying to get the gun and the bullets out. I don't understand why they don't keep the bullets in the magazine of the gun. It would be a lot quicker, a lot safer in the event of a bear attack. I shot at a piece of ice on top of a pressure ridge a ways away. Vasa went and looked at it, came back, and he was most impressed. I had hit it dead centre where I had aimed. I don't think they expected that I could do that.

MARCH 5. DAY 3

Max

The most frightening experience of my life took place as we started across a point where protruding pieces of the adjacent pans touched, bridging a lead. The grinding of one huge pan on the other had thrown the edges up into car-sized boulders. Three or four members of the team crossed the bridge without difficulty, but as Chris and I faced the boggy mass, it started to move. In the heat of the moment we were torn between dashing across or waiting and risking separation from the others. Chris dove for it, and I wasn't long behind him. I was halfway across when my ski binding released. I fell smack in the middle of the churning rubble. My ski tips went down. I spent an eternal second in purgatory before finding myself miraculously on the other side. Volodi had seen my plight and managed to nab the scruff of my neck, salvaging me from death by a combination of drowning, freezing, and crushing. My heart was in my throat, and the contents of my bowel were in my kamiks.

The whole area was alive with movement, and I became very conscious of the fact that we were travelling on water. It struck me that every day we spent on the ice was like a millennium of geologic time. We could witness the tectonic shifts, the formation of mountains and ridges and their eventual erosion and dissolution back into the liquid mass underlying the friable crystalline surface.

While traversing a pressure ridge, Dmitri broke his second ski of the trip, and we replaced it with the only other full spare we had. We were now dragging two three-quarter-length skis with jagged broken ends as spares. Richard and Chris could be heard snickering inside their snow house at night, while the rest of us, having opted for the wooden skis, were far from smug. These little sticks are starting to look mighty frail under the incredible bulk of our packed-out bodies. No more spares, and we have ten days to go across this rubble before we can get more.

We completed eight marches in all, and were camped by about 5:00 p.m. One of the marches I scarcely even noticed, as I immersed myself in thoughts about what to do with my life (and my girlfriend) following return to the real world. Marriage was a consideration. I was able to piece together how it might work for the first time.

Christopher

At 8:30 this morning, as everyone was milling about, we realized that there was an enormous opening a few hundred yards to our left which had not been there before. We decided to pack up and get out of there, as, if the ice was shifting, we wanted to be on the far side of it. We left at about 9:00 a.m., and by this time the lead had turned into an enormous pressure ridge. We could hear all this grinding going on.

We set off, and within thirty minutes came across our first lead. It was about a metre wide when we got to it, so we skied along to a narrow part and crossed there. There were quite a few leads until about 1:00 p.m., and then they just stopped coming. We found one that we had to follow for half an hour before we found a place to cross.

Falls are a regular occurrence. Usually, I fall about once or twice a day. Fortunately, my sleeping bag hits before my bum, so it doesn't hurt, but then I am stuck like a turtle on its back. I have to roll over onto my hands and knees and try and get up from there: these bindings are not made to give too much forward flex. If I can't do this I have to take my pack off before getting up.

I am on duty today. The three Canadian stoves melted enough snow for five litres of water, and the two Soviet stoves melted ten. So there are good grounds for keeping them – although we are still overweight on stoves and should dump a couple. Sasha Believ admitted today that he managed to forget the peanut butter and the Skaklee bars, which will be replaced by sugar. We think that he did it on purpose. It seems very odd that he would forget just the Canadian food and none of the Soviet food. We have galetties (small biscuits) three times a day, and everyone is getting kind of sick of them.

It is now minus 18°C, incredibly warm. We never expected this temperature this early. Richard and I are sleeping outside. We have built a little shelter out here. Hopefully the wind from the south is blowing us to the north.

Richard

Now we have a wind from the south, which is blowing us north, and it also tends to open up leads as the ice pulls away from the shore. The first lead was just two cracks about two and a half feet wide, just wide enough so you could bridge it with your skis, and we got across except for Chris, Misha, Dmitri, and a few others who were a little bit farther back. By the time they got to the place to cross, the ice had pulled apart a little bit more, and they couldn't cross. They eventually found another place nearby. With dogsleds you can bridge about eight feet quite easily, and then just take a running leap and jump across, but with a big backpack you can't do that.

If the weather is always this warm, no wonder the Soviets do fine with their type of clothing. It works quite well when it isn't too cold; it is at minus 40 and minus 50 that it will really fail. We even had to use some ski wax today.

This evening I finally convinced Dmitri and Toli F. that it might be a good idea to put some shells in the magazine of the rifle.

MARCH 6. DAY 4

Max

My brilliant thought of the day is that exploring a frozen ocean is hardly a worthwhile pastime, at least in terms of those who follow, because what's here is constantly changing. At least "fixed land" explorers can identify things of some permanence – rivers, lakes, mountains, and so on. On the ice, each landmark we are able to identify will have moved or disappeared long before anyone else's shadows darken these snows.

So ends day four. It was a good day all in all. We walked southward along our lead for several hundred metres before encountering what looked like a traversable bridge of slush. Mish demonstrated his ingenuity and bravery (foolhardiness?) by building a bridge of skis over the weakest area and then dancing gingerly across it to the other side. The rest of us eventually found a more substantial bridge to cross. After negotiating several small pressure ridges, fields of rubble, and generalized rough stuff for about an hour, we had smooth sailing for the rest of the day.

Christopher

Since about 4:00 p.m. yesterday afternoon we've been skiing on light, fluffy snow, It's been great. Now we're in about a foot of powder, and it's pretty impressive. Of course, every now and then you approach the edges and your ski pole plunges through – gives you quite a shock. So then you just drift back over to the right and firm ice. We're a bit slow at the moment, because the guys in the front are having to break trail, and also they have to figure out where to go, whereas back here it's nice, the track is set, and all the thinking has been done.

Yuri always has a saying for everything. Like "From our mistakes we learn," or "A bit of time here, a bit of time there, it doesn't matter." He also has very bad eyesight. He left his good pair of glasses in Sredny, that I call "Model Number 1," because I've seen about eight different people with those same glasses. The pair he has here has a broken arm, so he has a bit of neoprene that he stuck together with string that holds them onto his head. He was having a lot of problems because they fog up, and he has no depth perception. Today I noticed that he wasn't wearing them, but he was also going slowly. You can really tell when you watch him in the rough stuff, because he pretty well has to feel around with his ski pole to decide where he is going to go next.

Laurie is really having problems. He is the slowest in the group by a marked amount. I know his foot is giving him a lot of problems. I thought, why didn't I speak up and offer to take some of his weight, because I could certainly handle it. I feel that he is not competent to be on this expedition, and that if he can't handle the conditions we have now, he will never make it when things get bad. It's just a matter of time.

We skied until 4:30 this afternoon, when the lead that we were following north-northeast suddenly turned 90 degrees to the right, and thus went southeast. Of course, now, what to do? We had reached a crossroads, so to speak. So we decided to spend the night here, and wait until morning to see if we had drifted or the lead had frozen over. I dug a nice little snow cave into the side of a hill, with the help of Fiodor. However, Vasa came along and showed us up by building himself a one-man coffin-shaped snowhouse. He had a light on in the inside, and I couldn't see any holes at all. We had a lean-to, and he had a house.

Everyone has agreed that there is a big problem with moisture in the tent. I saw Fiodor's sleeping bag, and there was just nothing to it. Much thinner than my blue bag at home, which is really a summer sleeping bag. And his parka is the same. It is a non-vapour-barrier bag, for one thing. And it is soggy and wet and thin when you can feel it, with only about one inch of loft – maybe.

Laurie

This has been one of the hardest days I've ever had. Finishing last night I could hardly walk. My left foot was badly blistered and extremely painful. Misha bandaged it up this morning, but from the moment I started I was in pain. For four hours, every step was agony. I have often had pain running ultra-distances, and often had blisters, but I have never had this level of pain continuing with every single stride. As we rotate positions in the tent, tonight I find that my position is right up against the wall. As we were putting up the tent, I tried to guess where the door would go and where my place would be and I put my skis (used to support the tent walls) over in this area. I misjudged it slightly; but not far from the position I am in I can see the ski with Sheena's name on it and the ski with Andrew and Alison's names on it.

During the evening radio session, various people sent messages, and I asked if I could speak to Resolute Bay. I thought they might be able to put in a phone patch, but that wasn't possible, so I just left a message to let Sheena know that she could contact me through the radio, mainly if anything happened to my Dad.

Today I was hurting so badly that over and over again I felt that this was the last place that I wanted to be, that it was a mistake, that I was out of my depth. I was in the company of people beyond my own ability. Now that I am settled in my sleeping bag, I feel much better about things, but I realize how easy it is for even a small amount of pain to be exaggerated. Certainly, in conditions like this, pain is more debilitating than normal. Whatever, there is no turning back at this stage – if ever there was, in fact – and so, for better or worse, I have to press on.

Today was Sunday, but very different from any other Sunday that I normally spend. However, this morning, as I had finished packing a little bit ahead of most of the others, I walked a hundred metres or so away from the camp, behind some hummocks of ice, and did something that I rarely do. I don't usually kneel to pray, but on a hump of solid ice I knelt for just a few brief moments, and prayed for the family, my Mum and Dad, and the congregation.

Richard

Last night's camp was thirty kilometres from Cape Arkticheskiy, that is 81 degrees, 36 minutes, I believe. It was still only about minus 20 this morning. It snowed quite a lot overnight; now there is a lot of deep snow, and a lot of fresh drifts on the trail. If we get any strong wind it could be a real problem. By a lot of snow I mean a couple of inches – that is a lot of snow for the Arctic. The drifts are sometimes knee deep in places. As the day progressed, the wind picked up. It also got quite a lot colder.

This is an expedition "which consists of a long line of everybody" (from *Winnie the Pooh*). In the long line, there are Laurie and Max, and it seems they have developed shadows. Max has Fiodor, and Laurie has Toli Fedjakov, and these guys ski along behind them, and they are supposed to help them if they are in trouble, which is kind of funny because they stick to them like glue; and if Max stops, Fiodor stops, if Max goes, Fiodor goes.

MARCH 7. DAY 5

Christopher

Last night we received a message from Gorbachev. He wishes us the best of success, and he hopes that the expedition will stimulate better relations between the two countries, and wishes us safe passage. Apparently, our telegram to Mulroney also made the national news in Canada. So we're in the big time – this is great!

Woke up this morning, and it was very cold. The warm snap is over. It was minus 34°C this morning. I'm skiing back and forth to keep warm. I started out with one pair of Chlorophylle socks this morning, but my feet got colder and colder, so I added a second pair, and the good news is I can feel the end of my toes. The bad news is they don't feel so good. However, if they were frozen, I would not be able to feel them at all, so it's good to feel pain, so to speak. My fingers are also cold.

One thing that I wanted to make note of was that yesterday Fiodor said the first English words that I've heard him say. He came up to me and said that he would like to help build our house, and would like to sleep in it, if possible, but his sleeping bag was too thin.

About 11:00 a.m. we passed a field full of ice which was a bright turquoise colour. It was amazing. I thought, "At last, we've reached the Emerald City." But, of course, as we all know, this ain't Kansas.

We are now passing through an area of very old ice. It looks like a graveyard full of tombstones spread ten to one hundred feet apart. Small ones for the paupers, and some big ones for the rich bankers. And, of course, all of them get melted in the summer, and the edges worn and rounded with time.

I lived today in a six-foot-diameter world, because six feet is as far as I can see with my hood up. However, the day seemed to go quite quickly, and my pack is feeling lighter all the time. We are getting much better at our snow house building. It's more like a trench, I guess – about four feet wide at the surface; but we've dug down, so at the bottom it's about five feet wide.

Laurie

At least with the easier ice conditions today I managed to go through the day without falling. Up until now, and for the first couple of days in particular, I was falling at least every hour, and sometimes more than once per hour, but yesterday I think I only fell a couple of times, and today I didn't fall at all. Some people did, but that's inevitable. It just takes the ski to touch a knob of ice and cross over the other ski, or to be going down a little slope and one tip to jam at the bottom. Falling is just part of the game, and everybody experiences it. However, there were a few places today that involved stepping out of frozen channels onto the solid ice, which I couldn't have done without the assistance of a pole to pull me up.

Last night and tonight I am in the two bad positions in the tent. I finished moving up the one side, and crossed over to the other side, so last night one half of my back was in contact with the tent wall, tonight the other side is in contact, and everything is really very wet. From now on until it warms up, I'm just going to have to use the black vapour-barrier system, because my sleeping bag is becoming a soggy mass, even though I have been more comfortable sleeping in the bag without the vapour-barrier. Last night I woke up two or three times cold and shivering, and, even though I am lying half in the bag just now, I am still very cold. I am really tired tonight, so hopefully that will help me sleep through the cold.

Richard

Got away at about 9:30 this morning, and right away we were back at the lead that had stopped us yesterday. After a bit of investigation, we found we could get across. We crossed into an area that was quite broken up, and then the next hour or two we spent our time picking through it, climbing over little leads, slowly making our way through. We had to stop a couple of times so someone could go ahead and look for a better route.

All the Soviets' sleeping bags, and indeed everyone's who sleeps in the tent, are losing loft; the feathers are getting wet, and the bags are getting thinner and thinner. Vasa's sleeping bag seems still fairly fluffy. He did sleep out last night. The rest are getting really flat. Max and Vasa's bags are a little bit better because they sewed in the extra vapour-barrier layer. There is just no way I am sleeping in the tent. It is jam-packed, for starters. It is so humid; there are wet bodies, clothing, and sleeping bags everywhere.

MARCH 8. DAY 6

Laurie

There were many, many times today when I recalled conversations and interviews I had had before the expedition. I know I said frequently that the first month was not going to be pleasant, and that I wasn't going to enjoy the first four weeks or so. That was fair enough to talk about it then, but it's a different thing to experience it, to have to face the reality. The idea of getting up again tomorrow in minus 40°C, with a wind blowing, is too horrific. Many times today I looked at my ski tips with the names of Sheena, Andrew and Alison, and wished that I was there with them.

I am acutely aware of the unfeeling, uncaring power of nature, and sense my mortality and smallness, at times almost like a child. The Soviet members in particular seem confident, and, on the whole, strong. Of course, every day people fall, but today I managed to go through the whole day without falling, until the very last hour. I am frustrated with the problem of the freezing of the ends of my digits. A serious case of frost-bite could spell the end of the expedition for any member. While I am not enjoying this day-to-day experience, I am determined to go through with the expedition to the very end and would be heart- broken to suffer something serious enough to have to be taken out. At the moment, it is nowhere near that stage, and, in any case, it would be almost impossible to be extricated.

Richard

Today we had our first real day of winter – 40 below with a nice, stiff breeze. I enjoyed it. This is what travel in the Arctic is all about. I dressed up in all my clothes, my polarsuit, my Chlorophylle wind gear, and my sealskin kamiks from Broughton Island, and I was toasty and warm. Let it howl away!

There is a band of haze that runs all the way around the horizon, and today the sun almost rose above it. When the sun is in the haze, it's a large, orangey-red, glowing ball, and, when it rises above it, it becomes the normal colour of the sun. Today, when the sun was at its high point, almost out of the haze, it became quite a bit brighter for an hour or so. In another couple of days it will probably get above it, and maybe we will start to feel heat from the sun, a little, finally. At the moment, we see the sun, but of course it offers no warmth at all. In fact, there is really not much difference between the temperature at night and the temperature during the day.

As I skied along I spent a lot of time trying to compose some nonsense songs, but rather unsuccessfully, I am afraid. I really don't think I am very musical. In the end, I spent several hours singing "Plastic Jesus" to myself, over and over again.

This afternoon, Misha asked me if we had any more sealskin mukluks and Chlorophylle socks, and a few other people talked to me about them. Volodi was very impressed by our vapour-barrier "kitchen catchers" socks. He explained it to Yuri, but Yuri found it difficult to believe that they were warm. Everyone is starting to be impressed by the socks, along with the plastic bindings which haven't broken, and the skis which haven't broken either . . . yet.

MARCH 9. DAY 7

Richard

A note on our diet. We start off the day with a hundred grams of Shaklee muesli cooked up – well, sort of cooked – with some butter, freeze-dried meat, whole powdered milk, and lots of galetties (dry biscuits), which I carefully save for lunch because I prefer them in the middle of the day. For lunch we get a little silver package. Rip that open and inside is a treasure trove of goodies; two large chocolate truffles, two chocolate-coated halvas, my favourite of the day, dried apricots, a package of hazelnuts, and, of course, galetties and a lump of sugar. We are also supposed to get two Shaklee bars, but we have been receiving only one because that's all we have, some peanut butter, a lump of fat, which I usually give away or throw away because it is so salty.

Supper is a one-litre bowl of kasha, buckwheat groats, pemmican, butter oil, dry milk, galetties, and dry bread. I usually save some of my galetties from the day and from breakfast and put them in my bowl along with whole garlic, dry garlic, a bit of thyme, a bit of basil, and a bit of dried onions – all in all, an excellent meal. We top it off with Red Zinger tea, which is the most popular hit on the Polar Sea. I also save some of my halvas from the day for dessert, much to the chagrin of Christopher who gobbles them at first sight and then eyes mine hungrily while I eat them in the evening.

Today was such a beautiful day, with a beautiful Arctic sun, a sun you only see in the Arctic, nowhere else, a sun that hangs just above the horizon and works its way around, glowing various shades of red and orange. I guess this is the reason why I come back to this place. For me, there is excitement in trying to exist at 45 or 50 below and skiing along all bundled up, toasty warm, and looking at the beautiful sunsets, the shadows on the ice, the different colours of the ice, and the shapes. Today we came across one piece of ice – it was like an obelisk pointing right into the sky. Vasa stopped, looked, pointed, and said, "See, look, 82 degrees. There is the marker."

Laurie is having a hard time keeping warm; his toes and fingers are in constant danger of freezing. He has had lots of problems with blisters, which I believe are slowly healing. He is so wet. It takes all his effort just to ski; he has no energy left to keep warm. The clothing he has chosen to wear is really all wrong. He has not enough in some places, and too much in others. He is not wearing a polar suit. Instead, he is wearing two layers of polypropylene underwear, a Chlorophylle pile jacket, and the windbreaker. He has only a very thin woollen Balaclava, and a thicker woollen Balaclava, not really every much for 45 below. On his legs he has some Soviet pants. Again, they are not really the best thing for 45 below, since most of the Soviets are cold too.

This afternoon, Chris and I were wondering how long he would last. Chris figured he'd go till he dropped. I am not so sure, because he has a family. I don't think anybody should go that far. There is no reason for it.

MARCH 10. DAY 8

Christopher

Today, at 12:00 noon, an Aeroflot DC3 flew several passes over us, then left. Our first contact with so-called civilization since we left Cape Arkticheskiy. Once I thought I heard a telephone, because the snow makes all sorts of different sounds, depending upon its composition. It was cold all day: minus 45° to minus 48°C the whole time, with a slight headwind.

Yuri's nose *just looks awful*. I was talking to him today, and you can see it has been bleeding all along the side. His cheeks are bleeding, and today he had an icicle frozen onto his nose. Literally, it was half a centimetre long, and you could see the whole thing was white, red, and bleeding where it had frozen. So I told him about it and he said, "Bah, nothing." So I told Misha as well. I told Misha that I felt sick looking at Yuri's nose, and he said that at the end of his last trip no one wanted to look at Yuri because he looked so bad. He also said that Dmitri will probably look the same as well. Richard also told me that in another three to four weeks of this weather, everybody will start looking really ugly. My hair is really greasy, but the rest of me feels fine.

We came across an open lead about 4:00 p.m. Usually you can see the clouds of steam in the distance. We skied into the fog, and then suddenly we came across a few leads, which we managed to jump over. All the obstacles on the horizon look enormous, as they are all compressed together. You think that you'll never make it through, but, as you get closer, you can see a way through. Some time today we passed our 100 km mark. Only seventeen more of these to go before being home again. I have a cold. Blowing my nose is just awful.

Laurie

All of us continue to have problems, with hands and feet mainly, and every time we stop you see people in motion. Nobody actually "stops." During the ten-minute breaks, people often take off their skis and just stomp up and down and shake their feet back and forth, swinging their arms around trying to get the circulation into the extremities. Strange things happen in these temperatures. Our Shaklee bars, for example. In normal temperatures, you can bite through quite softly, but at minus

20 or minus 30°C they are extremely hard and difficult to bite through. However, at minus 45°C they bite much easier because they simply shatter! Even more simple, today, when I had my Shaklee bar, I just put it on the ground, stomped on it with my ski, and it broke into three or four pieces suitable for eating. Dried fruit becomes a solid hard lump which is impossible to break apart, and all you can do is bite a corner off as it thaws between your teeth. The hazelnuts, which we often have for lunch or for our snacks, are like little hard marbles. The peanut butter, which we have only had a couple of times so far, has been scooped into portions and put in small plastic bags. The problem is that the plastic bags are stuck in small creases with the peanut butter, and, again, it is impossible to get them out. Most difficult of all is trying to eat these things with mitts on. Small items are impossible to handle, and hands have to be bared momentarily.

Richard

Another nice, minus 46°C day on the Arctic Ocean. Another eight marches today, through varied terrain, some large old pans, some very broken-up areas. Just before camp, we came to an open lead. It was moving so that it wasn't freezing – quite surprising. There was mist in the air, creating an eerie atmosphere.

Today I tried using one of my last two rolls of 400 ASA film. I had a lot of problems trying to load it into the camera: four times the tab broke off the film before it stayed in the camera; it was 46 or 47 degrees below zero, but, still, every time I put the film in and then started to wind it, it snapped, and I had to take the whole thing apart and pull the pieces out with a pair of tweezers, and then re-insert the tab. Of course, this is done with bare hands.

Just before supper, the Soviets were asking me questions about temperatures we experienced during the Steger expedition and about the clothing we wore. Perhaps the polar suit is starting to impress them. When I took the kitchen catchers off my feet, and showed them the dry socks, boy! they were impressed! I think if the temperature dropped to 55 or 60 below there would be some serious frost-bite to some people on this expedition. Their clothing will not handle those temperatures. They are already at their limit.

MARCH 11. DAY 9

Max

Despite my numerous cold burns and patches of skin that don't transmit sensation normally, I think that I am beginning to acclimatize to this environment. My main concern is that we are not getting enough food. I was calculating our caloric intake today, and I'm sure we aren't getting any more than sixty-five hundred calories. Our requirements are much greater than that, and I am hungry constantly. Sometimes I wake in the middle of the night and eye up the flesh on the next body. . . .

I am sleeping better at night now that the heat wave is over. As it gets colder, the stoves are no longer able to raise the temperature inside the tent above freezing. Instead of waking up sopping wet, we wake up with a light dusting of ice on the bag that brushes off rather easily.

Laurie

The person on duty has to get up at 4:00 a.m., have breakfast ready for 5:00 to 5:30 a.m., and then allow two or three hours for packing. The temperature is still minus 45°C, and getting ready for the day takes three or four times as long as it would take in normal temperatures. We still don't get underway until 8:30 a.m. Today skiing was very good. We travelled almost true north most of the day. Of course, we had the usual pressure ridges and jumbled areas to tackle, and there were parts where open water had frozen over recently, but enough to allow us to cross over. We skied steadily for our normal eight hours, and then we put in a last half-hour at the end.

The cold is the single most dominating element in the environment just now. There is no stopping. We have our ten-minute break after fifty-minutes' skiing, but during those ten minutes everybody is in motion, hopping from one foot to another, swinging their legs to try and get the blood into the feet, swinging their arms, doing everything possible to try and keep warm.

Packing up in the morning is the worst of all. You see people working on their packs for a couple of minutes, then running in a circle for five or ten minutes, then coming back to do some more packing. Then they bend over double with their mitts tucked into their bellies.

Most of the time when skiing it's reasonably comfortable, but the trouble is that there is still a struggle with the hands. I find putting on the backpack worst of all. I can't really put it on with big, thick mitts, and once I have got it on, I have to fasten the sternum strap and the waist belt. It only takes half a minute, but, inevitably, my hands are cold because of having stopped, and because of handling cold food. For the first five or ten minutes after getting in motion again, my hands in the mitts are in pain. I can see them turning white. I can feel the flesh freezing, and I have to get moving fast to try to regain the circulation.

I find the conditions as fatiguing mentally as physically. The constant battle against the cold is debilitating. There is the ever-present uncertainty of success. There is the insecurity of the surface over which we are travelling. There are the tensions of communication among ourselves, and, for me, also with the radio. Because I must stay up working with the radio, I get less sleep.

Richard

Today we crossed very varied terrain – some quite rough areas. It was broken up and filled in with drifts, and the team was twisting in and out, up and down. There are also a few large, open pans. We have actually covered 13 minutes of latitude today, about twenty-two to twenty-three kilometres, which is pretty darn good. We are up to 82 degrees, 20 something minutes.

This morning there was a funny incident. Vasa usually wears a blue sweater over a couple of shirts and a couple of undershirts. The blue sweater goes under his anorak. He pulled off his anorak and started to put on a red sweater. He said normally the blue sweater is fine, but, with the people we are skiing with, we go so slowly he needs two sweaters. He is becoming more and more impressive. He is an extremely strong skier, very adept. He impressed both Chris and me when he built the snow house so quickly. He has good insight into a lot of different things.

We ski nine marches now instead of eight because our packs are getting lighter. Therefore we are getting up an hour earlier. It takes us three hours from the time breakfast is ready to the time we leave. We are very inefficient. Now we are only getting seven hours of sleep. Cutting back on sleep in order to increase the hours of skiing is not the best way.

In the tent this evening, I suggested some things that could cut down on tent time, such as not sleeping after breakfast, having an assistant duty person, assigning specific jobs to each person, so when you make and break camp everyone does the same job every day and becomes very good at it. We should have a specified time to leave and to start skiing, so everyone knows what time to aim for and no one is left standing around waiting for everyone else to get ready. Apparently they are going to keep discussing it, which is the normal outcome when we suggest something.

The primary reason that the Soviets won't use the Canadian skis is that they are just absolutely petrified of back-slip. They think all plastic/fibreglass skis back-slip. I have explained to them many times that below minus 30 or colder you don't need wax, and above that you just wax. Very simple. But it does not sink in at all. Now they have to face the fact that their skis are breaking up faster than they can replace them. The Soviets seem to have a fanatical pride associated with their equipment, even though most of it dates from the turn of the century. They think that because it is Soviet, it has got to be the best, and they somehow feel obliged to use it.

I just can't see what Laurie is doing on this trip. He can't ski, he can't keep himself warm, he can't function. But he is here . . . . Every time we have a discussion with the Soviets, he always sides with them because there are more of them, like he is trying to be popular.

MARCH 12. DAY 10

Christopher

The rift has started. There is a pack of ice that is floating away from another pack. On one are Richard and I and a few Soviet dissenters – we don't know who they are – and on the other are the rest. Two days ago, it was decided that in order to do an extra hour of skiing we would sleep one hour less. It still takes four to five hours to get ready in the morning. So, Richard suggested that perhaps we should be a bit organized – a novel suggestion in Russian society – so everybody would have their own jobs. When we stopped for camp we would get everything built (speaking from the snow-house construction business), get the food started, the radio started – so that we're not up until 10:00 p.m. talking on the radio.

We were talking about assigning everyone duties so we would get away in the morning in two and a half hours. The Soviets argued amongst themselves, and then during dinner we asked Misha what the outcome was, and he said that they hadn't decided: "But, by the way, we have decided that we will ski an extra hour tomorrow, so we will do without one hour's sleep." Richard and I flew off the handle, and said that *the Canadians* had not decided, perhaps *they* had decided, but we were not consulted, and we would like to be involved in decisions that we are affected by.

Richard took a good photograph today. Salt-water ice is flexible, up to a certain thickness. And so during that time, if there is a major shift in one of the plates around it, you get waves in it that can get frozen in. So we got myself standing on one of them, trying to surf on my skis down the front of it.

Laurie

It was my turn to be on cook duty, starting in the morning by giving out some of the rations before our trek. Right from the start it was a tough day; the temperature was slightly warmer, minus 38°C, but for the first four hours conditions were the toughest that we have had for the whole of the trip so far. We struggled through pressure ridges, over pressure ridges, around pressure ridges, over cracks, around cracks, inching steadily northwards, but making many digressions. Every few metres, somebody or other would fall, and getting up was often a great struggle. These four hours through the really rough ice didn't do my pulled shin muscle any good, and through the many slides and slips it gradually became more painful. By evening, the temperature was dropping a little bit more, and I was glad to get into the tent to start the supper chores.

It would have been very difficult if Anatoli Fedjakov hadn't come to help me. I am not familiar with the Soviet stoves. We had supper ready much quicker than would have been possible otherwise. Actually, Anatoli (Toli) has been a tremendous help to me all the time. He has skied close to me a lot of the time, and whenever I have been in trouble he has usually been at hand. He often skis just ahead of me and waits for me, or is right behind me, and if I fall he is nearly always available to help me up.

The night was one of the worst experiences of my life. Right from the beginning I was cold, actually physically shivering. I hadn't taken any of my socks off, but my feet were still cold. My boots were solid hard lumps behind me, so I decided to try wearing them, but eventually had to take one of them off because I thought it was freezing one of my feet. My sleeping bag is sodden, and I lay awake for hours shivering and shaking. I must have dozed off one or two times, but always woke up bitterly cold. The time seemed to just drag by, and I suppose I had a good dose of fear, lying in the dark. What if I couldn't get any warmer than this? What if I couldn't get any drier? What if . . . ? What if . . . ? I remember looking at my watch at 3:45 a.m. and thinking that I should start the stove for breakfast, just simply to get some heat into the tent, and then, finally, I did doze, and didn't waken until about one hour later.

Richard

Compared to the Steger expedition, the workload is not nearly as heavy. I am really not very tired at the end of the day. Even at the end of the harder days, when the packs were heaviest, we still had the energy to build a snow house. There was no way we would have been able to do that on the Steger expedition. At the same time, the living conditions are far more miserable. The tent is so disorganized, there are basically just people everywhere. Everyone is supposed to have a spot, and they do, in a way, except Chris and me. But there are clothing and sleeping bags everywhere; everybody is walking in and out like it is a regular throughway. Everybody changes jobs and location in the tent regularly, whereas on the Steger expedition we had one job all the time, we had one spot in the tent all the time, and nothing moved, nothing changed, and we became very efficient.

MARCH 13. DAY 11

Christopher

We dug our snow house into a nice drift, and just at the end was a very thin crevasse. All night we started hearing creaks and groans, and we would hear the whale sounds. Whale sounds are the noise the snow blocks make rubbing on the other snow, when you drag them around, while making the snow house. When we woke up in the morning, the closest lead, which was about twenty feet from where our house was, was now open water. This morning it was very cold, minus 42°C, and the wind started to pick up. It was announced that we would start off at 8:00 a.m.

This morning we were going through really rough stuff. Every fifty feet there would be a whole new pile of ice to scramble through, and we would have to pick our way carefully. Then we came across a lead or two, and then the whole thing turned into great big pans, with big pressure ridges in between. I was leading for a while, and not going very fast — I'm sure not over three kilometres per hour, over perfectly flat terrain, and I get complaints for going too fast.

Today we had cheese curds. I was told we weren't going to have any cheese curds, but, all of a sudden, there they were. I sat in my snow house and ate them, and then I went into the tent and had two enormous helpings of kasha. By this time I was starting to feel a bit sick. Also now that we have moved out of the tent, there is no space for us, so when we go in to eat, we end up sitting in the middle.

Laurie said today that we were making good time, because of all the flat sections. During the second half of the day his sleeping bag was taken by Vasa to reduce his load, but he's still having problems keeping up.

Richard

Today was another disastrous day for Laurie. He went from slow to slower. We are now waiting an extra ten minutes every hour for him. Apparently he has a pulled muscle or something. He is working so hard at his limit that he has become prone to injury, and now he has injured himself.

But Laurie doesn't think this is a race, and he doesn't see there is any rush. He doesn't realize that we are racing against time. We must reach Ward Hunt Island before it is too late in the summer to travel. He doesn't think there is any rush, and he is ready to go on plodding.

This afternoon we were discussing the possibility of a bit more food. Most of the Canadians, at least Chris, Max and I, are feeling hungry most of the time. We are never satisfied, which means we are not getting enough calories. After the airdrop, we will have a bit more peanut butter or another Shaklee bar, since it seems to be in the middle of the day when we are the hungriest. There was some discussion that perhaps we should have something extra. I suggested another package of pemmican in the evening meal; they suggested dry meat and butter. They seem convinced that there is a lot of water in the pemmican. I told them a long time ago exactly what it is made of. They say that it contains water because it gets hard. Well, it is 45 degrees below. Anything will freeze hard! There is an inherent stubbornness in these people – incredible. They are very polite, but they just don't believe you. They are absolutely convinced that anything Soviet-made is the very best that can be.

Vasa is quite amazing. He has managed to stay dry and stay warm when no one else has been able to. But if you watch him closely, he never stops moving. I think Fiodor is getting over what happened back in Dikson. He is coming back to life a lot more, more like the Fiodor we knew before. He has been joining in conversations instead of sitting like an exile in the corner.

MARCH 14. DAY 12

Richard

Up at five for breakfast as usual. Away by 8:15, if you can believe it. It takes that long. Laurie set off a little early to get a good start. We still caught up with him within five minutes. We did six marches. It was just a gorgeous morning. One of those mornings when you are glad to be alive, and glad to be up in the Arctic. The light is just gorgeous. Only the light in the Arctic is like this. Even though we only "trundled" along at a snail's pace, I still enjoyed it.

We went through many very old fields or pans of multi-year ice where the ice has melted down, forming strange and wonderful shapes. Huge blocks of ice, half the size of a house, sitting on tiny, thin, spindle-like columns. Once, we came across what I believe is probably an iceberg. It was probably fifty feet high, a few hundred feet wide, much bigger than any pressure ice we have found before, but it was very old. It was rounded from melting in the summer, and all covered with snow. We climbed it, and there was a great view of the surrounding countryside or icescape. Then I skied up and down, doing telemark turns on the steep sections.

Laurie's leg is still hurting him a lot, a sort of tendonitis. I asked

Max how much he thought was real, how much of it was in Laurie's head. He said probably a bit of both; the injury probably comes from his lack of strength. To keep up with the group, he has to put out a supreme effort, therefore he is prone to injury.

This afternoon he crawled into his sleeping bag in the tent with his parka on. His parka was all covered with snow and frost. He used the radio box as a pillow. He was just sort of lying there, half sleeping, half awake, shivering. He replied, "Oh I'm cold, I'm cold," when I asked him how he was doing. It reminded me of the last days of Robert Scott in a movie. He was really pathetic. It was sad to see someone degenerate to that point. He really came alive again in the evening when we got the stoves going, and heated up the tent.

Max

I am on duty, and it is 4:24 in the morning. I am watching the snow slowly melt into water, and also, unbeknownst to the rest of the crowd, thawing out my piss bottle in the teapot.I left it in my bag full overnight, and it turned into a new geologic formation.

Last night was probably the most miserable night I have ever spent in my life. The outside temperature plummeted to a new low of around minus 48, at least at the time I recorded it, and it is very likely that it got colder after that. The intense cold, combined with the deteriorated insulating capacity of my bag, kept me awake and shivering most of the night. I was reluctant to sleep, even when I felt it was possible, because I wasn't sure what minor appendages I might be sacrificing to the elements by losing my conscious vigil.

My protective instincts may be surfacing too late, however. There is something very strange going on with the toes on my left foot. They seem to be working all right, and I am not really experiencing any pain, but they have been totally anaesthetized for the last few days. It is almost like having tight rubber bands around them at the bases.

During the day, the skiing isn't so bad. It is just the morning and evening hours, when you are immobile and freezing your butt off. I guess waking is the worst. Every morning I wonder what the hell I am doing this for.

My toes. My goddamn toes. I don't mind the idea of losing them so much, but the idea of having to be evacuated revolts me. Thank God for travelling companions like Toli Melnikov, who are walking proof that Arctic trekkers don't need twenty digits.

Laurie

Right from the beginning, Richard and Chris have been sleeping "outside." They have each had maybe one night in the tent as a test, but then have returned to their own sleeping arrangement. It is good for them in that they immediately recognized that the heavy humidity in the tent would create havoc with our sleeping bags. With their method, their bags have retained their loft much better, and therefore they have kept warmer. Another advantage is that as soon as supper is over they can slip out and go to sleep immediately in peace. From their personal perspective it has been a smart move.

It is also good in that it relieves the crowding in the tent. Even with eleven of us (the original number intended) the tent is crowded; but with thirteen it is ridiculous! One disadvantage is that they have to spend time each evening cutting snow blocks and putting up some sort of lean-to shelter – quite a lot of extra work. The other problem is that the Soviet members seem to misunderstand their motives. I feel that they are more interested in personal ambition, and more concerned with number one than the group, but that is not the reason for this particular action. Their reasons for sleeping apart are practical and sound, and it is just chance that this also reflects certain characteristics.

Christopher

This afternoon I was skiing along and thinking, suppose these guys let us ski a hundred kilometres onto the ocean and then don't bring us any new supplies, and make it a test for us to ski back without any food.

To enable our resupply plane to locate us, we radioed them last night's co-ordinates. We also have a radio compass that they can home in on. Of course, we also have radio contact with the plane.

We stopped for camp about 2:30, so we could get radio contact up for 3:00 p.m., to establish our position for the airdrop. Shortly afterwards, an ice-reconnaissance plane went over us, and then a few minutes after that the AN 74 came along and began the airdrop. A pretty exciting day all around.

SUMMARY

To this point, at the first airdropped resupply, the skiers had travelled 194 km northward, just less than one-fifth of their way to the Pole. (The distance is 1000 km on the Soviet side.) They set up their camp at 83 degrees, 1 minute latitude.

The team had been on the ice for twelve days. Richard, Christopher, Vasa and Volodi felt that progress was slow. This pace at least provided Richard and Christopher time to take a lot of photographs.

Their physical condition was fair. All had frostbitten faces, but most of them were well. Laurie was suffering greatly from cold and was travelling slowly. Richard saw him as a liability on the team and seriously wondered if he could make the entire journey. Max had a frozen toe. However, it was not yet clear how serious this injury was. All the skiers had lost weight.

The trip had started gently, as far as weather was concerned. It did not become seriously cold until the second week, which was fortunate because the skiers were not well acclimatized. They had trained very little during the previous month in the Soviet Union. It had not been extremely cold during their week at Dikson, either, which was also unfortunate. The relative warmth had caused some of the skiers to underestimate their needs and use footwear and other gear that were inadequate.

The ice was new, thinner, and with smaller pressure ridges than on the Canadian side, which meant that travelling was not as difficult. Having passed this first high-risk area without encountering uncrossable open water the group decided to discard the larger of their two inflatable boats, to save weight.

Conditions in the tent were terrible. It was too crowded. Condensation that formed in the night and froze on the ceiling, melted in the morning when the stoves were lit. So each morning it rained on the sleeping bags, soaking them. Deeper cold in the second week made things wetter. Even perspiration didn't evaporate.

Christopher and Richard had been sleeping outside the main tent to avoid these problems, despite the criticisms they received from the Soviets for being anti-social. (In some ways this symbolized the differences between the two cultures – in one, communal values had priority; in the other, individualistic values.)

Voting on sleeping arrangements, or any other group matter, was something that had never happened on previous Soviet expeditions. It was interesting to see the Soviet's approach to democracy in the group. The previous expeditions were run with Dmitri firmly in charge: he always had the final word. The Canadians instigated voting on group matters, which was well received. However, if there was a question involving something (e.g., food or navigation) that was clearly a responsibility of one person, the Soviets tended to vote with the person in charge of that area, rather than for what they personally believed.

Three Soviet skis had broken, and there were no spares left. Everyone was finding the packs heavy. Some of the Soviet skiers were discreetly burying their excess weight (for instance, lifejackets). The Canadians were openly throwing theirs away.

But the biggest problem was organization. The Canadian skiers were feeling the effects of the fact that the thirteen expedition members had never trained together as a group. It was taking a long time to get away in the mornings. Some attempt had been made to standardize routines, but this was not working. What had emerged was that Dmitri and a majority of the Russians had a different sense of organization from the Canadians.

Everyone was hungry, because their diet was not sufficient. After the first rest break they asked for – and got – more food. The mood was not improved by the medical tests, which had to be done during rest breaks. At this point, the Canadian skiers were introduced to the Soviet-style rest break: after the food arrived via airdrop, the skiers ate enormous amounts of food. They tended to eat in the rest days more than they slept; in fact, the whole idea was to travel hungry, and then gorge and gain weight back for the next trek. The Canadians, for their part, wanted to eat more on the trail and sleep more on the rests.

Everyone was beginning to realize the magnitude of the language barrier. The Canadians would see the Soviets going on for ten minutes in what looked like a violent verbal argument, and then be told: "It's a discussion," and nothing more. There was not a lot of interchange between the two nationalities. This was partly because it was an effort to speak the other language, and the skiers were tired. Also it proved hard to hear any conversation on the trail, even in one's own language because of the squeaking snow and bulky clothing.

The Canadians were all learning bits of Russian, and vice versa, especially Dmitri and Misha, who worked hard with a dictionary right from the beginning.

Communications with the outside world had been limited, to this point, to radio communications through Sredny. Laurie wrote an article describing the strengths and attributes of each member of the team, but without glossing over the severity of the conditions, and sent it out to the Canadian management team. This article was never released. The managers thought that if its contents were known, there would be pressure from media or government to take the skiers off the ice. Apart from one poor recording of the wives in an interview, the Canadians had received no word from home. In this first airdrop, there were no media articles and no letters for them.

Overall morale at this first stop was fair. The relative ease of progress was reassuring, but the worsening cold was hard for many to cope with. The relations between the two groups had not been worked out and were causing apprehension. Most skiers wondered how it would all settle down.

Stage Two

MARCH 15. DAY 13

Max

It was our first airdrop today. After a successful resupply in which eight parachutes floated gently to the earth directly on target, the ninth failed to open, and its precious cargo came rocketing to the ice surface at a fresh-frozen lead. The few inches of ice were inadequate to sustain the impact, and the whole thing shot through to Davy Jones' locker. We ran to the edge of the crater in time to see a delectable Ukrainian cake surface briefly in a rainbow pool of gasoline before disappearing forever into the chilly brine. We stared at one another in awe, disappointment, and fear as we realized that the fuel we had been waiting for so anxiously was gone. We lamented our loss with the pilots of the AN 74 briefly, and they agreed to make a return trip with more of the precious golden fluid.

Of course, every cloud has a silver lining, and in this case we found that Misha's centrifuge batteries had gone down in the bundle. This would make it impossible for him to prepare the blood samples, and everyone was overjoyed that we had a delay in the phlebotomy proceedings.

In an amazingly short time, the AN 74 returned and plopped two more lovely bundles, each consisting of three ten-litre canisters, into the middle of our campsite. In minutes, the freshly charged stoves were spluttering brightly under the pots, boiling up a restorative meal of macaroni and canned beef under the auspices of the Soviet doc. And, yes, to everyone's dismay, his batteries were included.

Following a suggestion of mine, we are embarking on an experiment which could radically alter life within the tent. We are going to try arraying ourselves radially for sleep purposes, with our feet in the middle, instead of in the traditional rows. I think the new method will eliminate the unpopular corner positions, and create a new sense of equality, in the true spirit of socialism. It will also mean fewer bodies to step on in the middle of the night when the old boys have to get up to piss.

We voted on trying the system for a few days, and even that minor break with tradition yielded a seven-six split, but here we are. This is our first group decision made by popular vote.

After a brief layabout in the snow house this afternoon, I returned to the main tent for a more extensive layabout. I haven't had a day like this in a long time – maybe ever. Gorge and doze, gorge and doze, all of us lying about uselessly, half in bed like a third-class male harem: concubines of a perverted ice-queen, waiting drone-like for her arrival.

Misha is going to take blood, and he expects me to help. I have misgivings about yielding up even one of my own corpuscles, let alone trying to harvest thirteen vacutainers from each of my teammates. The scientific program is legitimately a case of the tail wagging the dog. The reams of paper which constitute the "psychological assessments" we ridiculed so heartily back in Moscow appeared in one of our parachute bags, and Misha passed them around in all seriousness. One by one they were tossed back into the centre of the tent where they formed a neat pile in handy proximity to the stoves.

Misha has even brought along a portable cardiograph machine. I'm sure that if he had access to one, he'd be dragging a CT scanner too.

After breakfast, we set up the sauna. We cleared everything out of the tent except for Misha's pile of test tubes, which he was still busily centrifuging. We spread out the available sleeping pads on the floor and sparked up the stoves. Before long it really was warm enough to start peeling, and bundles of stinky clothing began to form piles between stinkier bodies. A pot of boiling water sat on one of the stoves in the middle of the tent, and from it we extracted "boil-in-a-bag" towels impregnated with antiseptic solution. Everybody had a good scrub down, then sponged off with dry towels. I'm sure we were just moving the dirt around, but it created at least a transient illusion of hygiene.

In conversation in the sauna our mathematicians pointed out that our average age was thirty eight, and our ages, totalled, equalled just over five hundred. I could see what Volodi meant every time he said, "We have much experience."

Misha and I took advantage of the exposed flesh to perform cursory physical evaluations of the gang, including skin-fold thick-nesses, weights (a set of throw-away bathroom scales had been included in one parachute bag, courtesy of Andy Rode), blood pres-sures, and more detailed assessment of any specific ailments. Holloway once again won the "Skinny Minnie" award for the thinnest skinfolds, with me and Fiodor close behind. It was not something to be particu-larly proud of in these circumstances, and we eyed up the voluptuous folds of Melnikov and Ledenov with some envy, realizing that their reserves might be what would ensure their ability to endure.

I had a grand conversation in French with Vasili tonight, which I felt was a bit of a breakthrough. He's generally not a real open kind of guy, and most of what I've heard him say has been monosyllabic. He related tales of his previous travels, told me about his wife and his home in Kazakhstan, and inquired about details of my life. We ended up singing "Alouette" together, to the awe and amazement of the other members. The singing was not good, but the mood was positive, and I think we all hit the sack feeling restored and optimistic.

Christopher

While we were having the sauna, the AN 74 buzzed the tent. We wern't expecting it, so Volodi and Vasa ran outside with their boots on and little else. I imagine it was a pretty funny sight. First of all, they come along and the whole camp is deserted because we are all in the tent, and then these two nude men start running around. We are amazingly clean. There is no dirt here at all. Generally, it is a sterile environment. There are no germs, except for the ones we brought in with us. There are no animals. And the best part about camping is there are no mosquitoes.

Yuri has given me his Navy belt. The buckle is the neat part – solid brass, and it has a star on the front. I had admired his belt in Dikson, and at that time he told me that if we made it to Ward Hunt Island he would give me this belt as a token of friendship, and as a measure of the way we have come together. He said, "I was hoping to make this a bit more symbolic, but, as a matter of necessity, I will have to give it to you now, because I don't want to carry it." So I said, "I symbolically accept it, and now that I have done so, it means that we have to make it to Ward Hunt Island."

We had quite a discussion this afternoon about speed. We have been averaging twenty kilometres per day, which is not too bad. We are now at 83 degrees, 1 minute, I believe. If we keep this up, we will make Ward Hunt Island in exactly one hundred days.

Laurie

Somebody, I have no idea who, phoned each of our wives and asked for a message to be recorded and sent it over to Moscow, from where it was sent in our airdrop. However, it was a very poor recording, and there was a lot of background noise on the tape. Suddenly, Sheena's voice started to come through, but obviously the recording had only picked up the tail end of the conversation. I just got a few sentences where she talked about Andrew going to the Arctic Winter Games, and then Alison came on and said, "Hi, Dad," and that was all. Even so, it was an incredible experience to sit here and to listen to their voices.

At times, this is a surrealistic situation. Here we are, miles from everywhere, probably the most isolated people in the world, and yet we have this amazing contact through the radio. And we have planes flying overhead. I certainly see the potential, now, for the expedition to be completed successfully, and personally, I know I will perform better if I can get over my two main injuries, a pulled shin and frozen hands. It's going to be a long and painful process, but hopefully by the next airdrop things will have recovered enough, and I will be in relative comfort.

Richard

Our first rest day. At the moment, we are sitting, eating supper. We had rice and canned meat, again, along with a bit of onions and cheese. It was quite good and then we had some cold chocolate milk, left over from lunch. Now we are eating, drinking tea. Everyone has a tube of honey, a cosmonaut tube of honey. The Soviets are eating it straight! I got mine in my pocket. I am not quite sure what to do with it. There is also a bowl of jam that they eat straight, too! – sort of a jam sandwich without the bread.

Earlier today we had a discussion with Yuri about diet. I said that I thought theirs was a very strange method: to lose weight like that, skiing, and then try to put it all back on again during two rest days. It is not really agreeing with me right now. I said that they eat too much sugar and too much salt, and I said that on the Steger expedition we had no sugar and no salt. We had more calories for the same weight. Yuri said, "Oh, we have to keep the proportions of carbohydrate, fat, and protein." I disagree there. I told him what we had done, and he said, "Oh, very strange for Soviets, very strange, that is all I can say." Not that I am advocating the Steger diet, but I think we can do a little better for all the food that we have.

In the big snow house that everyone built I put one Canadian stove and one Soviet stove. I set up a rack and started drying Chris's and my sleeping bags. It heats up the snow house a little bit, making it a bit more pleasant. We sat there and did chores. I made two straps to hold up my plastic bags on my feet, and organized my film. Eventually, we had to shut the whole system down when the snow house started to drip – it was getting too warm. But my bag is a hell of a lot dryer now. In fact, it is almost completely dry, except for the top section, which I haven't tried drying.

The reason, I believe, the Canadian stoves, the MSR stoves, haven't been working well is because the Soviet gas is not white gas. It is something else. Over a period of time, about fifteen minutes or so, the stoves start to block up, and eventually they just stop. *

Laurie wrote a very good article for *Komsomolskaya Pravda,* which will also be forwarded to Canada. It is not at all what I would write; it was kind of flowery, but just what they are looking for. He talked a little bit about the good qualities of every member on the team. Actually, I am quite surprised. He is really a good writer.

MARCH 16. DAY 14

Christopher

Here's a description of what I do in a day – and night.

---

* Because our fuel was lost down the lead, they had to take what they could find in Sredny. The replacement fuel was mixed gas, containing oil. That is why it blocked the stoves. This we found out later.

During the night I have to wake up every time I want to turn over. Generally, my hands and feet are numb, either because they are in an uncomfortable position, or because they are cold. I sleep with my mitts on. (I haven't taken my polar suit off for the past six days.) Every time I turn over, the leaves of frost that have formed on the sleeping bag, above my face around the drawstringed hood, fall onto my face.

Then someone comes out and tells us to "stand up," which is what the Soviets say for get up. They repeat this until we convince them that we are actually getting up. I have to work the zipper on my bag back and forth several times before I can get it open. At this point I usually have a wave of panic about being frozen into my sleeping bag. Then the zippers open, the panic vanishes, I put my boots on, and sprint into the tent for breakfast.

Richard and I have been having a rough time trying to find a place to sit in the tent for meals. However, we have become pushy, and have been able to squirm our way in. I usually end up in the middle of the tent and have to distribute spoons and bowls. Then we have breakfast, which consists of muesli, milk, butter, and dried meat. After this, we have some tea.

When it is time to get moving, we spend twenty to thirty minutes brushing out our sleeping bags and trying to get them rolled up. This is quite an ordeal. All the ice that has formed on the sleeping bag has frozen solid, and it takes quite a whacking to get it out. Then I try and roll it up. On at least three occasions it has taken me three tries to get it rolled small enough to fit into its carrying bag. By the time I get it rolled up and in the bag my hands are freezing, because I have to do all this with my gloves on, because with mittens it is too difficult.

Then we take down the tent. The person on duty has packed up all the utensils, bowls, etc., and has given the big pots and stoves back to those who are carrying them. The tent comes down and then we do a two-step dance on it to get all the ice out of it. There are three parts to the tent: the outer orange layer, and an inner frost lining, and the floor, which is made out of Tyvek (Laurie had this made for us). And then there is the frame made of the skis, and the roof framework, which Fiodor carries. I have been carrying fat and galettes for the past ten days, so in the morning I distribute the day's ration of fat to each person. Actually it is half fat and half raw pork. Don't know about the trichinosis factor, but we eat it anyway.

I have to repack my backpack every morning, because the heavy stuff like gas and fat has to go at the bottom of the bag. We finish packing and try to leave around 8:00 a.m., but it's usually around 8:20 by the time we leave. Richard and I use our snow house as an outhouse before we leave. It is very tricky to time when to take off my big jacket and overboots to start skiing, because I don't want to stand about waiting in thin travelling clothes. Then we start skiing.

For most of the skiing time, we have to come up with things to occupy our minds. Singing songs is a popular pastime. Richard has been stuck on *The Sound of Music* for some days. Whatever pops into our heads. Richard said he had learnt during the Steger expedition that the secret to passing time is just to free associate and let things wander in and out of our minds. Before we know it, another fifty minutes are up, and it's time for a break again.

Then we ski on and on. Lunch comes along. The sun is at its highest around 12:30. For the last two hours it is really sunset. When we camp, it's starting to get grey and the light is fading.

To set up the tent, Fiodor puts the upper ring frame together and then stands with it over his head, and then the skis are jammed into the snow and fitted into the frame. Then the material is put over the tent frame. Then snow is shovelled onto the edges to anchor it. It has a few guy lines. If there is a wind, a small wall is built around the wind-ward side, just to protect the tent a bit. At this point the person on duty is inside starting to melt snow for dinner. Snow blocks are cut for water and placed near the door of the tent.

At this point I start building my snow house, which usually takes about an hour. I find a nice hard drift that I can walk on and that doesn't sound hollow. A hollow sound means unpacked snow beneath. I then begin cutting blocks from the drift, resulting in a trench. These blocks are usually about four by one and a half feet and eight inches thick; just big enough to make an "A" frame over the trench. Afterwards the cracks between the blocks have to be filled with loose snow from the outside. The maximum width for this design is about five feet, just right for two people. If we get company, we'll have to master the conventional igloo design.

By this time dinner is ready. On cold days, we have hot milk first, and then it is another hour before dinner, because we have to melt more snow for the kasha. Then we elbow our way into the tent and find a spot. Usually, there are garlic and spices in the kasha. During dinner I take off my thick Chlorophylle socks and put them inside my jacket.

Then I turn the thin socks and the plastic bags inside out so the next day the dry side will be next to my skin. I put these in the pocket of my jacket, and then the thin Chlorophylle socks I put back on my feet, because I wear those to bed.

It's necessary to keep track of absolutely everything. It is difficult to lose things, but things can be misplaced. Misplacing gloves, for example, can be rather critical, Generally, I open my suit and put my hat and gloves in my jacket. Being in a cold environment teaches patience and organization. Patience, for one, because it's no good trying to hurry anything along. When my hands are cold, I have to work on them until they are warm again, and then go back to what I was doing. Organization, because the longer it takes to find things, the colder I get. These are lessons that teach themselves very quickly, although some people are quicker to learn than others. That is related directly, I think, to the amount of frost-bite that they have.

Richard

We had a discussion on boats. They want to keep just the small boat, not take the big boat any farther. That sounds good to me. The big boat is twelve kilograms. It is quite a heavy thing to carry, whereas the small boat is only about two kilograms. We can only put one person or one backpack in it at a time. We can only jump narrow leads with it. I think a hundred metres is the maximum we can handle with it, but that would take care of most situations.

Laurie is giving blood and doing his psychological test because he always does what the group does, or what he is told to do. Laurie apparently said, "By the time we reach the North Pole, he would either be a good communist or they would all be Christians." Well, I think he is well en route to becoming a good communist, because he says yes to absolutely everything they say. The worst part is that the other guys, the Soviet guys, all agree with me, but they do what they are told.

The temperature today was in the upper minus thirties. There was a bit of wind, so it is still quite nippy out. But very slowly it is warming up. It is certainly warmer than it was ten days ago when it was minus 47. It is no longer dark out even in the middle of the night. Now it is 9:30 p.m. and it is still quite light. It never gets completely dark any more. But the sun doesn't get up very high above the horizon or very strong. I was outside, and I could just about read a book even though it is ten o'clock – there is still a bit of a red glow in the sky. In two and a half hours the sun will start coming back up again.

MARCH 17. DAY 15

Max

The last remnants of the campsite were gathered together in a heap, and anything that would burn was doused in gasoline and torched. Surplus food was picked over, and odd morsels of meat or condensed milk were sautéed "*en canette*" in the flames of the garbage-que. Richard and Chris snuck off with some of the cans of condensed milk and were having a clandestine feed of their own inside the snow house, which I stumbled upon and blackmailed them into letting me join.

Christopher

Finally, around two o'clock, it was time to go. We weighed our packs on the bathroom scales that we had flown in. Max's weighed 47 kg, and Fiodor's weighed 50 kg. Mine weighed 40 kg. This was without things like my camera equipment and my big parka. It was okay until I put it on. It was really heavy. After four hours, I was really having problems. I was sure that my pack was more than 50 kg. I went up to Sasha and made sure that I didn't have any more food than I was supposed to. I had to keep on stopping because my legs were seizing up. The extra straps I had put on the shoulders were very nice but didn't help my legs any. I thought of famous sayings from Pia. "You know you are just as strong as the rest. If you can't keep up, then obviously your pack is heavy."

After the second break, Dmitri picked it up and said, "This is not 50 kg, this is fine." I traded with Mish for a while, and he said, "This feels like normal weight." And he seemed to ski with it very well. Pia would say to me, "If it isn't the pack, since everyone else says it's normal weight, then it's you just making this up and talking yourself into making it heavy. So obviously you can handle it. You'll just have to work harder at it, and you'll manage." So, I worked harder at it, although I wasn't very pleased about the situation. I couldn't even keep up to Yuri. I guess this was divine retribution after being so nasty to

Laurie. I now am in the same situation he was in last week.

The first time Misha came alongside me I had an argument with him. I told him that I didn't like the reason for carrying the extra skis. He was really very good about the whole thing. I was quite impressed. Apparently, because of our complaints, they left behind the electrocardiogram. After the second or third hour, I apologized for being in such a bad mood. He said that it was understandable and not to worry about it. About ten minutes after that, he skied up beside me and said that in the airdrop he had been given some chocolate, and perhaps if I ate some this would make my load lighter.

I've never seen Misha mad at anything. He's very smart and knows how to deal with people, especially grumpy ones with heavy packs. In fact, his chocolate did make my load lighter. The crunch came when Laurie came and offered me half a Shaklee bar and said that his pack was feeling pretty good. He is carrying half his weight in a sled, like Mish, and is keeping up pretty well. He said he could easily take a couple more kilos from me, if I needed help. I thought to myself, "Things are really getting bad when Laurie starts to offer me help." I was quite impressed by his offer, considering how nasty we have been to him for being slow.

Laurie

Leaving our camp, we all had huge loads, most bigger than what we set out with from Cape Arkticheskiy. Max, for example, reckons that he has close to 50 kg. Even Chris, the largest of the Canadians, is finding it difficult, and was lagging farther and farther behind during each march. Part of the problem is that we all have our original personal equipment, with the addition, now, of more that came in the airdrop. Our clothing is also damper, and thus heavier than when we started. Most of the extra weight is due to the fact that we are now going to be travelling for a couple of days longer without a resupply than we were doing at the beginning.

Richard

What I am wearing now is: starting on the inside, Thermax underwear, polypropylene shirt, Chlorophylle polar suit; on my feet I have plastic bags, the "kitchen catchers," heavy wool socks from Wigwam, and three Chlorophylle socks and my kamiks. My feet today were just toasty. Just like when I am running in the summer on a hot day and my feet are just burning. Well, mine were just burning. In the summer it is not so nice, but up here it is just great! The unfortunate thing is that I actually wore through my plastic bag. It is a little disturbing. I am not quite sure what happened. I will try again tomorrow and see what happens.

We heard on the radio this evening that there are three other expeditions starting from Canada and going to the Pole. There is Ranulph Fiennes who just started today. He sent good luck wishes to us. There is Pam Flowers who has already started with three dogs. She should do well. I wish her good luck. Then, apparently, there is an Austrian fellow who is starting 350 kilometres southwest of Ward Hunt Island . . . perhaps Eureka.

Apparently, the bets in Resolute Bay are putting the money on us. Each man with Ranulph Fiennes has 350 pounds, and they expect to get to the Pole two weeks before us! I think they are dreaming. Personally, I just can't imagine pulling 350 pounds, especially through the rough ice at the beginning.

MARCH 18. DAY 16

Max

Today was a bitch. Most of the crew skims along with the usual effort, but Holloway and I are lagging.

Nature's high point for the day was a partial solar eclipse. I don't know if this was predicted – I certainly wasn't expecting it – but between 10:00 and 10:30 a.m. Dikson time there was a well-demarcated bite out of the left lower quadrant of the sun.

After dinner tonight, Richard and Yuri had a long discussion about the merits of Soviet dried meat and butter versus pemmican. We got more of the former and less of the latter in the last resupply, and Richard charged that what had been purported to be a "mistake" had been conspired by Yuri and Sasha. Yuri doesn't like the recognizable organ bits, and thinks that pemmican contains excessive water because it gets hard at minus 45. Even the choice of food is a matter of pride, for both sides. There are vindictive mumblings about how things will change when resupply is conducted from the Canadian side: "No more of this Russian dogfood mystery meat." If something as simple as menu can divide our camp, how can we expect to boost each other across this formidable ocean?

Laurie

We did eight marches today, which, I must admit, took us a little by surprise. In the past, the Soviets always said that for the first two days after an airdrop we would do seven hours, next two days eight hours, and then, if conditions were right, increase it to nine, but today we plunged straight into a full eight-hour day. While I feel there is potential in the sled system, as I mentioned already, I am not fully convinced it is going to work out.

For the first half of the day, I found that I was never too far behind the leaders, but after the coffee break after the fourth march, somehow I managed to get behind, and, at the next break, took off my pack, sat down, and immmediately it was announced, "Two minutes to go." So, I got up again, put it on, tried to keep up with the front, and soon found that I missed that little rest, and was getting farther and farther behind. For the next march, when I caught up to the leaders for the ten-minute break, I was so far behind that I only got a couple of minutes again, and after the next march, the second-last of the day, I didn't even stop. I just caught up with the leaders, walked through, and kept going.

Richard

Laurie did much better today. He has a little sled like Misha, in which he has about 15 kg, or so. This is fine, except that when he gets stuck, he really gets stuck. Fortunately, Toli Fedjakov. follows along behind him, and pulls the sled out whenever it gets stuck. The Soviets had a great joke, calling him the "Dexter Express" because he didn't stop for some of the rest breaks, just kept on skiing through.

This evening, Sasha and Yuri have substituted a package of dry meat for a package of pemmican, and whatever else, more butter, more milk. Yuri thinks that dry milk, butter, and dry meat is better than pemmican, and that it has more calories, and he said, "I will prove it to you," and he brought out a paper from Mike Rowlands at Shaklee. It was an analysis of the pemmican based on a list of ingredients that I had given Mike Rowlands. That list had been an estimate quoted from memory. Then Mike had extrapolated and made some substitutions. Here was Yuri, taking it as the gospel truth.

Vasa interjected, "Oh, why don't we just throw out all the pemmican, just use dry meat and butter." That demonstrates their idea of a "joint expedition."

MARCH 19. DAY 17

Laurie

During the day, as I was marching head down, my vision limited by my hood, I kept thinking someone was overtaking me, or travelling parallel. But it was an optical deception. Each time I looked up I discovered it was just a chunk of ice. Maybe the pattern of the surface is changing, with longer stretches of flatter ice, so that spikes sticking up are more eye-catching.

Richard

Misha called me to the back of the line and said, "Richard, I have to tell you something. I hope you don't take this badly, but it is very serious." In Dikson I received a cake from Josée. I put it into my personal bag that I was to receive in the first airdrop, and then I ate it at my lunch breaks. Everyone saw me eating. I figured that was fine, it was my cake, she made it for me. She *didn't* make it for anyone else. So I ate it, and gave Chris some because I knew he would give me some chocolate in return, so I thought that wasn't a bad deal. Yes, he did give me some chocolates.

Misha said all the Soviets thought this was very bad. "If I had a cake from my wife I would share it with everyone." He thought they might go so far as to write about it in the newspaper – I can't believe it.

MARCH 20. DAY 18

Max

We continue to slug it out. Despite the slight reduction in pack weight, everyone was wiped out by the end of the day. The temperature was minus 34, and with no wind, travelling conditions were as good as one could hope for. The sun still hangs impotently in the southern sky, but with tomorrow being the spring equinox, we certainly have all the light we need.

Physically, no one has sustained injuries that are slowing our progress. Laurie's leg has recovered miraculously, and he cruises along comfortably with the lead group now.

My conscious energy today was expended on thoughts of immediate physical discomfort, and psychic flight therefrom. I mentally identified each of the upcoming "pleasure points" in my life: the point at which I would take my next break and let my pack fall to the ground, followed by the somewhat greater joy of sacking out for the night, the even greater pleasure of the next rest days, the arrival at the Pole, and, ultimately, the homecoming and reunion with Nancy after four months. I thought about the first Niagara peach of summer, still warm off the limb, sliding obscenely over my tongue. A wave of feeling overcame me as an image of my mother formed in my mind's eye.

Christopher

We skied for nine hours, and today went very well. After the seventh hour, when we had our break, I fell asleep on top of my pack, and started dreaming that I was in Venice, being offered canal tours by female gondoliers. Then I heard Vasa say, "One minute left," and it was time to go again. I didn't know I could fall asleep quite so soundly, so quickly.

After dinner, Sasha got out the radio, and managed to find some American station, which was playing "Bridge over Troubled Water." I thought that this was very appropriate for our setting.

The ends of Laurie's fingers look like he's burnt them on a stove element. Richard burnt himself when he was on duty, both last night and this morning. In addition, he's tired and is fighting off a cold. Max seems to have had trouble getting through ice ridges and other things for the past several days. He doesn't seem to be able to move himself like he used to. Laurie, on the other hand, has really picked up. Today there were a few marches when he was never more than fifth from the front, which is quite an improvement.

Richard

Today was positively a shitty day. If expeditions were always like this I wouldn't do any. I don't know what happened, whether it is because I was on duty and missed some sleep, and that I have a cold still, or who knows what. But I just had *no* strength whatsoever. We went on and on, nine marches.

I was at the end of the line. I could hardly keep up with Yuri. That is getting pretty bad. There is something seriously wrong. So I thought about Josée, and that gave me strength. I know there are lots of people, everyone else cheering for us. Parents and Peter, and Danièle and Paul, and everyone else. Josée, she never wanted this expedition. She doesn't even like the bloody thing. All it does is take me away, sends my interests and ideas elsewhere, away from hers. I know she is cheering for me hardest of all. That sort of made me feel good, and I could think about that, and it kept me going. I thought about the things she would tell me when I wanted to go out training, and I would say, "Oh, I am gonna get out of shape." She would reply, "You will do just fine, you will ski out there even if you ski till you drop, you'll do it. You'll do just fine. Don't worry."

At the end I really thought I was going to lose consciousness and collapse during the last fifteen to twenty minutes. It was just terrible. And then I helped Holloway build our snow house. After dinner I went out to go to bed and there was no room in it. So there I was standing in the middle of the Arctic Ocean with no room at the inn. I was so mad that I almost made a new door through the roof. Then I remembered that Christopher and Fiodor both have reactive tempers that do not like being woken up, and I decided to sleep on the ice. So now I am in my sleeping bag directly on the ice out in the open. I have put my jacket over my feet, and I made a little tripod with two poles and a ski, and I put some windbreakers over it, and even though it is minus 35 out I should still probably be okay.

At least Mother Nature was kind to me today. The ice was basically flat all day. We went straight north, only a few pressure ridges now and then. Today, we probably did our biggest mileage. We did 13 minutes yesterday, which means that if we can do about 12 minutes a day, that means about five days per degree. It means we would get to Canada about the fifth of June, at the present rate.

Vasa is a pretty good guy. He saw I was having a rough day, and he says, "The day after your duty is always bad." Apparently, the third and fourth days are always the worst after an airdrop. I picked not only the worst day; it was also a day after duty day. We also marched very consistently today – fifty minutes on, ten minutes off, quite regularly, with no stops for waiting for anyone or anything.

We had one Soviet plane fly over us today – circled a few times, and then went away. A twin-engine aircraft, sort of like a 748 – same sort of deal. I guess they are reconnaissance planes. Vasa tried to talk to them on the radio.

MARCH 21. DAY 19

Christopher

An hour after our lunch stop, Dmitri announced that it was 84 degrees. So everyone whipped out their cameras, and we ended up with equal numbers of people posing and taking pictures. It took an awful lot of shouting and yelling to get everyone to stand in one place so we could use the timers on the cameras.

Volodi said that what he would like for the next airdrop is Red Zinger tea and *Playboy* magazine. So Richard said no problem, you can have it. Front page, *Toronto Star*: "Soviets Demand *Playboy* Magazine." One of the Russians told us that one of his fine pleasures in life is to take "young women" into the country. It was quite clear from his implications that they weren't going to talk about the Five Year Plan. We said, "This is disgusting! You're a married man."

We asked him, "Well, what does your wife do?" and he replied, "Oh, she cooks." He said, "Well, don't you like young girls?" Richard said, "I have my wife," and he said, "Yes, but young girls, young girls." Richard said, "I married a young girl, she is only twenty-five, she is very good-looking, and I have no need to go running after anybody else." He said, "Well, when you come to Moscow we will fix you up with something." Well, I really don't think I need that.

Richard

When we started out this morning, I remembered that yesterday I had not been feeling well – poorly, to say the least. I thought that maybe I should at least take it easy in the beginning and see how it goes. So I saw Toli Melnikov heading off, and I thought I would just follow him for a while. So I started off after Toli, and, to my horror, found I couldn't even follow him. From there, things just went downhill. By the third rest break, I just plunked down on the snow, lying on my backpack without even taking it off. I put my hat over my face, and went to sleep for ten minutes. Towards the end of the fourth march, Dmitri came to me and said, "Well, would you like that we stop after this march, put up the tent, have some hot milk, and then we can take some of your weight from your pack and keep going?" I said, "No, that's fine, you don't have to do that for me. I will be okay." He did it anyway.

We listened to CBC on the radio. Just the tail end of the news, which is kind of neat. We found that the dollar had gone above eighty cents U.S. and Canadian skiers had come sixth and ninth in a World Cup downhill event. With a few kilos less in my pack, and a short rest, I felt a lot better.

Laurie has been doing very well the last couple of days. Indeed, this morning, I couldn't even keep up with him. He is no Speedy Gonzales, but he moves along, and he is not holding up the expedition. So, I would now like him to stay, whereas before I wanted to see him go. I will tell him that the worst is really over, and that it would be a real shame if he left now. Politically, it is always better if there are four of us instead of three of us.

Volodi wants to do 15 minutes of latitude per day now, for the next eight days, and cover 2 degrees. He is worried that Pam Flowers might beat us to the North Pole! He is a great little guy, but he is so fixed in his ways. He doesn't like to change anything, no way, he just doesn't like anything to change. He is the most conservative of all the Soviets. He says that if a woman beats him to the North Pole his wife will say he is a bad man. Especially a woman with dogs. Oh dear!

Apparently the Austrians that were going to the North Pole have already given up. They have suffered a lot of frost-bite. So that leaves Fiennes, ourselves, and Pam Flowers. Three groups. All are experienced expeditioners; no one is going to the Pole for the first time.

MARCH 22. DAY 20

Laurie

Since the last airdrop, I am now often with the leading group. Richard has had a cold for quite some time now, especially troublesome over the last two or three days. He felt very weak. Max has got a big blister on his heel, plus being concerned about his big toe that froze, so he was struggling a bit during the day as well. Other people also have things wrong with them. Yesterday, Dmitri froze a toe, and during the stop for milk Misha was working on it to try and restore circulation. Various people have blisters. Sasha, for example, has blisters on his feet, and other people have frost-bite. So there is now a bunch of them finding it difficult to keep up, instead of just one like myself during the first week.

All the men have frost-bite in varying degrees on their faces, cheeks, and chins, and some have frost-bitten toes and fingertips. I guess I am the one who has got the worst fingers. So, when we set out this morning, strong members like Richard were lagging behind, and at the rest stops they were just lying flat out on their backs. Max was struggling so much with his blister that part of his load was shared out. Some others took part of Richard's load as well. When this happened to me for that one afternoon early on I felt really bad about it. But since then others have had to be helped in a similar way. Because I was the first, it seemed to be a bigger deal than it was.

At one point during the day, Vasili came and swapped skis with me. It convinced me that the Soviet skis are easier in these conditions where I am not using my poles very much. Tomorrow I should switch back to Soviet skis. I am also trying another experiment. I don't think I need the sleeping pad underneath me. Most of the other people don't have one. For tonight, I will put the sleeping pad between the two top layers of my bag, which means I have a solid sheet of insulation above me.

Richard

It seems that I have a new name here. It is Mr. President, as the president of Polar Bridge Inc. The Soviets started to call me Mr. President, and now just about everybody calls me Mr. President. I am not sure at all that I like it.

MARCH 23. DAY 21

Max

Fiodor and I spent a rather chilly night in our snow house, owing to a rising wind that sent curls of sandy snow dancing between the snow blocks. We responded sluggishly to our breakfast call and, when we finally made it into the tent, we were met with a mixed bag of news. First, despite travelling for only eight hours, we logged an impressive twenty-eight kilometres, presumably because of positive drift. Messages were relayed by radio from both Nancy and my mother, which gave my spirits wings. The content was minimal, but I didn't care.

The headwind was only a few kilometres per hour when we set out, but rose to about forty by the end of the day. My foot hurt like hell. I fear that the footprints I leave on the sands of time may be short a few toes. My guts churned and burned all day. I must be developing an ulcer.

Living inside layers of Goretex, as we must do in these conditions, results in some pretty severe introspection. I can see nothing more than the rhythmic thrusts of my ski tips most of the time. Looking up for more than a split second is tempting the wind to freeze my corneas, or at least my eyelashes. What seems like conflict revolves through my mind repeatedly, until it finally becomes clear that there really is no conflict – only resolution. There is no choice to be made, thus no basis for conflict. One foot, then the next, hopefully in rapid enough sequence that a decision is not required for each step. Keep the feet in gear, try to remove the mind to somewhere else, and hope for my body's sake that things get better soon.

Laurie

I find it hard to believe the things that have happened over the last few hours. I had the usual evening radio schedule, and there were personal messages for everybody, all with lots of humour and good wishes.

Last of all, I also received a message from Sheena to say that my Dad passed away on Saturday, and was being buried today, Wednesday. There is nothing I can say at this point. External conditions are bad enough just now, and, of course, this adds to my own personal burden. I loved my Dad. I respected him and often sought his opinion on things, and I feel devastated on behalf of my Mum and Anne (my sister), who was apparently with them for the last three weeks, and for Sheena with the children. It's on an occasion like this that I realize how terribly committed we are to this expedition. There is no way out no matter what happens. No matter how bad things get, we are here, dependent upon each other for our survival, dependent upon our skills to get us through everything, because there is no way out.

I don't feel most of the others have this awareness, but I may be wrong. I feel that for the most part they are individuals who happen to be travelling together, but with little commitment to each other. Again, I may be wrong, but I feel this is particularly true for the Canadian members. In my grief, I realize how dependent we are on each other, and how crucial team work and mutual concern and support are for our eventual success, but there is no one I can talk to. We are workmates, a team of skilled athletes, but we are not buddies. We are friendly, but not real friends.

One of the unexpected things after hearing the news about my Dad last night: I actually had my best night's sleep so far. I think because I was warm for the first time in ages; and tonight, as I record in my bag, I'm reasonably warm again. I think I will continue using this system, taking the pad from underneath, and putting it between the two tops, but actually, I don't think it's good for the bag. The top of my bag is little more now than a few layers of nylon fabric, with fist-sized or smaller lumps of frozen down scattered along the edges!

I find I am losing perspective on time and distance. I just seem to exist from hour to hour. During the day the object is just to complete the next march, and during the night the object is to get one more hour's sleep. Occasionally, when I am carrying the pack, I hardly dare let myself think about our objectives, such as the Pole itself. It seems so far away. Right now all I'm trying to do is keep positive until the next airdrop, which is only six days away, but how my heart goes out to my loved ones at this time. It is hard to perform well under such mental and emotional duress, but I am trying to maintain a healthy outlook. I did tell Max and Dmitri about my Dad having died, so no doubt the word will get around.

Richard

Now it has been three weeks. We are almost a quarter of the way through, time-wise and distance-wise. I noticed that my sleeping bag is starting to smell a bit. A sure sign of time gone by, and the weather warming up.

Today we covered an amazing 15 minutes latitude. That must include about 2 minutes of drift or so. Apparently, there is a Soviet ice station that is not too far from us, on the same latitude, and they have drifted 1 1/2 to 2 minutes. Today it was windy, so it was horrible skiing – straight into our faces at about ten metres per second, which normally is not that windy, about thirty-five kilometres an hour, but when it is 33° below it is kind of nasty. Definitely a day for the face mask.

MARCH 24. DAY 22

Christopher

There was a hole in the snow house above Richard last night, and by the morning he was completely covered in snow. Nobody is in a terrible hurry to move this morning, because the weather is so bad.

The tent is flapping in the wind. When I breathe out, my breath moves with the wind, and I can see it make violent zigzags across the tent. All the knapsacks have horseshoe-shaped drifts around them about one and a half feet high. However, the ice hasn't melted underneath us, and we haven't been hit by lightning, so eight hours of skiing it is. It is one of those days when it is doubtful how much we are going to get out of this for the energy we expend.

The first hour was awful conditions. There was a head wind of forty-two kilometres per hour. I was five feet away from the person in front of me, and his tracks were disappearing. The temperature was minus 33°C. Dmitri didn't screw the lid properly on some of the thermoses when he filled them this morning, and as a result, some of the coffee ended up on my red Goretex wind jacket. Fortunately, the only result was that my pocket filled up with coffee, which froze, and then I had to chip this frozen lump of ice out of my pocket.

I was talking to Max and Laurie at dinner about sending messages home, which I haven't done much of. Actually, I do think of Pia an awful lot. I said that I was going to send one to my father, saying that I was being treated a lot better than he was in Poland. (My father was a Soviet prisoner of war in the Second World War.) I thought that was kind of funny, but then Max said, "Do you really think we're better off?" I said honestly that I thought it was pretty good here. The skiing is good, I sleep well at night, we're not starving; in fact, except for the frost-bite, things are going pretty well, and I was having a good time. Max gave me this sour look in response. I guess when every step causes you pain it changes your perspective.

Max

We inched along, leaning at about forty-five degrees into the wind. It was from due north; we just turned our faces to the most painful orientation and marched on.

At the first rest stop Toli M. appeared carrying two packs, with Dmitri limping along behind. He described having wrenched his ankle while crossing a pressure ridge, and it seemed like a good opportunity to set up the tent for an assessment of the injury. I dug into my pack for my thermos and found that it had leaked its entire precious warm contents through my clothing, my harmonica, and even my tape recorder. Richard's had done the same. Misha and I both had a chance to examine the afflicted foot, which didn't appear either swollen or tender. I suggested we ice the injury, given the availability of the materials required, but Misha felt that might increase the risk of circulatory impairment to the rest of the foot, and I could see his point.

While all this was going on, Richard was diddling with one of the MSR stoves, trying to generate a little more heat. It was spluttering inefficiently, so he picked it up and started pumping it in the middle of the tent. Suddenly, a jet of flame shot from the burner and seared eyebrows and beards off at least three faces before he pitched it at the tent door. The latter vaporized instantly and took a good bit of the surrounding tent and liner with it. Smoke from the burnt nylon and hair was soon dissipated by the tempest raging through the smouldering hole. Mercifully, no one was hurt, and Vasa and Volodi were able to refabricate a door over the following couple of hours with an extra vapour-barrier liner donated by Laurie. It was obvious that this day was never meant to be, so we decided to delete it from the calendar.

Laurie

I really have not been able to mourn at all. It's not a case of control or discipline, it's just a matter of struggling so much for survival that I haven't had the emotional surplus in order to go through the grief process. When I heard the news, it wasn't unexpected. Strangely enough, I slept well after it; and again last night, because I was warm, I slept well again. I have tried to pray for everybody, I have tried to think about things, but I have had no chance really to express any of my feelings. I don't know how many times I have wondered just how much combined physical and emotional stress a person can bear, but, of course, in my case there is no option.

I don't think we did much more than a couple of kilometres or so today. We are really going to have to push hard over the next four days, assuming that Dmitri is able to do so, and also assuming that the weather allows us. We really shouldn't have been travelling today, and, as the Canadian members thought, were asking for trouble.

MARCH 25. DAY 23

Max

The most discouraging news of our unscheduled rest stop came this morning when we got our co-ordinates. Our lack of activity, combined with severe backdrift from the north wind, left us over five kilometres farther south than when we had started two mornings earlier. Damn nature anyway.

With the weary rested and the wounded bandaged, we again headed off into a horrendous head wind, but shortly after setting out the sun burst through, the wind subsided, and we were left with the most pleasant ski day so far. The Goretex lids came down, and Holloway and I had a grand old chat skiing along side by side. This was the first time we had been able to communicate on the trail, and the diversion made the hours fly by.

Christopher

I just want to describe the scene in the tent.

I am sitting in the middle, in my Goretex pants, so I don't get wet from the sleeping bags. Everyone has a bowl in his lap with a cup in it, because the cups have started leaking. Toli Fedjakov is playing with the radio. Everyone is sitting up in his sleeping bag with his feet pointing into the centre. Yuri has a very nice angora wool sweater on, which must weigh a ton because it is caked with ice and frost. Most have sweaters of some kind on.

It is minus 38° outside, with a slight wind. The Soviets are going on and on in Russian. Every now and again we hear words like "peanut butter" and "Pam Flowers." An assortment of dead animals is hanging from the roof – fur hats mainly, face masks, scarves, socks also. Misha and Max usually take this time to dispense various medicines – creams, pills, etc.

Toli asks each person if he wants more coffee, and they all say no. Then he says, "That's too bad. There's only a little bit left." And then all these cups are thrust forward, and voices say, "Oh, I'll have some." Then after the coffee is finished the vitamins are passed around, and we all complain about not having anything to wash them down with.

Richard

Last night I decided to sleep in the main tent. I thought that I would try to be more sociable. I suggested it to Chris, as I thought it might be politically a nice gesture, but he says he doesn't like sleeping so close to so many people. It turned out to be a big mistake. During dinner, frost kept falling off the tent into my bag. This morning it rained on my sleeping bag, but the worst was when I awoke in the night. My feet were jammed tight amongst the others' feet and no matter how hard I pushed, I couldn't straighten them out. I do not feel any more or less part of the group because I slept inside. Indeed just sitting here and listening, I think our little experiment in social integration is failing. The conversation is entirely in Russian; only a tiny bit of it gets translated into English, really not very much. Maybe we will end up working together as a team because we have the common goal of reaching Ward Hunt Island, but we will never really be a team. I think there will always be an "us" and a "them."

We have failed to learn Russian, and most of them have really failed to learn English, except Misha, and perhaps Dmitri has a smattering of English. We have nothing but a smattering of Russian, so we can communicate if we have to, but we can't sit and chit-chat. So the chit-chat goes on in Russian because there are more than twice as many of them as of us. We just sit here in silence.

Today we had a further argument about Canadian muesli. They

now claim there are no calories in muesli, that the carbohydrates have been removed, and that the Soviet guys are hungry very soon after breakfast, but if they ate rough oats, ordinary porridge, this would not be so.

Dmitri hurt himself yesterday, and today he was going to have less weight in his backpack, and he wanted someone to ski close to him in case he needed some help. Chris chirped up and said, "Oh, I'll do it," and they laughed at him. You can't have a Canadian doing anything serious, you know. So they got Misha to do that, and Toli Melnikov to ski last. As one of the weakest skiers, he is not the best candidate for the anchor position.

MARCH 26. DAY 24

Christopher

I am going to have one hundred grams of peanut butter a day in the next set of marches. I am going to carry the extra. I am also going to "steal" some butter in the rest break. (The Soviets do not approve of picking up excess food from the resupply and keeping it.) I figure that I can carry a personal supply of two kilograms of food to compensate for the negative caloric balance of our diet. More than that weight would start to slow me down. Sasha came up with this claim that pemmican is 20 per cent water. Sasha's head, on the other hand, is 20 per cent air.

Richard

Yesterday we heard that the Austrians have dropped out of the race to the Pole, and that it has hit Pam Flowers rather hard because she was to be splitting resupply charters with them. We heard today that her camp got attacked by a polar bear, and the tent got ripped. And she lost her glasses, so she is going to stop. She is waiting for a pick-up by plane. Fiennes is badly frost-bitten, and is also waiting for pick-up by the same plane as Flowers. This takes us from four groups to just us on the ice now. It will be a lonely year at the Pole.

We are tired because we are now towards the end of this leg of the expedition. We will soon have an airdrop and a rest. We are hungry because we have been underfed for the past two weeks. I even ate my bacon fat for the first time. All these factors really add up when the weather gets cold. Fortunately, the skiing was pretty good. The sun came out quite strongly, strong enough that I could actually feel it on my face if I turned into it with my eyes shut. This was the first time, so it is a good sign. The wind dropped right off towards the end of the day.

MARCH 27. DAY 25

Max

Leaning into the gale march after march, dragging my deadened toes beneath the symbolic existential burden, I realized that I was probably experiencing suffering for the first time in my life. I wasn't thinking then of how expanding the experience would be, or how my character would profit. My mind was playing games of escape. Summer time, flowers and trees, and the glorious weightlessness of swimming. I felt like an insect that had flown inadvertently out to sea where it could only perish. I needed to get back to where humans normally live, and do human things.

Richard

A cold, nasty day, minus 45 this morning, but the wind has swung around to the south, which means it is pushing us north. So, actually, it is quite warm skiing. It is just when you stop that it is really nasty.

We received good news on the radio: we are at 85 degrees even, which is great. It means we went 17 minutes in the last twenty-four hours. We only walked eight hours today, which means we are drifting – that is due to the wind, of course. It means we are probably drifting 3 or 4 minutes a day.

Today was the first time I have really felt good since I have been sick. When I first got sick I could only keep up with the slowest. And I was wondering, Am I sick! Am I wimping out? Am I psychologically backing down? What is going on? I questioned myself a lot as to whether it was all in my head and I was imagining it, or whether there really was something physically wrong. I didn't actually feel all that bad, but I just couldn't ski, I felt so weak. Eventually it became clear that I was sick.

Slowly, my body is trying to rebound, bounce back. Every day it is trying to get better, but every day I beat it back down by skiing ten hours, not feeding it enough, and not sleeping enough. My body is fighting back, and I am just knocking it back down every day with a shortage of sleep, food, and too much exercise. But today I felt good.

Then we came across the most bizarre thing I have ever seen. A log. Vasa, Volodi, and I were standing there, and I looked ahead, and I thought I saw something, but what the hell could be out there? There is nothing out here. If you want a place that is devoid of all life, then this is where you come. Occasionally, we hear an airplane in the distance, but apart from that there are no bugs or birds or animals – there is nothing. But this time, there was something out there on the horizon. I didn't say anything because my eyesight is not all that good anyway, but they seemed to see something too, so all three of us marched side by side up to it without saying a word. It was a log. A tree. A large spruce log or pine or something, sticking out of a pressure ridge. Vasa took out the snow saw and carved thirteen notches, one for each.

MARCH 28. DAY 26

Christopher

Misha is on duty. He is the ultimate efficient person on duty. He orders everyone around, serves up food, then tea, and out of the tent you go. The plan was that we should ski for ten hours today. There was a big argument this morning about how we should organize our skiing. Should the fastest person wait for the slowest? Should the slowest only have five minutes instead of ten minutes to rest? What should happen? Laurie really spoke up, because he has a vested interest in this, being one of the slowest people. He said that the fast people should slow down, and not go too fast, so that the slow people can get lots of rest in the breaks. I told him that he should ski a bit faster. The fast people should get ten minutes rest, the slow ones at least five minutes, and the leader should slow down so that he can always see the last person – for safety. I felt I was proposing a compromise solution, but nobody seemed interested.

Richard

This evening we started cutting blocks and they all started breaking again, but this time we got smart instead of freaking out. Once again, I could hear the people in the tent talking, it sounded joyful, it sounded warm and comfortable, and then I thought, yeah, just wait till the stoves are turned off, forget it! We made a real igloo with blocks that slant inwards and go round and around, a couple on the top to close it off, and a door. The door is a little unorthodox. We used Misha's sled, but apart from that the top part is round, the bottom part is rectangular, but it looks like an igloo from the outside. It is starting to blow hard outside, but we are comfortable in here, so, if we are not going anywhere tomorrow that will be just fine – we will sleep.

Fiodor has problems with his backpack. After each break, he is one of the first people to put on his backpack and start skiing, and then every once in a while he has to stop, bend over, and rest his shoulders. He has one of the old-style Soviet backpacks. It has only two thin shoulder straps, and that's it. He finishes each march at the end of the line. His backpack looks very uncomfortable, and I'm sure it is. Especially when it weighs 50 kg. So we offered him one of the Karrimor backpacks, and he thought about it and he said, "I'm scared." That was his answer: he had never used one before, and he had never tested it, and he was scared.

The guy is suffering in agony ten hours a day because of his backpack, anything would be better, but no, he is not going to try it, it might even be worse!

But he did take the sleeping bag from us. Considering his own was only about a quarter of an inch thick, and most of that ice, he really didn't have a lot of choice. This is the Western Fibres Qualofill bag, two-bag, inner bag-outer bag system. He says the inner bag is very dry. There is a little ice, but not much for two weeks' accumulation. I am quite impressed.

This morning Misha and Max discussed exactly what was happening with Max's foot and toe. They decided that as long as there was no infection, he was okay, but if his foot became infected and it spread, he would really be in trouble. Dmitri said, "Look, we are not very far from a floating ice station, if you went out now, you will probably save your toes, if you go on you could lose your toe or more." Toli M. added that Max's toes were now in the same condition that his were in before they were amputated. But Max had no hesitation. He said, "No, I'm going on."

Max feels that there is nothing that can really be done anyway, so he might as well just keep on going. It wouldn't make any difference; Dmitri said it would take at least a month in hospital or a month of rest or more in order for it to heal, but rest is not what it gets here.

MARCH 29. DAY 27

Richard

This morning it was blowing quite hard from the north, a bit of blowing snow. It was about minus 45 I would say, but we broke the thermometer, so I don't really know.

We really are an ugly bunch. We all have scabs and stuff clinging to our faces. Yuri is the worst; his whole nose is a scab, looks like it has been through the blender. It is various colours of black and grey, with dead white skin clinging on his nose and his nostrils. Dmitri: the end of his nose and one of his cheeks are a grey-white death colour, with big crusty parts. Everyone has some frost-bite on his face to a greater or lesser degree.

There are an awful lot of bandaged fingers, too. What happens is that you freeze the end of your finger, and the skin goes hard. The new skin forms underneath, but the old, hard skin splits.

About the tent, it never fails to amaze me. It is *so* horrible in there. Every meal it is the same. We sit down and get rained on. Chris wears his waterproof Goretex pants to keep dry. This morning I brought my Caribou sleeping pad into the tent to sit on. It slipped, and I ended up on Yuri's sleeping bag and completely soaked my suit right through to my bum. When Misha makes his medical rounds, he puts on waterproof boots to walk on the sleeping bags so that he doesn't get his socks wet. They all take it in stride. The door of the tent is always coated with frost. When they dive out of the tent to piss in the morning, they get covered in frost. Coming back in, they get covered again, and climb straight into their sleeping bags. They don't even bother to brush themselves off. Amazing! Then they wonder why their sleeping bags are wet.

Today we came across some more wood. This was a tree stump, with all the roots attached, quite a large stump; the roots were about ten feet across. The nearest place with trees of that size has to be a long way south of 85 degrees! Where we camped there was a small piece of wood sticking out of the ice, too, which is very peculiar. No one has ever seen that before.

Max

There is some consolation in knowing that I'm not the only "patient" in the group. Most of us have had bouts of diarrhoea and cramps. I'm sure that we are just physiologically unable to digest the seven-thousand-plus calories that slide down the tubes, most of them in the form of fat.

In the 1986 trip Will Steger observed what he called "cold diuresis"; frequent urination induced by cold. I piss at every rest break, even if only a few ccs. Maybe I'm just exhibiting territoriality.

Severe dry skin is another universal problem. We pass the bottle of Nivea cream every night, but there are pretty deep cracks in some hands.

The art of Arctic defecation has become highly refined. When the urge strikes, it cannot be ignored. Wind direction is briefly assessed, and the ice formation providing best protection is cased. Often, if the "stooler" has chosen a popular time of day, he will find either another happy camper crouched in the lee of his iceberg, or the residue of a previous visit. As is the case with most jobs, the difficult part is the paperwork.

We do not sleep well. Some days are worse than others. Two nights ago, I was "on duty." I got to bed late, and the alarm was set for 4:00 a.m. In between, I remember the passage of every minute. It was one of our colder nights, with the temperature hovering around minus 45°C. Inside my sopping bag I lay rigid, unwilling to release my hold on consciousness in case the frost were to invade one of my limbs unnoticed.

We are not an overly chatty group. On the trail, the physical barriers to communication are insurmountable, and at dinner time eating takes precedence. We have made some linguistic progress, but most conversations don't bridge the language barrier. Few of us seem to have enough extra energy to think, let alone speak, and attempting to make small talk in a foreign language is not a priority. Unfortunately, I think that our non-involvement in important conversations weakens our political voice and creates the impression for both Russians and Canadians that the four of us are "passengers." Perhaps even worse is that the issues that do bridge the gap are usually trivial conflicts, which assume inappropriate importance. Richard always seems to be battling it out with someone or other about plastic versus wooden skis, pemmican versus dried meat and butter, muesli versus rolled oats, and on and on and on. It all works, and it all fails, and it seems to me that it's not worth busting the morale of the group over.

Integration has been impeded by the tendency of the Soviets to see everything that we do as having symbolic significance, and by the failure of some of us to respect that. Sleeping apart from the group outside the tent and declining the scientific testing are both easily justifiable in our minds, but are taken as an insult in some Soviet quarters.

My role as the Canadian physician is ancillary to Misha's, but only partly because of experience. Mish represents the very much more aggressive approach of the system in which he was trained. Many of the ailments that I would leave to the healing power of nature meet with much more invasive therapy, my own frozen toes being a case in point. In my own little bag of tricks, though, I have a variety of pharmaceuticals that make his eyes bug out. I am in part redeemed by my pills. Misha takes great pride in his expertise in Arctic medicine, and looks a trifle hurt when I provide treatment even for the Canadian members without consulting him. I commonly "do rounds" with him after dinner each night, and I think our "professional" relationship is improving.

Today is the day we've all been waiting for – "parachute day." We skied for seven hours, managing to knock back another twenty-four kilometres before stopping to erect our "weekend" camp. On schedule, the old reliable '74 swooped in like a hawk and popped life-sustaining supplies onto our campsite with amazing accuracy. The only casualty this time was a box of jam and preserved fruit, which blew up on impact with the hard snow.

Watching us running bundled up with stubby little arms stretched skyward reminded me of the candy toss at the Santa Claus parade.

SUMMARY

At the time of their second airdropped resupply, the skiers had travelled 451 kilometres northward, nearly half the distance to the Pole. Their exact location was 85 degrees, 19 minutes latitude. They were well away from land, in the middle of the Arctic Ocean. In terms of their hoped-for arrival time, they were on schedule. In this second leg of the journey, their pace had picked up: they had crossed 2.5 degrees of latitude, as opposed to 2 degrees in the first leg. In part this was because their physical condition was on the whole better. Laurie had improved dramatically and was skiing with the leading group. Max was experiencing great pain with his frozen toes; but though Soviet doctors in Moscow had recommended his evacuation, he was not holding up the expedition and elected to stay. Dmitri had asked if Max wished to be taken to a Soviet drifting station, which was at one point only two kilometres away, but Max did not wish to give up. As for the physical well-being of the Soviets, while they always said that they were fine, it was apparent that they were also experiencing problems. During the sauna, their blackened and scarred toes could be seen, but they never complained.

Skiing at this stage was unpleasant, because of headwinds and cold temperatures. The ice conditions were better than in the first stage. Vasa and Volodi were doing an excellent job of leading, even in bad weather.

The problems in the tent of space, noise, and condensation remained. The only improvement occurred when additional members moved out. Fiodor and Max occasionally joined Christopher and Richard in snow houses. Misha also said that he would be moving out after he had dried his sleeping bag during the rest days. By now it had been accepted that sleeping outside did not signal rebellion or disloyalty.

Routines in general were better organized, and the skiers were pleased that they were wasting less time getting away in the morning. However, different styles of behaviour in the Soviets and Canadians were becoming more of an issue. Certainly at least two of the Canadians felt that the Soviets avoided discussion, especially Dmitri. This did not aid in mutual understanding. (An example provided by Richard is that the group stopped for a few hours, putting up the tent for lunch, when Dmitri claimed that Richard needed to rest. Only later did Misha confirm Richard's suspicion that Dmitri himself wanted to stop because his feet were cold.)

There continued to be many arguments about food. The issue of pemmican versus Soviet supplies had died down somewhat; but now there were differences over "personal food." Richard and Christopher picked up some of the extra food left on the ice after the airdrop. They carried this to eat during the day and were no longer hungry. The Soviets did not do this, considering it "wrong." But they were hungry. (Since the last resupply, while Christopher was still the thinnest he had gained some weight. Max, Richard, and Misha had stayed the same, and the rest had continued to lose weight.) All the Canadians had arranged to receive small "care packages" at each resupply and received a few gifts from home, although the Easter packages they had been looking forward to had been re-routed to Sri Lanka. These had been intended for them specifically. The Soviets also received larger packages intended to be shared amongst the group. They never carried any personal food after the rest days.

As part of the medical program, the team had several heart monitors. The skiers wore these during the day. The data would then be transferred on to paper in the evenings.

Radio communications were now more regular, and Laurie spent many hours working at the radio. Messages from immediate family had begun to come through for the Canadians, but as all the radio broadcasts came from Soviet bases, the Canadians were beginning to feel isolated from the outside world. They had heard nothing from Conexus, their managers, nor had they seen any Canadian media reports. In general, however, apart from Laurie's personal grief, the team morale had improved since the first airdrop.

Laurie wrote a very good article for *Komsomolskaya Pravda*, which was also forwarded to Canada.

Stage Three

MARCH 30. DAY 28

Christopher

We got up at noon. Set up our drying shed, an eight-foot by ten-foot place with snow walls and a parachute roof. Here we would dry our sleeping bags with some of the extra stoves. Misha is intending to move out of the main tent, but he is very busy with his medical stuff, so we are drying sections of his bag for him. This has caused some controversy among the Soviets, who are indifferent when Richard and I sleep out, but feel that Misha should stay in the wet tent with them. Some of these guys feel that it is too complicated and too much work for every one to do this, and since we should all be suffering equally, nobody should dry his bag, especially not one of the Soviets.

Had dinner at 6:00 p.m. I decided to leave behind my big red parka. I took all the useful things off it, like the zipper, the Velcro, etc. Offered it to Fiodor, who is going to use the sleeves for slippers. While I was doing this, Yuri said something in Russian, which, by the tone of his voice, I realized right away meant, "Holy shit, am I in trouble." I jumped up and saw that he had spilt some gas in the kitchen area of the tent, and his legs were on fire, as well as the kitchen, and he was saying, "Ah, *balet!*" in a disgusted tone of voice. He was just sitting there and looking at all this stuff burning. So he grabbed the stove and threw it towards the door (our nice new door). We saw this, and Toli Fedjakov said, "Oh no! Not my door." Misha pulled the stove away from the door. I grabbed my old insoles and started wapping everything in sight. Gave Yuri a few waps just to keep him in line. Eventually, we managed to smother the fire.

Max

I bounced the concept of a polar wedding off Laurie, and he ate the idea up with gusto. It wasn't long before he was on the blower trying to make a connection with the bishop of the Northwest Territories to determine the feasibility and legality of such an event. I feel a little sleazy popping the question over the wireless, but maybe if we can organize a phone patch, it'll seem a little more personal.

Today marked the beginning of "Polar Day." I met Yuri outside at around midnight, and the two of us stood and clapped as the sun shrank to a thin line of orange on the horizon, then began its glorious resurgence. A full moon hung in the opposite sky, creating a rare and beautiful contrast.

Richard

Yuri has been "on duty" today. Being on duty during a rest day is really not the nicest activity. You are supposed to be relaxing, eating, resting, and making equipment repairs. But if you are on duty you are endlessly cooking, making tea, and refuelling stoves. It is awful.

Yuri is definitely the worst cook of the group. Every time he is on duty you can be sure that the kasha will be burnt, the muesli will be burnt, the coffee will taste like dishwater, even more than normally. Today was no exception. He almost burnt the tent down. There is stuff spread everywhere in the tent. At one point during the day, we had a little snack. We each had a can of mystery meat. I ate the meat, but I didn't drink the juice because it was really salty. I accidentally dropped the can and spilled the juice all over Yuri's feet, and all over the kitchen area. He looks at me and says, "Normal, normal, no problem." He is a really good guy. He says what he thinks and believes, and he doesn't beat around the bush. He is a very straightforward guy.

All photographs by Richard Weber and Christopher Holloway unless otherwise indicated. Color film courtesy of BLACK'S 🏃

JERRY KOBALENKO

The four Canadian members of the Polar Bridge expedition (*clockwise from top left*): Max Buxton, Laurie Dexter, Richard Weber, Christopher Holloway.

Overleaf: During the first part of the expedition, the day was half sunrise and half sunset. The low sun produced colours of orange, yellow and blue on the old pack ice.

One of the enormous Aeroflot helicopters that took us to the starting point of our expedition at Cape Arkticheskiy. The temperature was minus 43 degrees Centigrade.

Although we were often spread out, we always kept within sight of one another for safety.

Opposite: After almost eight weeks we reached the North Pole, and were visited by personnel from the nearby Soviet ice station.

The tent was an ingenious Soviet design using the skis as part of the framework. Over this were placed two layers of parachute cloth.

Max Buxton on cooking duty doles out the daily ration to the other doctor on the trek, Misha Malakhov.

After the first month, when the sun rose higher, rest days afforded us an opportunity to dry our equipment in the sun.

This was open water, then a south wind caused the ice plates to drift together. The crossing was still treacherous.

It took thirteen weeks to travel the thirteen hundred miles to this stretch of gravel on Canada's northernmost shore on Ward Hunt Island.

The team pictured at 88 degrees north on the Soviet side of the Pole. *Back row, left to right:* Richard Weber, Dmitri Shparo, Laurie Dexter, Fiodor Konukhov, Mikhail (Misha) Malakhov, Vasili (Vasa) Shishkarov, Volodja (Volodi) Ledenov. *Front row, left to right:* Anatoli (Toli) Fedjakov, Christopher Holloway, Anatoli (Toli) Melnikov, Alexander (Sasha) Believ, Yura (Yuri) Khmelevski, Max Buxton.

MARCH 31. DAY 29

Christopher

Fiodor has cut off the arms of my big jacket that I'm throwing away. He now has them on his feet as slippers. Over them he is wearing two sacks for holding sleeping bags, and in this fashion runs about on the snow. Here we are with custom-made footwear.

We just checked the temperature. In here it's pretty toasty. Outside it's minus 46 now – no wind at all, it's perfectly calm. It's 1:00 a.m. and the sun is still up. This is our first day of twenty-four hour sun. Unless we hear otherwise, we are farther north than anybody in the entire world.

I'm sitting breathing gas fumes from our smokehouse. My sleeping bag is definitely a lot drier – no lumps around the head. The pressure ridges all around us are crunching and grinding. It's kind of like being on the ocean – well, of being on another ocean where you have breakers on the shore constantly hammering away. Only these sort of come and go.

I noticed that Misha was wandering around with his do-it-yourself dentistry kit. Suddenly he started putting a filling into Volodi's mouth. He said he taught himself when he was in Antarctica. He had lots of patience, lots of time, and no competition. He had his little kit and his little book. He said he practised a bit. Now he's working on Toli Fedjakov. He does it without freezing, too.

APRIL 1. DAY 30

Max

I did it last night. I composed a little message, got down on one knee in front of the radio, and proposed to Rick, the ham operator at the drifting station. The idea was not to see if Rick would marry me, but to have him relay the message to my beloved Nan back home. Realizing the confidential nature of the communication, he decided not to transmit it on the open airwaves, but to call her himself directly from Moscow where he is headed tomorrow.

It's not really a spur-of-the-moment decision. The idea had been rolling around my mind with increasing energy in the weeks leading up to our parting. On our last night together, I couldn't sleep, and I'm not usually prone to insomnia. The Question was on the tip of my tongue, but it never came out. First, I didn't think it was fair to lay that on somebody just when they have their first opportunity in months to start hanging around in the singles bars. And what if I really didn't make it? Widowed before the poor woman was even married. That hardly seemed right. But what really shut my mouth was the fear that she would say no, and that I would have nothing to inspire me across the icecap.

Christopher

This morning Richard and I presented Dmitri with a problem that we would like to have solved immediately. Sasha Believ traded in his red Chlorophylle parka for a green Soviet parka. Now there are four people dressed in green, and the number is increasing. This is of real concern to us because of all the trouble we went to get the equipment.

Dmitri promised us in Dikson that only two people would not be wearing red. Now we've got four. We pointed this out, and he said, "Don't worry; by the time we come to the North Pole there will only be two people not wearing red."

The Soviets say, well, you know, you can't make a person wear something because they didn't have enough time to test it. That's fair enough, but why did they ask for the clothing in the first place? Look at the skis: only one person tested them in Dikson.

Laurie, who was sitting beside them, said, "You can't force a person to wear something." Richard replied, "Yes we can. They made an agreement with us that if we got the stuff they would wear it. We got the stuff and they're not wearing it, so they are not living up to their half of the bargain." Laurie kept saying, "Well, it's not really a problem; I'm sure the clothing manufacturer would understand."

We said, "Well, listen, we want to live up to our agreements with our manufacturers. We're the ones who did all the work, and we didn't see you help." To this Laurie (this is the first time I heard him swear) said, "Fuck off, Richard, you don't know what you're talking about." Richard said to Laurie, "For somebody who lived in Pond Inlet, you seem to be completely ignorant of winter, and aren't in a position to say anything because you don't even have a clue how to dress yourself, or what even happens in the winter in the Arctic. It is pretty amazing for somebody who claims to have spent so much time in the North."

In any case, we agreed that these guys should still carry their red Goretex parkas. We don't care about the pants or polar suits; however, we're very concerned with the jackets and windbreakers, because those have the sponsor's advertising on them. They are also the most visible, with Chlorophylle written right down the arms.

Max was very quiet during the actual argument, which petered out with Richard and me yelling away and the Soviets agreeing because they're so polite. Afterwards he said, "Well, I'm not sure you can blame them; after all, look at the society they come from. Contracts are not really a major part of their system. When you haven't grown up with business ethics, it's kind of hard to develop the habits, isn't it?"

The problem is these guys don't see it as lying and deceiving. They say one thing and they do another. It happens regularly. It happens with equipment. They say, oh yes, we'll do this, and then they go and do something else. They said in Moscow, oh yes, only one press conference; it's been nothing but press conferences in Moscow. The longer I spend with them, the more vicious and nasty I get. It seems to work.

Laurie

This being Good Friday, I gave out some Christian literature, a few small tracts, which I have carried with me, written in Russian. I said that I didn't want to be offensive to anybody, that if they didn't like them they could chuck them out, but this was the most important time of the year for Christians, Easter time, and so I wanted to share some of my beliefs.

Today we will continue our travel over the trackless frozen desert towards an invisible destination. Every day becomes a fraction more rewarding, although it will be during the next stage that the days take on more meaning as we approach the Pole. While I hate the thought of carrying a heavy pack, I am keen to get going again to try to make some more distance northwards.

It was a beautiful day, about minus 38°C, and a slight wind from the north. Ice conditions were excellent, fortunately, because if we had had to negotiate rough ice with those packs it would have been abominable.

Actually, while we were packing, I found that I was getting quite chilled. I was dressed for travelling, not for standing around. Also, my packing was almost complete, and I knew I was well ahead of many of the others, so went for a little run two or three times around the area, and during that time I was able to pray for the family and everybody else. It was a very opportune moment to have that sort of worship as I jogged over the beautiful ice formations. Then, as we got underway, I continued to be intensely aware of this being Good Friday, and, as I struggled under my huge burden, I thought of Jesus carrying the cross.

APRIL 2. DAY 31

Christopher

The second rest break ended with a bang. Well a flare, actually. Vasa shot one off over our heads to get us moving. Max and I had been carving up some of the butter that was going to be left behind, and succeeded in breaking two knives in the process. Our band also left a pile of equipment on a high piece of ice, in case someone came by and could use it. You never know.

It was minus 39° last night, and today I think it's about minus 36°. It's sunny and no wind at all. It may sound cold, but really it's very nice. Sun's high in the sky, and I slept on the last rest break, which was very nice, very refreshing; you can keep on going a long time after that. I'm wearing the heart monitor today. I cinched it up really tight and put a strap over my right shoulder which is now bugging me because it is right underneath my knapsack shoulder strap. In any case, I'm getting results. My pulse is about 115 when I rest, and 125 to 130 when I ski.

Max said I look like a cabbage today because I've got so many scars on my face and I'm peeling. The corners of my mouth have cuts through them, so I can't open my mouth very wide. My bottom lip on the left hand side has a great big ulceration from where it froze. Lips freeze differently than the rest of you. Both cheeks are red. I had a look at myself in the mirror during the rest day – not a pretty sight. But, anyway, it's all superficial stuff. I've got scars about the size of silver dollars, except they're triangular, on my cheeks. The bottom of my nose all around my nostrils and the end of my nose is scabbed and peeling. I don't think I've frozen it yet, so it's not too bad. The bridge of my nose has a scar on it.

This morning I got rid of my Balaclava, which has been bugging me. I've worn it about two times since we left Sredny. It ices up really quickly, and it's always nice to get rid of something. I said, "Who wants this?" A number of people said they did. Then I thought, great, time to make a little profit here. So I said, "One Soviet chocolate bar for my Balaclava." With a bit of bickering I managed to get one Soviet chocolate bar from Volodi. Although we had attempted to auction off our sugar each night with little success, this idea of auctioning clothes seemed to be a new concept for the Soviets. They seemed to like the idea, though, when I divided the chocolate in thirteen for the group.

We have now abandoned our snow houses in favour of sleeping under a parachute saved from one of the airdrops. When we finish a hard day's skiing we don't want to start building snow houses. It's kind of good to warm us up, and when it's really cold it was something that I would look forward to. But now that it's warm, all I want to do is lay out my sleeping bag, go inside, do a bit of sewing, have dinner, and go to sleep. We put up our parachute tent. Fiodor started digging trenches and blocks of snow. So here we are sitting in a very low-walled structure with a parachute over the top, and my skis holding up the centre of it, which falls down every now and then as soon as I touch the poles.

Richard

We were off to a good start at about 7:30, a beautiful morning, just gorgeous. Skiing along, the sun coming up, climbing higher and higher. It never set, but in the wee hours of the morning it is still only a red ball on the horizon. Today the sun was actually quite hot. You could feel the heat of the sun on your face, it was really warming, even though it was still minus 37°C.

APRIL 3. DAY 32

Christopher

This was one of those days I would really like to have missed. First thing in the morning I got up, no problems. We had breakfast, that was fine. Then I checked over my skis, and I found that my right ski was broken; not completely broken, but the edge was cracked and blistered in one place right under the heel where it usually breaks. The tip was really twisted. When my foot was flat, the tip of the ski would angle to the right. It bugged me all day. I didn't do anything about it, first of all, because the camber is still there, and it didn't really slow me down skiing. But it's one of those things; after having said that our skis are so wonderful, and no, they never break, what should happen?

I've come up with a cataloguing scheme for the arguments of the day. This way I figure we can save a bit of time. Instead of having to listen to the Soviets argue, we can just call out numbers then they can all bring out the same reasons – pros and cons.

Argument number one is the new system of sleeping in the tent versus the old system. The new system where everybody's feet are in the centre of the tent and everyone's heads around the outside of the tent, which sounded reasonable in a round tent, is no good because when you sit up in the morning to eat breakfast you get a cold draft down your back. Volodi figures this causes back pain to people, and they should go back to the old system where everybody's heads were in the centre.

Argument number two is what is wrong with the food. If something is wrong with the food, usually it can be traced to: (a) the muesli, or (b) the pemmican. It can't be traced to the vitabars any more because the Soviets have eliminated them from their diet. The exception is Misha, who still has one a day.

Argument number three is "Where is my place?" When somebody comes into the tent they say. "Where is my place?" The person on either side of them where they're supposed to be says, "I don't know, but somebody on the other side of the tent has so much room; look over there." This is, I think, founded on the fact that if you're sitting elbow to elbow with somebody on one side of a circle, i.e., a tent, and you look across, you can see more space on the other side of the tent than you can on your own side of the tent. So it is your impression that they have more space over there. Hence, argument number three goes on and on.

Argument number four, which is less common, so it is ranked near the bottom, is "Where shall we put the tent?" Today we skied into this place, which, if it hadn't been absolutely white, could easily be on the face of the moon. It had really nice large blocks of old ice about fifteen feet high with green bits jutting out and a nice flat little crater in the centre. I thought it was just perfect. But these guys came along and said no, this is no good, and tried to look for a flat spot. However, because their hour was up, they could go no more than about fifty feet in either direction. In the end, they decided that, yes, in fact they had no choice, no option whatsoever, but to stay here.

Max

We just wound up two days of very good travelling, eight hours each, with temperatures ranging between minus 35 and minus 40. There was enough energy in the sunlight that we could dry clothing by hanging it on our packs. With everyone's laundry hanging out, we looked like a real rag-and-bone show.

The short-wave radio is tuned in to an upbeat station from Melbourne, Australia. The reception is remarkably good, but is interrupted every few minutes by an odd pattern of clicks and beeps. Vasa tells us that we are intercepting transmissions from a nearby submarine.

The last couple of days have been a bit of a turnaround. I think my outlook has improved with the resolution of my nuptial intent and the gentle tail wind and brighter sunshine make me feel a good bit lighter on my feet. Out of sympathy for my toes, the group has reduced my share of the group equipment, so I'm travelling lighter both physically and mentally.

The main topic for conversation after dinner tonight was Argument number two with the usual polarization (pardon the term) between Richard and Chris on one side, and Yuri and Volodi on the other. The rest of us are somewhat less fanatical in our allegiance to pemmican or dried hamburger.

Laurie

This is Easter Sunday.

It occurred to me that on Saturday, March 19, I had those optical illusions, caused by the ice formations, of someone being close to me. Not until four days later did I find out that was the day my Dad died. Now I know there is a simple explanation. The area we were travelling was fairly flat, with isolated chunks of ice sticking up, and, as these came within range of my peripheral vision that was limited by having my hood up, they were easily mistaken for another member of the expedition stopping for some reason, or overtaking. I know that, and yet it hasn't happened on other days!

This weekend I tried to think about the Easter story, and I have tried to pray, but I find it very difficult when having to concentrate so much on the physical effort. Later on, when the packs get lighter, I find that I can do better; but I did think a great deal about the family. In fact, I had one quite bad fall because of daydreaming. I was actually thinking about Andrew's hockey, of all things. Usually, a fall consists of sliding in rough ice and more or less falling on the spot. This is the first time I have taken a tumble skiing over a ridge, coming down the slope on the other side. My skis took off ahead of my centre of gravity, and I went flat on my back. Even though it was a really hard fall, the backpack had a cushioning effect, and I didn't hurt myself.

APRIL 4. DAY 33

Max

Quite frequently we ski by little patches of particulate matter that look for all the world like sand. No big deal anywhere else, I grant you, but how the hell does sand end up here? I guess old icebergs could have impinged upon a land mass and floated the stuff out here, but I wonder about the possibility of airborne pollutants being precipitated by the cold. Nuclear fallout perhaps? I can see why the Soviets vetoed snow sampling. More paranoid conjecture. Richard says that he's seen bits of seaweed frozen into the surface at times, so likely there is a benign explanation.

Because of a tendency to drift westward, we've had to angle our course slightly to avoid being swept out into the north Atlantic. Nevertheless, we made 12 minutes' progress northward yesterday, delivering us at 86 degrees, 7 minutes.

Christopher

We've been listening to Radio Australia from Melbourne, which sure has a bit more objective news than Radio Moscow. Also, they have better music. It's now 24° in Melbourne. A hot spell has come through here too: it's minus 35°. Unfortunately, the wind has picked up a bit as well. Last night I just slept under my parka, and it was very comfy and warm, even though when I woke up this morning there was a reasonably stiff wind; probably about three metres per second.

Today we skied for eight hours. I think we made pretty good speed, although we were heading 15 degrees east. It was minus 35° this morning; it's now minus 33°, and we had a head wind all day. I had to wear my face mask, to which I've made a great improvement by cutting out almost all of the mouth. The only problem was that after about four hours I got a layer of ice inside, which you always do. Anyway, this frost-bite on my lower left lip got stuck to the ice a few times. It's just like putting your tongue on metal. Then it started ripping off the fine layer of scab that I was so delicately nurturing. My face mask had not only icicles off the end of the nose, but also blood dripping down out of the mouth.

As I was skiing today. I was thinking that *perestroika* in the Soviet Union really hasn't got a chance. You're taking an idea which is based on individuals' thinking for themselves (i.e., capitalism, individual companies, entrepreneurship, etc.) and trying to apply it in a society where individualism is really wiped out.

Toli M. gave me extra kasha for dinner, which was very nice. I've chopped all my fat saved from the day's rations, too, for a veritable feast. Fat is pretty good; you can chew the bacon rinds and swallow them. There's a bit more meat on them. I'm going through lots of garlic because there's still lots of it. I'm averaging six cloves a day for dinner. Maybe that's why I'm sleeping out here alone.

I said the other day that what we should do at the North Pole is have our sauna and run outside and have pictures of us all standing nude. Then I thought maybe we should have our flags just covering up our vital parts so that we could tell who was who. Volodi thought that this was just hilarious; then I told Misha and Vasa. Vasa said, "You can wear your flag wherever you want. I wear mine on my chest because my flag is my god, my country is my god." My country is my country, but fortunately I have a sense of humour.

APRIL 5. DAY 34

Laurie

Last night's radio reception was much better, and I was able to get out the other messages that Chris and Richard had prepared. We still haven't heard from Sheena concerning the marriage at the North Pole, or from Nancy whether she accepts Max's proposal, which he made during our last airdrop. If there is no message tonight, I will send off another one to find out what's happening.

There is a big discussion going all the time just now about what to eat at the Pole and afterwards – Canadian or Soviet food. Personally, I think it's very simple. We eat Soviet food up to the Pole. At the Pole we eat Canadian food supplemented with Soviet food, and after that we eat Canadian. But Richard is griping because of the extra Soviet members, and saying that if we order food then the Soviets should pay for their extra two men.

Personally, I disagree with this. I think as we are on the expedition together then the cost of feeding the extra two is going to be relatively slight, and the generosity of the Soviet members to us, and also travelling to the Soviet Union, as well as on the expedition, has been immense, and we can't afford to be stingy. Richard and Chris are both making loud and angry demands for payment, and I find it embarrassing. I hope the Soviet members make allowances for the special circumstances we find ourselves in, and do not jump to hasty conclusions or generalizations about the character of Canadians based on this display.

Richard

During the last set of rest days, I made the suggestion that Max carry less weight. After some discussion, we decided that Max would not carry any food. This is to help him so that he does not get as tired. We want him to save his energy to heal his foot and make him less prone to infection. He cannot get well if he carries a full weight and exhausts himself. Yesterday he started to get some feeling back in his foot; he seemed more chipper and said he felt stronger. So I think it was a good idea.

I am sure we are going to have problems about food at the North Pole. The question is, whose food do we eat, and if it's Canadian, do we pay for the two extra Soviets? Dmitri said, "We are a family and we must all eat together, and they need to try your food." My plan was that the four Canadians put up another tent and eat there. They do not want that because it splits up the expedition in their eyes.

We are not communists and do not have a collective mind. We have individual minds. That is one of the true differences; we are four individuals and like to think of ourselves as individuals. They are part of a collective whole and think of themselves as part of that whole, and not as individuals; whereas we think of ourselves as individuals working together. If you want to get ahead of your neighbour, you have to think of something else that nobody has done before, whereas these guys do not want to improve their lot, they do not want to get ahead of their neighbour, they just want to be the same as everyone else.

Yuri is a good example. He says that he does not like to own things, he does not want material things, and he does not really care where he lives or how he lives. It is the quality of his feelings which is important to him, not really the material quality of life. This is probably a rationalization. Since it is very hard or it is impossible to get ahead, they can then rationalize it by saying we will improve the quality of what we have, read more books, go to the theatre, get my Ph.D., study hard, improve my mind, etcetera, because I cannot improve my living situation materially.

Chris cracked a ski about four days ago. Today Max broke one, not in two but close. This worries me considerably that two of them would go within four days. Max has had considerably less wear and tear on his skis than Chris because he is lighter. That they both break at the same time is a little unnerving. One of the interesting things that happened when the ski broke is that Vasa took control and, assisted by Volodi, had in five minutes mounted another ski. He is really amazing at that. Thirty-five below and zippity-do-da, five minutes and the ski has new bindings. He drills the holes with a pair of scissors and screws on the bindings with a Swiss Army knife. And he gets it straight.

I was standing around, admiring the view, because we had just gone through a rather rough spot that was fairly picturesque, and Dmitri came up and said, "Beautiful view." I said, "Oh yes, it is really nice." He says, "Yeah, that does not matter," turning back and pointing to the broken skis. "It does not matter at all, what matters is we are here, it is beautiful countryside, and we are right in the middle of it." He was so sincere, no doubt he really enjoys the scenery, the changing ice, and the changing light ofthe polar sea.

APRIL 6. DAY 35

Christopher

When I came out after breakfast I found Fiodor burying his parka. I said, "What are you doing burying your parka?" He said, "No, no don't say anything, don't say anything at all. Dmitri wants me to keep it, and I don't want to keep it, so I'm burying it so nobody will know."

Our expedition has turned into a slow, lethargic animal. Going around each pressure ridge is a new excuse for slowing down. Every morning it's taking longer to come out of its drugged stupor to hoist its mass onto the trail. Thirteen is just too many. The problem is there is no incentive to go fast. As long as you stay ahead of Misha, you're going to get there. As long as you stay part of the group, essentially, then everyone assumes that we're going to make it to the Pole.

This afternoon I skied with my vest and my anorak, and I was still getting cold. It was taking me forty minutes before my hands were warmed up after each ten-minute break. I decided I was going to sleep in a snow house as opposed to under a parachute, I was so cold last night; and also just so I could get a bit of exercise in order to warm up after skiing all day. Pretty sad state of affairs when you have to shovel snow to warm up instead of being able to work hard on the trail. Today was a breeze. I think I could manage eleven or twelve hours with no problem.

Richard

I'm tired of being woken up at 5:00 and not leaving until 8:00 when we're supposed to leave at 7:30. This morning Chris and I were announcing the time every ten minutes as agreed, and at 7:30 I put on my pack, and left with Vasa. We were followed shortly by Volodi, then Christopher. Then there was a large gap. We skied for exactly fifty minutes and plunked our packs down. Vasa and Volodi thought this was a great joke. Slowly but surely people started to turn up, but after twenty minutes, everyone had still not arrived, and I was starting to get cold. So I put on my pack and off I went, followed by Vasa, who still thought that this was a great joke. He kept saying "This is a good lesson, a good lesson indeed." At the next rest stop, I plunked my pack down, and after twenty minutes Dmitri turned up and said, "Well you were right, we should leave at 7:30. We also have a problem with speed." I don't know what he exactly meant about the problem, and he never really said. I waited thirty five minutes on the second break, and was *quite cold* when we left. But if we can start on time in the future, this will have been worth it.

As the day wore on we went slower and slower. Laurie had a rough time. He did not sleep much last night because he was cold. At a couple of rest breaks, Laurie lay down on his pack and within a minute he was snoring gently. Vasa would wake him up when it was time to go.

Laurie

Things started badly because Richard and Chris kept shouting at everyone that we had to get ready and be away for 7:30 a.m. It is rare indeed for either Chris or Richard to be ready before me, but 7:30 came and only Richard and Vasili were ready. So they started, and Richard took off. But by the time they had finished waiting at the first stop, some of the members still hadn't arrived. So Richard and Chris took off, saying that anyone who couldn't keep up shouldn't be on this expedition. Eventually everyone caught up at the second stop, but it was a bad atmosphere to start off the day.

Of course, they were trying to make the point that if we say we are going to be ready by 7:30 a.m., then we should be ready by that time. I agree with this, but do not appreciate the abrasive manner with which they frequently approach problems, discussion, and differences of opinion. They see their approach as being an aggressive businesslike method. I see it as uncouth.

The day was very good in terms of the terrain, with not too many ridges or anything difficult to hinder our progress. It was minus 43°C, but calm. I must admit it doesn't feel the same as minus 43°C did a month ago, because of the sun being up now and the calm weather today, but it still is incredibly cold and dangerous as far as hands and feet are concerned, and people are refreezing bits of their faces again. However, we travelled fairly well.

APRIL 8. DAY 37

Max

Word came by radio last night that Nancy is willing to tolerate a lifetime of my idiosyncrasies. "Yes," she said. "An unqualified yes." As for the concept of hitching up at the old Pole, she was a little less certain. "Dependent upon circumstances," was the cryptic reply. True, much is necessary in the way of arrangement, but I wonder if she is not subtly trying to describe some official resistance back home from either managerial or political sources.

So I'm going to be a married man. Just where the proposed event will transpire remains to be seen. Of course, I still have to get there, and again my body is manifesting its many flaws. My entire left foot went numb today, I think because of the abnormal way I'm walking on it to protect the delicate bits. A Tylenol 3 with breakfast helps a lot. I've never had occasion to use these little gaffers personally before, but I can see why they're so popular. "Polar marching pills."

I'm on duty this evening, and the meal was pretty good if I do say so myself. I had the brilliant idea of adding the spices (thyme and basil) while the kasha was cooking rather than after it was served. They certainly have more effect, and everybody likes them. We're a spicy group. A one-kilo bag of fresh garlic usually lasts about five days, and much of it is consumed as whole buds, eaten like candy.

Everybody has cracks and erosions on their fingers, probably initiated by frost-bite and perpetuated by intermittent cold-induced circulatory impairment. They heal very slowly, but mercifully are numb rather than painful, for the most part. I'm sure all 128 toes are frost-nipped (Toli M. only has eight), but mine are still the winners in terms of severity. Faces are pizza-like and swollen, and the three Ottawa Valley lads seem pretty sensitive to the sun. We must be getting a lot of reflected rays. Whereas Laurie and the Soviets seem to brown up nicely, the three of us respond with an almost urticaria-like rash on exposed areas.

From a psychological and psychiatric perspective, I can't believe how well we're doing. On Dmitri's 1979 polar trip, he described week-long periods during which no one would speak, and animosities ran rampant. They required daily communication with a Moscow psychiatric facility, and team failure almost spelled the end of the expedition on more than one occasion. We have our beefs, but I think the group is large enough to defuse the interpersonal tensions, and the importance of diplomacy is recognized by most for reasons which extend beyond the thirteen men on the ice.

Laurie

I was up at 3:30 a.m. and got things going. We had finished breakfast by 5:45 a.m., but still had a struggle to get ready for 7:30 a.m. So, once again, Richard and Vasa took off, with myself and a couple of others close behind. We opened up a huge gap before the last members had even left camp. So once again there was a big discussion about it, with angry words flying between Richard and the Soviets. Personally, it doesn't worry me. If we start five minutes late then we just finish five minutes later in the day. Whatever it takes we must be willing to give. But Richard is very insistent on the discipline of starting on time.

As usual, I understand his reasoning. Discipline is necessary. But I do not feel that we are in fact lacking discipline. Having gone through that period of injury early on, when no one else was injured, I know how necessary it is to be sympathetic to those who are struggling now. Richard also went through two or three days when he was struggling, and had some of his load shared, but, having recovered, he does not seem to have any feelings for others who are finding it tough just now.

Whether or not it was the effect of Richard's tirade, during the rest of the day people kept much closer together, and really worked hard. It was a glorious day, about minus 30°C, with a slight wind, which meant that we still had to wear all our clothing; but we started off fast and never slowed down all day – nine solid hours of fast skiing, over the best conditions we have ever seen, no pressure ridges, no open water, reasonably flat, and a reasonably hard surface.

Richard

We were supposed to start at 7:30, which has been our agreed starting time, but some people can't seem to be ready on time. Some, like Vasa, usually sleep in and are always ready on time. Others like Toli M. are never ready on time. It means that those who are ready on time must stand around and wait for those who are not. An unpleasant occupation at minus 35°C! So we left on time.

I threatened the Soviets with setting up my own expedition. The only person who fully understood was Max. He was horrified. He said that this was not in the spirit of the whole expedition and that we were missing the point entirely. I tried to calm his nerves by explaining that this was only a threat to shake them up a bit.

Max, I think, is quite a pacifist, but the only way to get through to the Soviets is by hitting them hard. If you want to go into a Soviet house, you don't knock gently on the door, you kick it down, and then they might say, "Oh, good gracious, you want to come in? Well, do come in and don't worry about the door." But that is the way it is. If you hint gently, they will miss the point entirely. You have to come out very strongly or they won't take any notice. Or perhaps they will say, "Let's have a meeting about it," and then nothing will happen.

Most of the time we were going across very old pans of ice. Lots of crusty snow, making it hard to control our skis. It has warmed up a bit, too, so our skis tend to be a little bit more squirrelly. Yesterday we had a couple of good-size pressure ridges to scramble across.

We got our location. We are at 87 degrees. This morning we were at 86 degrees, 40 minutes. That is 20 minutes in one day, that is almost forty kilometres. This is amazing! I am sure we are not skiing more than three kilometres an hour. We did nine marches. That only makes twenty-seven kilometres. I don't know where the other eleven or twelve kilometres came from, unless we are drifting north really quickly.

APRIL 9. DAY 38

Christopher

Two more days and we will have had our forty days in the wilderness. I haven't had any visions yet, but I have seen an awful lot of ice. This morning we decided that we would try an experiment at Misha's suggestion. We would get up one hour later. That way the radio would be just before and just after dinner. Then Laurie would get his eight hours sleep instead of six hours. The way it is now, pretty well every rest break he just collapses on his pack and snoozes. He starts snoring in the middle of our ten-minute rest break.

There's no reason why they can't change the radio hours. We're flying these operators in and out. They're there solely for us, and now that we have twenty-four-hour sun there's no peak time for transmission.

Misha suggested this two days ago, and Dmitri had no comment; just didn't say anything, and brushed him off. Misha was quite put off at this. Today he brought it up at breakfast. He asked everybody in turn. Everybody said yes, we think it's a good idea. Why in hell wouldn't it be a good idea, and why don't we do it? When he asked Dmitri, Dmitri was the only one with no comment. He said he had not decided yet. We all sat around and waited for a while. Finally, after seeing that everybody was in favour of this,

Dmitri said yes. Anyway, because this was resolved, we got an extra hour's sleep last night, which was good.

The big problem today was food. At the beginning of every stop I was hungry; I'd eat and then be full for forty minutes, but our next break would be fifty minutes away, so at the end of each ski I'd always be hungry.

Richard

This evening I inspected Yuri's sleeping bag. It's quite solid. It consists of baffles separating icy lumps of down. There is really no insulation. He would probably be better off with a few garbage bags, since they would be lighter to carry, and just about as warm.

APRIL 10. DAY 39

Laurie

Gradually, my various aches and pains have been healing. My fingers still require protection, but every few days another one heals enough to leave it bare. Soon I'll have four fingers completely clear, and the others are beginning to improve quite well. One of my biggest discomforts is still my toes. I think the nerves have been damaged. The toe is sort of prickly and affects my balance a little when skiing in difficult places.

The sun is beginning to have quite an effect. The air warms up slightly during the day, but also we are beginning to burn on our faces, and we are going to have to be very careful to start wearing glasses soon, as protection against snow blindness. However, we are never actually travelling facing the sun. In the early morning the sun is on our right-hand side, and gradually it swings behind us until it is on our left by evening.

The weather was marvellous: minus 33°C when we set out, and rising to about minus 30. I was able to take off my red Chlorophylle windpants and top and ski just as I was, feeling just right. Everybody was shedding clothes, mostly inner things. The ice was good as well, mainly large rolling fields bordered by pressure ridges. When the pressure ridges did occur, some of them were amongst the worst that we have experienced so far, in fact so bad that some people took off their skis and walked across; but on the whole we kept up a reasonable pace. As before, I stayed right up with Volodi and Vasili, and while the pace wasn't as fast as some previous days, it was steady, and I felt that we should have covered at least as far as we did with the ten-hour day.

Richard

I even put on suntan lotion today, which is pretty amazing; yesterday we froze our faces, and now we are burning them. Mind you, it is still 30 below out, but, after living at 40 below and colder for a month, it feels quite warm, especially with the sun.

What a difference in the tent now from only a few weeks ago. Now it is bright, it is sunny, and if you stand up, it is hot. Items of clothing dry very well up by the ceiling, and sitting here it is really quite comfortable. The temperature ranges from probably minus 10 on the floor to probably about 25 degrees in the roof. This is while the stoves are going, preparing the meals.

We just got our co-ordinates in. We are at 87 degrees, 32 minutes. Yesterday we were at 87 degrees, 14 minutes. We have gone from 91 degrees to 93 degrees longitude because we were angling 15 degrees towards the east today. I can't believe the speed we are going. There must be a very good drift. This is definitely the correct side of the ocean from which to go to the North Pole – flatter ice, good drift, can't get anything better.

APRIL 11. DAY 40

Max

We just got something on the radio from the bishop stating that "It would not be practical" to perform a wedding at the North Pole for the following reasons:

1) It was feared that the place would become more important than the event;

2) Geographically the Pole was not within the Christian community;

3) No premarital counselling had been conducted with the parties concerned.

Laurie was not impressed, nor was I. Of course, it's not "practical" to get married at the North Pole. It's not practical to go there. It's not practical to get married. And most of all, as all good communists know, it's not practical to get involved with religion.

In essence, Laurie had been denied permission to perform the ceremony by his church superior. He quickly pointed out that he was still legally qualified to do the job, though, and flashed a mischievous radical smile.

In defence of the bishop, I must admit that he suggested the alternative of bringing a justice of the peace in from Resolute. The idea seemed a little silly with Laurie sitting next to me, and the expense of bringing another body to the Pole would be considerable.

Christopher

Yesterday we had an interesting discussion. It seems that Max, Laurie and Richard did not remember their responsibilities as shareholders in a company called Polar Bridge. They all seemed to have forgotten that they could not pay themselves until, or unless we made a profit. Something about basic economics that I thought was self-evident. Max said that he had a lawyer and an accountant, so he wouldnt need to know. Laurie probably prays to God, so he wouldn't need to know, and Richard claimed ignorance.

Laurie came out with this short red jacket that we'd never seen before. He's been complaining about how heavy his pack is, and he comes out with a jacket like my Goretex jacket. It's lined Goretex with a ruff, and it's got to weigh at least a kilogram. He's been carrying this around and not using it. He's not using the skis or the poles; he's not wearing the hat. He's wearing the Chlorophylle jacket, admittedly; however, he's planning to dump the red one. About the third march, I went out and spoke to him for the whole march. An hour went by very quickly. I explained to him that he, personally, had responsibility to the companies that we, Richard and I, had made commitments with, because we made them on his behalf. In Iqaluit he had said specifically that the clothing was fine, and by not asking for any changes he had consented to wear it.

I also called him dishonest and a liar. I had to retract my liar statement. I said if he says one thing and does another, then in fact he's being dishonest. I also said that the Soviets did this sort of thing, and it was one of the big things that we had against them. If we're going to provide an example for them, especially with clothing, then he, as one of the Canadians, has to be responsible in this regard.

This evening I told him that I would sew a zipper into his red parka if he would like me to. Thinking that this might be a problem for the Soviets, I made a similar offer to Yuri, and Toli Melnikov.

Misha worked on Volodi's cracked tooth again last night. Volodi said that he has a new life, he's a new man. He sure was in a lot of pain for a couple of days. However, he continued to lead, and never complained.

I also made a bet with Yuri that I may regret. Three litres of Canadian Club says that the temperature will not hit minus 40° again. Two bottles of senettata [a Soviet liqueur] says that it will.

Laurie

I took off my Chlorophylle jacket for the first time and replaced it with the red Goretex one I have been carrying, which has much better fur trim around the hood, and also a zip which allows me to ventilate more. Chris was highly incensed. He accused me of telling lies, of being deceitful, of breaking contracts, and all sorts of things like that. He made the outrageous statement that I had agreed to wear the Chlorophylle suit and I was liable for legal action if I did not live up to that contract. It seemed to make no difference that Goretex is one of our sponsors, and that I was now wearing a Goretex jacket. So we come to the end of our fortieth day in the wilderness!!

APRIL 12. DAY 41

Max

While skiing today, I thought about how this whole experience has been the equivalent of going to war for me, something my generation of young Canadians fortunately avoided. Obviously, this is a much more pleasant event than war, but we have left the comfort of our homes to do daily battle in a foreign environment. Our enemies are not human, but are the elements of distance, time and climate. We have good allies both amongst ourselves and on the outside, and we haven't really lost many of the battles. But the more time I spend here, the less I feel in conflict with the Arctic itself. On days like this, when you can actually see around, the ghostly beauty of blue-anmd-white forms is awe-inspiring.

APRIL 13. DAY 42

Richard

When we got up, it was really nasty out; it was blowing about ten metres per second. But the sun was still visible. The sky was still blue directly overhead, but there were clouds all around, and the snow was blowing somewhat. We took our time packing up. Max even came over and said he thought that we shouldn't travel, but by the time we started travelling it was already better, and throughout the day the weather continued to improve.

I was feeling sleepy. We talked until late, and I didn't get a lot of sleep. I didn't want to overheat, so the first march I led, and then the second and third I skied with the slowest people. I was almost able to fall asleep on my skis. I was nodding off a couple of times, and after that I started to pick up. In the evening, our position was confirmed, after five marches, 88 degrees, 10 minutes, so we did ten minutes. It amazes me how we seem to go slowly but still proceed fairly quickly. It almost seems that the slower we ski, the more ground we cover.

We put up our tent in the lee of a large pressure ridge. A couple of hours later, along came our beloved AN 74 out of which popped all sorts of goodies. The pilots were very good. The first package landed a little far away, and a couple of the boxes burst open, spilling galetties all across the Arctic Ocean. But, apart from that nothing got damaged, and most of the drops were rather close to the camp. In fact, one of them just missed Laurie.

We spent a couple of hours running around, picking everything up. It is always fun. It is like Christmas with goodies dropping from the sky. The best goodies, of course, are letters from home. The letters confirmed that all our mail for the second airdrop ended up in Sri Lanka, including goodies from Josée and Pia, chocolates and Easter eggs from my parents. I did finally receive one letter from my mother that was due for the second airdrop. All the rest, including letters from Pia Josée, along with the edible stuff, had vanished.

This time, both Chris and I received cassettes from Pia and Josée respectively, and this is just great. Mine had Chris and me in stitches, it was so funny. Afterwards, there were a few quiet words from Josée, and also recordings of the birds in the backyard, the cat, the dog, or at least she tried to get the dog to say something.

The food in the airdrop was the best yet; it was really good. We had good ham, good bread, English cucumbers, fresh carrots, oranges, apples, not frozen, not bashed or smashed, boiled eggs, cake galore, cheese, and jam. Unfortunately, there was no real information. There were no letters from Peter Baird [of Conexus], just a short note saying that we should be more careful of what we say on the radio, and that was it. I am a little distressed, a little disturbed, that our managers do not send us any information on what the heck is going on in the outside world. What is happening with the ceremony? What is happening with the organization financially? organizationally? What is going on about the resupplies? It is almost like he doesn't exist any more.

Something happened yesterday as we were sitting in the main tent "pigging out." We heard an aircraft, so Chris and I ran out of the tent. It flew a large, low loop around the camp, and on the way back the pilot threw something out. There were no markings on the wings. It was a black and yellow plane. We ran over and retrieved the package. It was a plastic bag with a little parachute attached. The plastic bag was from the Thule Air Base in Greenland. On it was printed "Top of the World Club," and inside were eleven donuts and chocolates, toffees, M & Ms, and a note from this guy whose address is in Fairbanks, Alaska.

The only other thing we saw written on the side of the plane was "Polar Air." So we are assuming it was some private guy with obviously a lot of money in order to fly his plane around here. He must have been in Thule Air Base, picked up the package, and then decided to fly his airplane to visit us. He must have found his information on our location from the radio or SARSAT.

We have been hearing planes all day. One flew over the camp and dropped a set of bathroom weigh scales for the medical program which they had forgotten. I just heard another one fly by. Apparently, we skied by one of three drifting ice stations the Soviets have at the moment: NP29. We passed within two kilometres of it. We didn't know. We thought it was about ten kilometres away. If we had stood up on a high pressure ridge we could have probably seen it. Apparently, about ten or twelve kilometres from here is an unidentified camp with probably ten to twelve people. They said there are five huts. It is not Soviet, so we don't know. Maybe it is American?

Volodi found a very small piece of red plastic bunting/tape on the ice yesterday, so maybe it blew over from them. I wouldn't have thought anybody would dare to inhabit the Soviet Arctic, so to speak, without permission, but then again, the Americans don't even think that the water between the Canadian Arctic islands belongs to Canada, so I am quite sure they don't think any of the water this far offshore belongs to either Canada or the Soviet Union. They probably feel they can do what they like.

I got the list of ingredients for the pemmican, including the percentage of water. There is no water in it. I listed all the ingredients to our bunch of "doubting johnnies," and they were still a little doubtful, but they really can't say much any more. Yuri said, "Yes, I like the list, it would make very good pemmican, but that is not what we are eating." I said, "Perhaps in the Soviet Union you can be told you are eating one thing when it is actually something else. This is not the case in Canada, and it certainly would not happen with André Moreau." Dmitri said he was very glad that I had taken the trouble to get the list of ingredients, and he now felt much better.

SUMMARY

By the time of their third airdrop, the expedition had travelled 769 km northward. They were almost exactly three-quarters of the way to the Pole. They made camp at 88 degrees, 11.5 minutes. During their three-day rest period, their camp drifted twenty-three kilometres in a southwesterly direction. The drift had begun to get stronger because of currents in the Arctic Ocean beneath the ice. They felt capable of reaching the Pole, although there was still concern among some members about being late for the ceremony that was scheduled for their arrival.

The skiers' physical condition was remarkably good. Max's feet were still causing him pain, with frozen toes on one foot and an enormous blister on the other, but he was clearly going to recover; there was no further question of his leaving the group. Volodi had a broken tooth. There were a number of rashes, bacterial skin problems, and frost-bite injuries, but these were minor. Laurie was keeping up with the leading skiers. His commitment to complete the journey was proving to be his strength.

The medical tests showed mixed results. On the (roughly) seven-thousand-calorie diet some were fatter, some thinner. Some had gained weight, while a few had lost.

The skiing at this point in the journey was a bit dull. The landscape was chiefly composed of large flat pans of ice. The weather had "warmed" to minus 30, comfortable for travelling if not for standing around. This made an enormous difference. As well, the April sun was higher in the sky, which meant that it was strong enough to dry things out. This eased all the problems with the condensation in the tent, and with sodden and cold sleeping bags and clothing. Skis glided with less effort for the same reason.

It was a surprise to the Canadians that their skis started to break. They were guaranteed for long use, but were simply fatigued, as they were intended to carry a person, but not the extra weight of a forty- to fifty-kilogram backpack. The snow house where Richard, Chris, Misha, and Fiodor slept had been replaced by the parachute tent, with its wall of snow blocks, that they had devised.

Group dynamics were close to their low point. However, comparatively speaking, the group was faring better than others. As Max had learned, in Dmitri's 1979 all-Soviet North Pole trip, it had been necessary for the team members to be in daily communication with a Moscow psychiatric facility, and at one point the skiers didn't speak to each other for a week. The constant airing of differences, sparked primarily by Richard and Christopher, may actually have helped the group by preventing similar extremes of introversion.

Now that the ice was flat enough to allow skiing side by side, skiers could talk to each other, which improved their relationships and also made time pass more quickly.

There were still a great many arguments, particularly between Christopher and Richard on the one hand and Yuri and Volodi on the other. One issue revolved around wearing clothing from sponsors so as to fulfil agreements that had been made on behalf of the team. The Soviets and some Canadians did not feel compelled to wear clothing with visible labels all the time, while those taking photographs were sensitive to what showed up in their shots.

There had been much discussion about food for the North Pole ceremony. Some of the animosity surrounding this issue dated from the addition of two extra Soviet members to the expedition at the last moment, and the extra costs involved. Personal food was also a point of contention. The Soviets noticed that the Canadians' personal food sent in from Dikson – chocolates and baked goods – was prearranged by themselves and put into their parcels for the plane drops.

Although the Soviet airdrop brought good food for the rest days, during the travelling days many skiers, both Soviet and Canadian, were hungry. Toli Fedjakov, in particular, talked all the time about food. Some Soviets were ready to go against their tradition and take a personal food reserve, but they needed an authorization from Dmitri. Misha felt it a good idea that the men each carry a personal reserve, but had not yet actually done so. He felt that the Canadians were becoming stronger than the Soviets because of their extra food.

The issue of the caloric and nutritional value of muesli and pemmican had been partially resolved, and partially argued into the ground.

One of the Soviets later claimed that Yuri had never intended to honour the diet agreement made in Iqaluit. At the time it was easier for him to agree to Richard's suggestion and avoid a debate.

At this point in the expedition it was becoming obvious that Dmitri was failing to give effective leadership. The team still had a great deal of trouble getting away in the morning. When there were conflicts, Dmitri preferred to avoid them. He did not like to take hard decisions, as was demonstrated before they left land, when the extra skiers were included. Arguments, some of which were inevitable under the circumstances, dragged on for a long time, because neither Dmitri nor anyone else stepped in to stop them. Although he himself did not wish to take charge, he didn't want anyone else to do so either.

It seemed to the Canadians that avoiding direct conflict was the Soviet style, and that it was also Shparo's personal style. However, he had begun by this time to ask the Canadians for their views on matters such as how far they should ski, and how long, and he sometimes called for a formal vote.

Communication with the outside world had improved considerably. The skiers got letters and food from home, and this made them feel great. But the Canadians still had no news from their managers about their financial situation or the press reaction to the expedition.

The radio system worked well for the Soviets; all had contracts with the media in their country, and had to transmit articles word by word maybe once a week. The Soviets spent hours every evening on the radio. This became so important that the camp schedule revolved around the radio and was dictated by when operators would be available, and for how long. As the Soviets sent out far more reports than the Canadians, this information was translated for use by the Canadian media.

By this time radio communication was with the station NP 28 (a Soviet ice station drifting near the Pole), rather than Sredny. The Canadian Barry Garratt was at NP 28, and his presence made getting messages from Canada easier. Laurie and Toli Melnikov often spent long hours listening and writing messages with numbed fingers while others slept. But there was some uncertainty still about radio messages. Because they were handled by ham radio operators, the messages went out via hams and could be picked up by the media. Once a personal message sent by Richard to his wife, Josée, was broadcast on the radio in Toronto. After this, Canadian spouses were careful not to answer personally. Unfortunately, this meant that the senders did not know for certain whether their messages had been received. The Canadian wives had also been led to believe that the radio was not available to them to use.

Stage Four

APRIL 15. DAY 44

Max

Christmas time again! An opportunity to pig out with family and friends, have snowball fights, and open presents and mail. Included in my care package was a copy of a very official letter from Peter Baird to Nan, outlining the impossibility of a North Pole wedding. The implication was that it would not be acceptable to the sponsors, but no specific source of opposition was noted. The reasons matter very little. If Conexus is unwilling to assist, the exercise becomes impossible.

We're still alive, and we've made it to rest break number three. As a group, we've had an uncanny combination of good support, good experience, and good luck. Of all the expedition members, I've probably fared the least well to this point. The combination of huge blisters and frozen toes has kept me limping since the first week.

There is a single-mindedness within our ranks that has buoyed me along through the tough bits. It is manifested in such things as the redistribution of group equipment so that laggers like me can keep up. I think the worst is over for me, but we've all been subjected to incredible physical and mental stress.

The cold alone is stress enough, but it is compounded by sleep deprivation, physical exhaustion, injuries, illness, a rather unusual diet, lack of privacy, communication and cultural barriers, and absence of women. It's taken its toll. Even after we dealt with the diarrhoea, many people continued to have bowel cramps, and I have had heart-burn almost constantly. The antacid tablets deal with it short term, but I'm afraid that I may be at risk for peptic ulcers, so I've started myself on Tagamet.

This feast-or-famine approach to nutrition is pretty weird. I have lost up to five kilos during a two-week stage, but two days of solid gorging usually recovers most of it. I've noticed the stress affecting me emotionally as well. I'm not generally a hysterical kind of guy, but I often find myself swinging between inexplicable laughter and tearful-ness inside my Goretex prison.

Our single-mindedness is not universal, though. I guess I feel more a part of the Soviet group than the other Canucks; maybe more than I feel a part of the Canadian group. Laurie is my closest confidant, but I have no trouble interacting on a personal level with any of the Soviets. Chris and Richard's pre-existing bond has done a good deal to isolate them from everyone else, as Dmitri feared. Neither of them is disposed toward diplomacy, and though I enjoy Holloway's company, I find both of them selfish. We all have selfish motives for being here, but they deny any more altruistic aims, and indeed their isolationism bears this out.

So there are conflicts, both international and intranational, but the interpersonal and internal ones are definitely more significant. At least we are single-minded enough that we're all going in the same direction – 313 km in the last stage. This kind of progress virtually assures us of arriving at the Pole on schedule.

APRIL 16. DAY 45

Laurie

We found the day began to slip by until, at one point, I asked Dmitri, "What are our plans for the day?" He replied that we would try to get ready and do a couple of hours' skiing just to get moving. However, they all lay around until about 5:00 p.m. Chris was on duty by this time, and was being given a hard time. He was finding it difficult, because rest-day duties are extremely busy and tiresome for the person on duty. There are so many extra things to do, and the Soviet members in particular were asking for more and more food. Chris just could not keep up with their unreasonable demands and was becoming annoyed and curt.

About five o'clock I said, "Even if we start packing now it is going to be seven or eight p.m. before we leave." Everybody was galvanized into action to get the food distributed and get packed, but of course by that time it was too late, and so we just stayed for our evening meal and continued working on the radio, and thus ended up having a third rest day. What gets to me is that I have the feeling Dmitri had already decided to have a third stop day, and probably the other Soviets were in on it as well, but did not inform the Canadians, probably thinking it would be opposed.

I re-read the letter that Sheena wrote on the twenty-first of March. It is a long time ago, but in it she talks of my Dad's death, and I found out today I was able to grieve a little bit more than I have been doing, I suppose. It hurts, but I realize that it is all so necessary.

Richard

This morning, Dmitri informed us that the mysterious camp about five to six kilometres south of us has been identified. They have four flags flying there – two American, one Canadian, and one N.W.T. flag. So we can assume that the people there are from those countries and territory, but why and who remains a great mystery.

APRIL 17. DAY 46

Max

It's a beautiful day now, the overcast sky having given way to brilliant sunshine. The temperature is around minus 30 and will warm up as the sun rises higher behind us. This diary entry has been taken en route, courtesy of high technology. I'm dictating on the trail, the new office on the move. This is the first day I've been able to wear sunglasses without them frosting to the point of opacity. In the nick of time, too, I'd say. The sun is powerful, and even with it at our backs, the reflected rays were enough to give me second-degree facial sunburn at the last stage.

We're travelling through an area of very old ice: many seasons' accumulation of snow covers the thick pans, and formations are large and worn smooth by the forces of nature. It's spectacular, but there are no trees. I like trees.

It looks like our first fifty-minute march of the day is up. I can see those ahead of me grouping and dropping their packs. Another minute and I'll be able to do the same. It'll be great. God, it's amazing the things that will make you happy up here. Six months ago, all I wanted was a red Mercedes. Now, to sit for five minutes is my main goal in life.

Christopher

Today we skied eight hours with our post-airdrop heavy packs. The first day after the airdrop is the one you always dread. It went fairly well. We are now at 88 degrees. We did 12 minutes of latitude. Twelve is the magic number because, in order to reach the Pole by the twenty-sixth, we have to do 12 minutes every day. Now, if we can do 12 minutes on the first day after the airdrop, with heavy packs, then we should be able to do more later on . . . .

APRIL 18. DAY 47

Max

There will be no wedding at the North Pole. For me a disappointment, if only because it will mean another month before I see my bride-to-be. It's a strange concept, marriage. Not that I haven't thought of it before, but I've actually been able to suppress the idea, or redirect my thinking before this point. On the ice there are no distractions, no focus for redirection. Straight across the Pole to the altar.

I thought a few months would give both of us a chance to reflect individually on our lives before committing ourselves. For me, the reflection didn't require months. The power of isolation, the clarity of this huge "tabula rasa" to sketch one's life upon – the inestimable value of suffering. Such decisions make themselves under these conditions.

I have never really suffered before. I was born into a world of abundance, and good fortune has followed me reliably through the years. In such a world, most, if not all, hardships are self-inflicted, and

I guess this is a prime example. To have the opportunity to suffer was one of my main motives for participating in this folly. For a typical spoiled North American of the 1980s, maybe it will be a source of strength, of enlightenment.

Christopher

Minus 35°; only 5 degrees from minus 40°. I told Richard that as I went on his recommendation to make the senetatta bet with Yuri, I was hoping he would contribute to the fund if I lost. He agreed, on condition that I also split the winnings. Fair enough. A bottle each it will be – I hope.

The second day of skiing after our third airdrop. There is absolutely no wind, and the sun is shining. I am wearing the pants of my polar suit, my Chlorophylle jacket wide open, with long underwear underneath, and I am still sweating. So I thought I'd celebrate the fine conditions with a little ditty.

They say I've got a habit
They say it's kind of sad
I never really noticed
Until it got this bad

It started off in high school
With camping trips and such
But who knows, maybe this time
I've bitten off too much

'Cause I'm out here with the Russians
We're outnumbered two to one
We're freezing on the ocean
And frying in the sun.

I've had forty days in the wilderness
With sixty more to go
With a monkey on my back
And my little sled in tow

We've got bug eyes coloured green
And rubber on our face
And each night in the tent we cry:
"Hey, where is my place?"

Laurie has been losing sleep because of the radio and noise in the tent, so today he kept us moving by being the first one up and about after the rest breaks. So tonight we should get to sleep at a reasonable time.

I'm still amazed at how badly Laurie skis. If he or Dmitri is in front of you at a pressure ridge, you might just as well find another spot to cross, rather than wait. He does zip along quite nicely on the flats.

Today we celebrated Vasa's thirty-ninth birthday with a bottle of senetate. The usual one tablespoon each. Tonight he will again be sleeping outside. I find this a surprising habit for him, as he was so adamant about us sleeping in the main tent at the beginning.

Laurie

Fortunately, this was a very cold day again, minus 35°C with à slight following wind. I never thought I would use the word "fortunate" in connection with cold temperatures, but I say fortunately because that meant that I had to wear my full travelling gear of windpants and parka, and, of course, it is easier to carry this extra weight on one's body than in one's pack.

A lot of the time I am able to daydream and think about different things, whereas earlier in the expedition, carrying a heavy load, my total concentration was on the weight and on the pain, and on the problems with balance, and so on. So one of the things I daydreamed about for one pleasant hour was putting together a choir again for Fort Smith, and putting on another cantata, and also the possibility of putting on a program of mixed sacred music with testimonies, especially if we could take it on tour to Yellowknife and Hay River.

APRIL 19. DAY 48

Max

We're now 32 minutes away from 89 degrees, 5 minutes on the Soviet side. That's the halfway point of the trek. We should be able to get there by the twentieth of April. The estimate of a hundred days to reach Ellesmere seems reasonable.

I don't know what I'd do if my tape recorder ever crapped out. We've become quite intimate. Nothing perverse, you understand, but old Micro-Dick, as he's come to be known, is privy to all my most personal secrets. I lie semi-conscious at night, with the snores roaring in the background and we exchange pillow talk.

Christopher

We passed through some spectacular pressure ridges this morning. One had ice blocks piled thirty to forty feet high. We had to walk through one particularly nasty stretch. We had a break on the other side. We had to wait for Dmitri and Yuri. They refused to take off their skis to get through this stuff.

Then we came across some huge leads, about a kilometre across, which had frozen only about a week ago. It's stuff like this that we want to hurry for; as the weather gets warmer, these won't be refreezing.

Richard

Today we had nice pressure ridges, the biggest and most beautiful and picturesque yet. Lots of good-sized blocks of ice, the size of cars or maybe even small houses. They are all piled up, nice and green. But they make life interesting, climbing over them, especially with the sled. I only needed help about once today, so I was getting better. I'm not as good as Mish, but he has had more practice. Bumps his little sled around a lot better than us. Chris put a hole in his sled today. I also cracked mine a little bit, too. They sure are good, because after eight marches I could have gone for another two marches easily, not really the slightest bit tired.

APRIL 21. DAY 50

Christopher

Seven forty-one p.m. It was an awful day – really windy – a headwind, too. It was about minus 25°, but the wind was twelve metres per second. I almost fell through a lead. Everybody had skied across, and Toli Fedjakov was standing on the other side. I managed to get the tip of my ski on the far side, and my foot was in line with the near side, my little sled in tow, on the near side also. So I stepped off to the far side, so now my right ski was in the middle of the lead. Put both poles on the far side. At this point, my left ski slid backwards, and the tip went right into the water. I wasn't braced very well with my poles, and so I started to fall head first towards the far side. Except I knew that I wouldn't make it to the far side. So I sort of jumped off my right foot, and did a nice shoulder roll onto the far bank, with my knapsack. While I was doing this, my sled, I thought, was in the water. There I was lying on my stomach, with my pack on top of me, tangled up in the sled cord. As I was tangled up, I asked Toli Fedjakov if he wouldn't mind moving my sled out of the water.

Later, I was standing in line waiting to cross an ice crack, and suddenly the ground opened up beneath my feet. I heard this great big *crack!*, and then the crack formed right underneath my feet. I waited a while, so that it would become large enough to actually call a crevice. After a minute or so, it got to be about an inch and a half wide, and by then I was holding up the line, so I had to ski on.

Trying to ski when the light is flat can be a real problem, especially if you are in the front. Not that I've done that much. But I have it on good authority from those of us who do. . . . Okay, so I avoid it. I don't like skiing in the front, because you have to work. I just like cruising behind the first few. You ski in front, you have to work hard. You might even sweat, and I don't like sweating. So I just sit in the back. Usually, I stay in back just in case there are any good photo opportunities. When the trip is over, it will have been more important to have good pictures than to have said that I made the first tracks. I got a good one of Mish falling in. A historic occasion, because it's the first time he's ever fallen through the ice, and he has been on all sorts of polar trips. He is a really good skier, too, He is called "thin ice Malakhov," because what happens is we'll come to a tricky part that no one wants to cross, and Dmitri calls on Misha to go across. And then the rest of us follow.

Laurie

The stoves are going, everything is in hand. I have the water on, the milk added, the dried meat in; all I have to do now is to wait for the water to boil and put in the Shaklee muesli after it is taken off the stove. The water in the other pot will soon be boiling and ready to add coffee. Then I will fill up the flasks for the day, and we are ready to serve breakfast. Everything is well in hand, and it is still only 3:25 a.m. I have already taken my sleeping bag outside, but I had to put my packsack on it because the wind is blowing very hard. What is more, it is blowing from the north; not good news in terms of the drift, and it's going to make travelling uncomfortable.

We set out in a blizzard. As we were packing, we could hear the rumble and growl of moving ice. About a hundred metres from the tent we watched huge slabs of ice very, very slowly being pushed upwards, tilting and grumbling and cracking. A pressure ridge was being formed. Shortly after setting out, we came to open water. It is hard to know exactly what it was, but there was a large area of open water with the waves being whipped up by the wind on it. We had to travel sideways, but very soon it turned and we were able to find a way around it. This happened two or three times in the morning, but, after a couple of hours, conditions began to improve. Once again we found ourselves crossing a number of danger zones, places where the leads had come together and were forming pressure ridges, making noises even as we moved across them. A couple of people almost had accidents.

This was our fiftieth day on the ice, and we passed 89 degrees, 5 minutes, which is the halfway point, so actually we are absolutely on schedule for our hundred-day crossing. We are hoping that the first half will have been the harder, and that the next half will go faster than fifty days. Of course, it is hard to estimate all the possible factors. We have been running into open water even though weather conditions are improving, and if this continued, or the ice deteriorated, it would slow us down considerably, and certainly with winds like this it would make travelling extremely difficult.

Richard

A very windy day, twelve to fifteen metres per second – according to Vasa, a very experienced man – from the north-northwest, so basically straight into our faces. Right off the start we encountered a large lead, and we spent about an hour getting around. We came to a spot where a large piece had broken away from the edge and turned sideways. We managed to use it as a bridge, and jump across. Then, after that, throughout the day, we kept running into minor small leads, anywhere from four feet to six feet or eight feet across. We had to work our way across these small cracks. It kept us on our toes, made the day interesting.

Just as I was leaving the tent after supper, bound for our tent, Dmitri said, "Richard, we have a problem." And I thought, "Uh-oh, now what?" He said, "Moscow thinks that Fiodor should leave the expedition at the North Pole because we don't have the money that we agreed on. What do you think?" I said I thought that it was a very bad thing, and that if someone started on an expedition they should finish it. I thought that if thirteen people reached Canada it could be a very successful expedition because with so many people there is a very good chance of someone getting injured and not making it. If you send him out we will have partially failed. But if we can reach Canada with all thirteen people, it will be a significant achievement.

Dmitri agreed with this, and Laurie agreed with this. Then Dmitri said, "Well, maybe we can come up with the money. But I have another variant idea, how about if you and your wife, Chris and his wife, Max and Laurie and their wives, Peter, Paul, and Danielle all come to the Soviet Union and have an expense-paid holiday?" I said that if we have to pay for air transportation, that really doesn't help a lot. Max and Laurie said that if we were paying for the resupply and pick-up aircraft anyway, what was the difference having two extra people?

The point is we had a deal. We agreed to the extra people, and they agreed to two-thirteenths of the Canadian expenses. We have been learning about their deals.

APRIL 22. DAY 51

Richard

During the seventh march, the sun went behind some clouds, and it became just a red spot. I had to look behind me to see the sun in order to navigate, because there were no shadows. The light became so flat that I had a really hard time skiing. A couple of times I tripped over some drifts and fell. It was awful.

We only did 9 minutes of latitude, so we are up to 89 degrees, 21 minutes. The ice station drifted south so it is very likely that we drifted backwards (south) a little, and we did drift west a full 9 degrees; we are at 80 degrees longitude. This is rather interesting. If you plot where we should be located by calculating with the direction we are heading and the speed we normally go, and then look at the drift of the ice station for the last twenty-four hours, then superimpose the ice station drift onto our theoretical movement, it is exactly where we are now!

From now on we could end up fighting the ocean currents, not simply wind-induced drifts. We have drifted from 89 degrees to 80 degrees in twenty-four hours (a degree of longitude here is approximately three quarters of a nautical mile). We drifted west about thirteen kilometres in twenty-four hours. That is an awfully long way, almost farther than we can ski in one day. It means that if we find ourselves on the downstream side of that drift, we could not even ski against it. Even if we skied all day, and then camped, we would drift back farther than we skied. We have to be careful what we do or we will be swept past the Pole.

APRIL 23. DAY 52

Laurie

Yesterday, after being on duty the day before, I was sleeping at the side of the tent close to the door, and my bag kept getting covered with snow. However, to add insult to injury, I woke up cold in the night to find the door wide open, and a lot of snow blown in. It is somewhat amusing – if it were not so annoying – to get my bag covered, and it shows how blasé people are getting about the cold and wind. The environment is still incredibly hostile, and anybody who suddenly dropped in on us would be appalled, but for us it has become a normal part of our world, and even in 25 below temperatures and a whistling wind the guys don't notice or bother if the door of the tent is left open!

Richard

We came to one lead which was a little bit more open than the rest. We had a rest break there, and afterwards Dmitri said, "Oh, let's bridge across here, Richard," so I took a ski pole and I poked it and it really didn't look very thick or very solid. I said, "No thanks, it is too thin for me." So he contemplates it for a while, and he looks around and he says, "Malakhov, get over here. Try it." So Misha pokes it a bit with his ski, climbs down, throws a few skis across, climbs on top, and runs across, on the skis, to the other side, no problem! Eventually everybody crossed on these pairs of skis. On every occasion when there is thin ice, everyone comes up, stops, and looks at the ice. Up comes Mish, he looks at the ice, and walks out onto it, no problem.

When I was leading the last march, we came to an area of leads, like many narrow creeks with black water partially covered with drifted snow. At one lead, Volodi came up behind me and said, "Let's go around." I looked around. It was a shattered area, small splintered leads going everywhere, little pressure ridges, chopped up ice, just nowhere to ski at all. I was getting tired because the light was flat, and I couldn't see where I was stepping.

Then I thought, if Misha was here he would probably walk right across this. So I took off my pack, and I walked right across it, no problem. My heart was in my mouth a little, but it was not too bad. The only thing was that my backpack was back on the other side, so I had to return.

APRIL 24. DAY 53

Christopher

Lately, we have been getting quite a bit of open water. There's an elasticity in the ice, so the ice will crack and open up, freeze in the middle, and then close back up just a bit because the ice springs open and closes. I got a few pictures of that with the ice in the middle that has refrozen and then gets compressed. It sort of bends as much as it can, and then starts cracking. There is not an awful lot of intellectual stimulation here, and so I look at the ice a lot.

The ice around here is really impressive. I've seen black ice, although there's not very much of that. You hold it up to the light, and it's black. Full of mud, or something like that. There's gravel up here too.

Richard

We are in the region of the North Pole. Compared to the Steger expedition, it hasn't been very hard getting here. Except when I was sick, I was never really tired. There have been lots of expected discomforts, like frost-bite, icy sleeping bags, and having to shit outside. But we've just skied to the North Pole. It is supposed to be hard. Well, it hasn't been.

This puts me for the second time at the North Pole in less than two years. Also, I am the first person to go from Canada to the North Pole, and from the Soviet Union to the North Pole, to approach it from both sides.

APRIL 25. DAY 54

Richard

I was talking to Volodi yesterday. He wanted to know how many millionaires there are in Canada. I asked him, "How many millionaires are in the Soviet Union?" and he said, "I don't think as many as in Canada, but I guess there are some." Then he continued: "Money really doesn't do a lot of good because there is nothing to spend it on." He said, "Even if you have the money to buy a car, you might not be able to find a car to buy." He said he is going to buy a new car in the fall. I said, "If we get to Canada?" and he said, "Yes," and he laughed. I suppose that one of the perks he receives for going on this expedition is that he is going to get the money, or the permission, or both, to buy a new car. He is the only Soviet who owns a car.

Max

I had always pictured the arrival at this final pre-polar campsite as the point at which we would start whooping it up, but instead I found the mood of the group to be strangely sombre. Holloway and I had been skiing along singing sixties rock-and-roll favourites, and arrived feeling celebratory. As we slalomed down the final ridge into camp, I pulled an "Eddie the Eagle" and imploded into a knot of arms and legs, which launched us both into hysterical laughter. I crawled out from the tangled mass of packstraps and skis, and clutching my poles just above the baskets like ice-picks, dragged my wasted hind limbs back to the top of the ridge. I slumped melodramatically as I planted one of my poles erect in the snow. Though no one else seemed impressed, Holloway accommodated me with a picture.

Tonight we sent out the official announcements and telegrams to heads of state. The ceremony was scheduled for midnight Dikson time, or noon Ottawa time, on the twenty-sixth, so we had a day to prepare documents and speeches. Yuri, Sasha, and Dmitri concocted a statement or "appeal to the world," as they called it, and Laurie and I offered minor modifications.

Richard

This morning, the Soviets, Yuri, Dmitri, and company, prepared a public statement to be read from Moscow. Piotr Strezev translated it into English to be released from the Canadian Embassy. It was titled, "An Appeal to the Peoples of the Earth," and it went on to say that our common goal in doing this expedition was to unite the earth in peace. Chris and I did not agree with it, Laurie liked it, and Max didn't mind it too much. These are rather grandiose ideas, and that wasn't really the reason why we are here. The main goal that united us was the fact that we all want to get to Canada, and that – that alone – keeps us as one coherent group.

So, we managed to delete the one sentence, and change the title from Ski Expedition Soviet Union-Canada, to Soviet-Canadian Transpolar Ski Expedition. It said that we joined our lives and destinies together entirely in doing this expedition, which really is not true, so we deleted the word entirely. It said our common goal was a first step in making the Arctic Polar Region a region of peace and co-operation. That wasn't bad. But generally the whole thing makes me feel very uncomfortable.

During the morning, helicopters from NP 28 dropped in, and the first unscarred faces we had seen since Arkticheskiy popped in through the door of the tent. Strezev and the illustrious Snegirev lifted the mood within our ranks with hearty congratulations and promises of crates of Soviet ice cream after the ceremony.

Laurie

The question is, do we announce we are at the North Pole or not? Most expeditions consider anything within five minutes as being accurate enough to be considered the North Pole. We have such fine-tuned scientific methods of measurement that we can actually be more precise than that, and so we are camped about 1.9 minutes from the precise position of the Pole – in other words, about 3.5 kilometres. We know that we are drifting down to the Pole during tonight and tomorrow. The radio has been in use pretty constantly since we camped, and I sent messages to Bishop Sperry, to Archbishop Michael Peers, to my Mum, and to Andrew and Alison, but when I asked if I could send an official message on the radio to Canada, Dmitri replied quite emphatically, "No, we are not at the Pole yet."

So that was fair enough, and I thought, "Okay, I'll do it tomorrow, by which time we will probably have drifted over and beyond the Pole." But then, to my chagrin, in talking to the other Soviet members I discovered that he had already sent a message to Premier Gorbachev and to *Komsomolskaya Pravda*, and they have already received messages of congratulations from this newspaper and various other groups in Moscow. I felt that this was unfair and that he should have sent official messages to his people and yet suggested so curtly that I should not consider it official for us. So I ignored his opinion and got back on the radio and sent a message through Barry Garratt saying that the first span of the bridge is complete and that our expedition reached the North Pole today at this particular time.

There was a lively discussion among the Soviets after supper tonight led by Volodi. When we asked what it was about he said that they were discussing whether God was with us. Of course, most of these men would claim that they don't really believe in God, but some do not seem so sure about it. Volodi was saying that he believes that God must have been with us because the water that could have stopped us had been frozen over, and other conditions had changed, such as the contrary wind and things like that. I am not quite sure how serious the conversation was, but at least it occurred. Obviously, I, for one, do believe that God is with us.

I sent a message to Archbishop Michael Peers, starting off with a quotation from Acts, "And you shall be witnesses for me in Jerusalem, in all Judaea and Samaria, and to the ends of the earth," and I said that perhaps the "ends of the earth" doesn't literally mean the North Pole, but it can be taken in this way, and we have indeed fulfilled this quotation today.

It has been a long time coming, I suppose a lifelong process, but in many ways this is the culmination of all the expedition work I have done in the past, and the fulfilment of a childhood dream. Yet there was very little excitement. Everything went just as normal. We pitched camp as normal, and made supper as normal. There was a lot of interest taken in waiting for the location transmitted through the radio, but otherwise things have gone on just as always.

Around 56 minutes, very close to the North Pole, we came across polar bear prints. They were well frozen over, but because of the wind and the snow that we have had over the last few days, these prints couldn't have been more than a week ago. It boggles the mind to think of a polar bear right at the North Pole, 750 km from the nearest land. How it lives, I don't know.

APRIL 26. DAY 55

Max

Some time in mid-afternoon word came over the radio that the Canadian contingent was weathered in at Eureka. In the early evening, we broke our camp "in the wings" and struck out to complete our victorious arrival at the Pole.

It was a wild feeling. At about two kilometres from the site, we could see something that looked like flags rising above the horizon. As we got closer, we recognized them as balloons decorated with brightly painted greetings. Soon we could see Soviet and Canadian flags flying among them, and, not to be overshadowed, McDonald's familiar golden arches. At this moment, more than any other, for some inexplicable reason, I felt a wave of emotion.

I would never have believed that seeing a hamburger sign at the North Pole could be a numinous experience, but I think the realization that life in the "real world" was unchanged was enough to send my limbic system into spasm. As we slid dreamlike over the final pressure ridges into the ceremonial site, we were greeted by various members of the Soviet support team, including Valera the cosmonaut, and Sasha Shumilov, both of whom we had last seen in Dikson.

A large circle had been soaked in the snow with blue dye to represent the Arctic Circle. At its centre, "the Pole" itself – a cyclindrical piece of ice about four feet high – gleamed brightly in the sunshine. Sundry temporary structures lay about, among them a radio communications tent, an equipment tent, a tent for the staff from the drifting station, and two large inflatable buildings, probably five-by-eight metres each. These two blubbery domiciles lay with doors facing, and would be used to house the journalists and *"oochesnikum expeditse"* (expedition members) after the ceremony.

It was already close to midnight, and it was obvious it was going to take at least six or seven hours for the Canadian plane to get here, if it came at all. We decided that we might as well sleep, so instead of putting up the tent, we just used one of the big inflated buildings.

We were awakened at about eight-thirty by the flap of helicopter blades, but we weren't exactly galvanized into action. We lay stuporous, half-cringing in the bottom of our sleeping bags, reluctant to face the music.

Laurie

We started to get dressed, and during the process a few heads began to poke into the tent – people like Vladimir Snegirev and others, and it wasn't long before, lo and behold, Joe Womersley comes in, and, spaced out behind him, one by one, others came in – Jill Cob, the Grassie brothers, Jo Wells, and others whom I knew. I can't begin to name everybody who was there, but it was really great to see all these old running friends. We shared lots of hugs, and then the door opened again, and to my absolute consternation, in walked Sheena.

Of course, I was delighted to see her, although I don't know that I showed it quite as I should have, but I was also dumbfounded, as we had been told quite categorically that no wives were coming as it would cost too much. It turns out that Joe had called her up and made all the arrangements. When she protested he told her it was too late as he had paid her fare and made all the arrangements all the way from Fort Smith to Ottawa and to the Pole! I guess it didn't take too much persuading after all that! And there she was. Later on, I was just passing by Peter Baird, and he happened to say, "When I get back I'll phone your wife and let her know that you are well." He didn't even know that he had travelled up in the same plane as her. Apparently, it was done in absolute secrecy. Joe had booked her under a false name, and when they were at Iqaluit airport, for example, Sheena was made to go off into a corner, wearing dark glasses, so that people wouldn't recognize her and spill the beans.

Max

When we stumbled into the bright light of day, there were hundreds of people milling around – well, 189 to be exact. Most of them were press. Canadian reporters carried out some informal interviews, and Holloway and I made a brief television appearance in which we were unable to put together a coherent sentence and broke down giggling like schoolgirls.

Soon the ceremony began. The press and members of the "audience" gathered in one end of the blue circle, and the dignitaries in the other end, with all of us surrounded by enormous flag banners provided by The Polar Pacers. Snegirev acted as the master of ceremonies, with Mr. Nyet (Peter Baird, as christened by the Soviets) wedging in a few words of diplomatic rhetoric at intervals.

The first address was delivered by Uri Israel, the Soviet minister of hydrometeorology, with excellent translation provided. Next, Marcel Masse, looking dapper in his caribou-skin parka, spoke with equal eloquence in French and English. His talk included some excerpts of Robert Service's poetry, though he never spoke about the "strange things done 'neath the midnight sun." I had taught some of the Soviets the first few lines of "The Cremation of Sam McGee," and was hoping that we could all join in the chorus. Masse's words were a heart-warming welcome back into Canadian waters. Dennis Patterson then spoke about similarities between northern peoples of our two lands and the necessity for the development of strong friendships between not only newcomers to the North, but the indigenous peoples as well. Part of his address was delivered in Inuktitut, which he then translated himself.

Dmitri followed with a moving appeal for world peace and acknowledged the individual strengths of each of the expedition members. His speech struck a chord with the audience.

He was followed by Mr. Albert Reichmann. By this time, everyone was cold enough that the arm flapping and jogging on the spot obscured his words. The microphone had mysteriously shut off, and the translator completely ignored him until Snegirev, sensing Reichmann's plight, elbowed the translator in the ribs. Startled, the translator admitted in two languages that he hadn't been paying attention. I felt badly for the poor man, who had travelled so far under such adverse conditions, and had sponsored the trip so generously.

After Reichmann, a Soviet cosmonaut named Axionov rambled at length about the similarities between travel in space and travel on the ice. By now, the audience was flapping and writhing and jogging violently in an attempt to stay warm. Richard's speech was mercifully short and to the point, and Laurie's and Yuri's appeal to the peoples of the world topped the event off.

Upon returning to the inflatable shelter, we found a voracious hoard dining on the delicacies that the Polar Pacers had brought up for us. It seems that with all the delays and excitement, someone had forgotten that 189 people would need to eat. The gastronomic orgy that took place resulted in the disappearance of several kilograms of raw bacon and sausages in seconds. A robust Soviet journalist whose name escapes me, but whose dimensions linger in my mind, had her face completely immersed in her hands which were cupped full of raw bacon. We watched in horror as the last strands disappeared down the massive eating machine.

But as quickly as the locusts had appeared, they were forced to depart. News of worsening weather conditions drove the first groups back to the whirlybirds before they could wipe their chins. One could sense rising panic among those who remained, awaiting the second shuttle to the drifting station – the gateway home. I shared a few brief parting words with Paul Larocque and Mr. Nyet, and at twelve-thirty Dikson time the event was over.

The unfamiliar intensity of social interaction left all our heads spinning. Don't forget, we're agoraphobics – that's why we're here in the first place. Having all these people around, if only for four hours, was enough to make most of us want to bolt for our skis and scurry off over the nearest pressure ridge.

Laurie

In other circumstances the speeches would have been fine, but for this setting some of them were just a little bit on the long side. For people suddenly to find themselves stepping from the cocoon of twentieth-century technology into the middle of this bitter primaeval world was quite a shock, and many of them got cold. The Polar Pacers, for example, were dressed for running, and they did eventually manage to set out a loop over the rolling ice and run for half an hour. We were cold as well, because we were dressed for working, and our clothing isn't really suitable for standing around.

On the other hand, I suppose that is what it was all about, and we hope that it really will have ripples of effectiveness that will help relationships between our two countries. So, eventually, I am not sure exactly of the time, I wasn't checking my watch, possibly around 1:00 p.m., I walked with Sheena to the helicopter, and she got on, and that was it. How I would have loved to have had even half an hour by ourselves to talk, but we never had more than a few seconds of hastily snatched conversation, and never a single moment alone. However, she was able to give me some letters, ones that my Mum had written and that Anne had written to us in Fort Smith, and this gave me a lot more information about by Dad's death, and about how things are progressing since then, and what my Mum's plans are.

Now I find myself torn between emotions. One moment I wish we could have had more time with our visitors who dropped in from outer space, and the next I have a sense of relief that they have all gone and left us to our own familiar world of ice and snow.

SUMMARY

The skiers had reached the Pole by the date expected. They were now more than halfway to Canada – because their starting point in Soviet Siberia was farther from the Pole than their landing place in Canada would be. The team had stayed together, no one had been taken off because of injury, and the worst of the cold weather was over.

However, they faced what lay ahead with uncertainty. The ice was expected to be more difficult to cross on the Canadian side. Canadian ice averages twenty years in age, whereas Soviet ice averages five years; the currents in the Arctic Ocean cause ice on the Canadian side to loop around, growing rougher and thicker, whereas Soviet ice fans out into the Atlantic Ocean. Also, as the season progressed, they could expect to encounter open water.

They were in good physical condition. Max's foot was improved, and all the skiers were feeling strong. Some of the skiers – both Soviets and Canadians – were actually gaining weight, as they were eating the same diet as earlier while skiing more efficiently and expending fewer calories to keep warm.

The latter half of April, during which they had completed stage four, afforded optimal conditions for Arctic travel: it was still sunny, with little wind, and temperatures were relatively easy, averaging minus 25 to minus 30°C. The ice had been relatively flat thus far, but they were now starting to see what the Soviets called "Canadian ice" with bigger ridges.

The various opinions about the tents, equipment use, and diet had been argued to death. In the articles they sent out by radio, the Soviets asserted that their equipment was better; but Misha ceased to believe this, and because he did not want to lie or be censured, stopped writing articles. Richard and Christopher were insistent that the Soviets have sponsor patches on their clothing. This went against the grain for some, for instance Vasa, who was a Leninist. But Dmitri made members sew on patches showing the sponsor's name, to honour their commitment.

Group relations were at a low point. All the members were tired of arguments that were never resolved, but simply abandoned. For the homeward (for Canadians) half of the trek, the issue that became contentious was how many hours they would ski each day. It had become clear that the Soviets had much more relaxed attitudes about deadlines, but their positions had yet to be stated clearly.

The North Pole stay represented a high point in diet. The skiers had a veritable feast during the rest period on top of the world, although it was not quite the feast that the media described. Twelve loaves of homemade bread from Christopher's mother, Dorothea, and twelve cases of Molson's beer vanished as the resupply equipment and food made their way through N.P. 28 to the Pole. So the *Maclean's* magazine article that referred to "Beer and lobster at the Pole" was in error – the beer never made it, and there were only a few small morsels of lobster in André Moreau's delicious appetizer.

The sense the Canadians had had until now of being cut off ended at the Pole. Manager Peter Baird from Conexus arrived with good news regarding finances and media coverage, which eased their minds. They also received letters and care packages from home. Radio communication was much easier now that they were using NP 28, rather than Sredny, as the base.

The Canadians summed up their feelings at this point in a speech that Richard delivered during the North Pole ceremony:

"As our group approached the Pole, it was evident [to us] that the polar ice was not dramatically different from what we had been travelling on for the past fifty-four days. So what draws us to this unique point? The Pole holds a powerful secret which has fascinated mankind since its existence was first revealed. The secret is different for all who rediscover it. To earn its familiarity requires time, unswerving motivation, and considerable hardship.

"We have not conquered the Pole; indeed, any surrender or any

Stage Five

APRIL 27. DAY 56

Richard

There is definitely something to be said for the simplicity of life on the trail in the Arctic. Maybe it is prolonged discomforts and the little things that are sort of a pain in the ass, such as shitting outside. But you are always eating, sleeping, or travelling, and life is very simple. None of the complicated complex worries of the South such as mortgages, traffic fines, parties, entertainment, jobs, whatever.

Chris and I made breakfast. We made scrambled eggs in the new pot, and it started to burn at the bottom. There was not much we could do because the pot is very thin. So the next time, in the future, it would be better to use boiled eggs. Then all the radio people came in, Sasha Shatokhin, Piotr Strezev, and company, and, by that time, we had twenty-three people in the tent. So breakfast didn't go very far, needless to say. Eventually, they climbed into the helicopter, and off they went. We were all alone, with just our little tent and the few odd bits of garbage left behind.

APRIL 28. DAY 57

Richard

Six fifty-five in the evening. We have finished breakfast, which took three hours. Now we are heating water for the sauna. We are going through our pre-sauna routine. Max goes around and measures with the calipers how fat everyone is getting or not getting. Misha goes around and checks everybody's body for lesions, bruises, and other abnormalities. I was pretty good this time, nothing except getting fatter. We also got weighed. We didn't have the bathroom scales, so we had the Soviet weigh scale up on a tripod outside. We all ran outside in our underwear, got weighed, and then ran back in. I was up to seventy-two kilos. I have never weighed seventy-two kilos in my life. I can also tell by my stomach I am fatter than I have ever been, and my numbers on the calipers were way up. It is definitely time to cut back on my food. Chris is also getting fatter, Max is getting fatter, Laurie is getting fatter. A lot of the Soviets continue yet to get thinner. Why? I am not quite sure. Chris and I pulled sleds the last time. We don't work as hard, because we are more efficient, because of better skiing technique and physical conditioning; hence we get fatter and they get thinner.

Misha is doing an operation on Yuri's nose. He is removing all the dead material. He has a little spray bottle; he freezes the nose, covers it over and around with some gauze, and removes the dead material.

Max's toe is coming around very nicely. You can see all the pink coming through now. His toenail came off the smaller toe, and it is all pink underneath, and I presume the same thing will happen with the big toe shortly. So he has been very lucky with that. He has been changing his footwear regularly. He does not get enough support with the kamiks, so he will try the Soviet ski boot without the overboot.

APRIL 29. DAY 58

Max

Laurie and I were engaged in a conversation about religion, which Toli Melnikov joined. It evolved into a general discussion about problems inherent in Soviet and North American societies, respectively, though we really didn't get into anything too specific. Nonetheless, it was a pleasant change because we haven't had many conversations of this genre, and hopefully it is indicative of a new state of relaxed communication.

Christopher

During our sauna we heard the snow creaking outside the tent like someone was walking around, but of course, after a quick head count, we found that all were accounted for. So the next thing we thought of was where was the gun? No problem, it was near the edge of the tent. Volodi went outside to have a look around and said that he could see nothing. After the sauna, Fiodor had gone out to our tent, and he came running back saying that a lead had opened up between the two tents.

I guess that it is literally the rift that has figuratively divided the two camps. We all stood around it for a while laughing and trying to get a good photo angle. It missed our parachute tent by about three feet. Dmitri fell in it; Misha pissed in it, and everybody laughed.

The Canadians' personal food bothers the Soviets. The rationale is that everyone should have the same amount of strength, the same pack weight, the same skiing ability, and the same metabolism, and consequently require the same amount of food. Of course, none of these is true. My pack is under 40 kg, and some of them are carrying over 50 kg because of personal clothing, which is spared discussion; but Dmitri said that if I eat more food I will have more energy. Sasha Believ accused the Canadians of eating two hundred grams of personal food a day, like cakes baked by wives, which is bullshit except for Richard's case. Misha had wanted to take some personal food, but others won't let him.

I am incredibly pissed off, because this so-called leader of ours, Mr. Shparo, obviously had no intention of getting our group moving today as he had promised yesterday. Why I ever believed him, I now cannot understand. He just seemed so sincere. I can't see why I should ever trust him. I have been on duty with Richard, cooking our Canadian meals now, for three days because we wanted them to turn out well. This also makes it the third break in a row that I have been on duty. Since we stopped before the Pole, it has been five days. And still there are complaints that we need more rest. Well, I have been working, and I am much more tired after their "rest" days than after travelling days, even when I'm off duty.

Laurie

I went for a short walk, and took the Russian New Testament which I have carried with me right from the beginning, found a large chunk of pressure ice, opened up the New Testament at John, Chapter 3, and placed it on the ice. I took some photographs and left it there. I had inscribed in the flyleaf, "I leave this Russian New Testament at the North Pole with the prayer that God's word and love will continue to move as naturally as the Polar ice, drifting southwards to all nations through which the lines of longitude pass from this point," and signed it: "Rev. Canon Laurie Dexter." I imagine it will last there for a few days before it falls off its icy shelf, and, for many months or even years, will lie buried in the ice before eventually disappearing into the ocean.

Not far from where I left the New Testament was the helicopter pad which had been decked out with flags for the people arriving from the South, and, as I stood on the helicopter pad, I thought again about the almost total lack of communication between Sheena and myself due to the extremely hurried events when we never could get alone together, about the disorganized conversation snatched in brief moments as we walked from one piece of business to another, about my Dad who did not live to know about this moment, about my Mum now alone. I felt the hurt, and I must admit that I cried quietly by myself there, well away from all the others. I think most would understand, especially Dmitri, who told me how he also had received word of his father's death during one of his earlier expeditions, but I do not want to let them see my grief in case they misinterpret it as looking for sympathy.

Richard

We have been "on duty," Chris and I. During the past three days we stopped, literally, for two hours. All we do is make food. It's one meal after another meal. No rest, just eat. We have had three stove fires; it seems that the stoves are getting hot enough now because it is getting warmer. Then when we have the stoves on the table, gas heats up and expands and shoots out of the safety valves, and catches fire. We have these big blow torches shooting across the tent. We are getting quite used to it now; it has happened three times today.

I had ten litres of water, just warming on the stove, it was just warm, and one of the three support arms that swing out to support the pot on the stove wasn't out. Chris just touched the pot a little and it tipped over on me. Soaked me. There were about three inches of water on the floor of the tent, so we cut a hole in the floor to let it out. Of course it melted the snow under the tent, so there is this big hole there. Luckily, I was wearing my sealskin kamiks, which, with their tight stitching, are as waterproof as rubber boots. I was standing in the water, and the Soviets were yelling, "You're standing in it, you will wet your feet, you're standing in it." "Ah, no problem, no problem." "*Zabies, zabies,*" (Amazing, amazing).

We fed them granola, which received a mixed reaction. On the average, I think they liked it. They were a little bit surprised. We passed around some nuts and dried fruits that Josée sent. We had to explain what were Brazil nuts, dried papaya, dried pineapple, dried pears – a lot of the things they had never seen. It was a real show and tell. I said, "So why don't we have just orange juice and go to bed." Yuri pipes up, "I cannot sleep without tea." So, I am making tea.

We are drifting south rather rapidly. As of last night, we were at 89 degrees, 51 minutes, and longitude 109 degrees west.

There is some talk of not going tomorrow and resting another day. They say that Misha has too many medical tests to do. He wants to do another whole round of psychological tests. We have to start to make miles, and they are not in any hurry, as usual. They said "Let's have eight hours of sleep, get up, have something to eat, and see where we are." So we will do that.

It is 3:00 in the morning. It doesn't really feel like the middle of the night. I am not very tired for 3:00 in the morning. It is just that when the sun is spinning endlessly around you at the same height, and it is just as bright at 3:00 a.m. or 3:00 p.m., there is no reference for time. We have our watches, but they don't really mean much here. There is nothing to tell you that it is daytime or nighttime except your watch, and that becomes irrelevant. You really lose track of time, lose sense of time.

I supplied the Soviets with Ziplock bags. I suppose they can't get plastic bags in the Soviet Union very readily. Every time they come across any good, solid plastic bag of any sort, they keep it. If you give them, say, a Shaklee plastic bag, which is a good one with handles, three months later you will see some of them are still using the same plastic bag! And Ziplock bags are real treasures.

We had lots of ice cream on this rest stop. Chris sent a message to Snegirev asking for ice cream, and this produced ice cream! That was well worth a telegram. First of all, we had lots of little ice cream bars and cones, so we ate all those. Then, during one meal, Chris went out to fetch some more. He came back and said, "There aren't any more plain bars, but there are these." They were little bars about two inches wide and four inches long. They had fancy icing, made of cream and ice cream, on the top. It was strawberries and the bottom part was different sorts of ice cream, vanilla and coffee, and pretty darn good. It turns out that Toli Melnikov's wife went to the factory in Moscow where they make ice cream and told them that we had a request for ice cream, and they made these special creams for us.

Fiodor just came in with his new hat. It started out as a piece of wool, from a sock or something. He made a headband, and then he added ear flaps, and then he closed in the top and added another piece all the way around, and a visor for the sun, and it is made entirely from various kinds of socks with different colours and shades, and one large Nikon patch.

APRIL 30. DAY 59

Max

This morning we spent two and a half hours posing for photos at the "North Pole" –the cylinder of ice in the middle of the ceremonial grounds – before getting underway. My Canadian counterparts got impatient, and this set the stage for the usual day's-end confrontation. Richard and Chris virtually demanded an eight-hour day, which they did not get. Dmitri's attempts at diplomacy only fan their anger, and the whole situation gets pretty uncomfortable for the moderates like myself. Richard and Chris meet the strongest resistance from Volodi and Yuri, who are less disposed to placate them. Sasha, Toli Melnikov, and Dmitri prefer to avoid direct confrontation, while Vasili, Fiodor, Toli Fedjakov, and Misha usually linger in the background and avoid the issue completely. I find this approach out of character for Vasili, who on other issues has proven himself to be the most capable decision maker of the group.

We skied today through the infamous "*belli meglaw*," or "white-out" as we say here in the Canadian sector. Distinguishing features of the terrain was almost impossible in the flat light, and we spent a lot of time falling down and getting up again. The temperature at lunchtime was the warmest we've had so far – minus 12°C. The ice was "lively"; pans were fragmented and moving, and there was quite a bit of open water around. We got through it with minimal casualties.

Several times today I got "freeway fever," that feeling that you just have to pass the slowpoke in front of you. I'm sure I could have led the line all day, but for political reasons I mostly hung back in second or third position. The hierarchy of the trip is now established, and disrupting it would cost in terms of morale. I am a cripple, and a passenger, and will be perceived as such until the end of the expedition, even if I ski up on land with a body slung over each shoulder. Laurie faces the same problem of definition. It is now six weeks since the first stage, when he suffered all his setbacks. He has been at the head of the pack since then, but he's still seen as the guy that needs help.

Richard

In the morning, the sun disappeared and it was cloudy, making it difficult to ski, and very slow. Now it is not just Chris and I wanting to go faster and do more, it is also Laurie and Max. Laurie was very pissed off yesterday when we didn't get moving. He also thought we should do more today, because we didn't do anything yesterday. Max also thinks the same. It's all the Canadians who want to do more – and the Soviets: no hurry, no rush, the packs are heavy.

The going was extremely rough: the first three hours we hardly went more than a couple of hundred yards without running into a lead.

MAY 1. DAY 60

Richard

Today the whole world around us is shades of white, grey, and a bit of blue, the new ice being very blue, light blue, turquoise; the sky being shades of blue and grey and white, and the snow also being white and shades of grey. Everyone was falling everywhere. The Soviets' skis are getting very skiddery; they don't have very good edges. They all have new skis, which they received at the North Pole. Vasa was leading, and even he slipped and fell on the flat, which goes to show that it is getting very tricky.

We ran into a lot of leads that were mostly frozen, but we could work our way across them, on sometimes very thin ice. I went across to this place, and stepped on a large chunk. The whole piece immediately started to settle into the ocean. With a very great shot of adrenalin, I double-poled hard and went shooting across to the other side, safely.

When we cross leads, it reminds me of penguins in the Antarctic. They will form a big crowd and approach the edge of the water, and they will all push and push until one falls in. This is to test the water, to see if there is anything dangerous in the water that is beneath them. We come to a lead and we crowd along the edge and push and push until finally someone steps onto the thin ice. If it holds, then everybody follows! Only one thing wrong with this. This ice wears out, so if you cross and it flexes a little, the next person to cross it flexes it a bit more, and by the thirteenth person it is more likely to break. So really, in order to cross, it has to be quite solid or one of the last people will go swimming.

Our backpacks weigh about forty kilos. When I first started training for this trip, twenty-five kilos was so heavy. Now, forty kilos is light! Anything over forty kilos I still find hard. Of course, I knew today at the end of the seventh march the big question would come up again. How many marches, eight or nine? I knew the Soviets wanted to do eight, but I wanted to do nine. I was thinking the best thing would be to have the four Canadians just keep on skiing, if the Soviets don't all agree on nine marches. This is a very antagonistic approach, but I couldn't think of anything else.

First, I had to win the support of Max and Laurie, so I swung by Laurie. Laurie said that we have to negotiate this kind of thing. I said that it seems that every time we negotiate, they say, "Yes, yes, yes," and then do whatever they feel like doing. Max said, "Well, I actually don't mind doing only eight hours, but I will wait and see how I feel." The following hour I gave them each a halva. Laurie said, "Well, if I eat it," (which he did), "then I suppose that I am bought."

On the seventh hour Dmitri came around and asked the question and I said: "The Canadian guys want to go nine and the Soviet guys want to go eight. Yesterday, the Canadian guys wanted to go eight, the Soviet guys wanted to go seven. We went seven. This time, it's the turn for the Canadians." Dmitri said, "We will have to check the opinion of all the guys." I said, "Yeah, but there are nine of you and there are four of us, which means we will be outvoted every time." He said, "No, no, no." I said, "Dmitri, this is supposed to be a joint expedition, how about taking our opinion into account for a change?" "No, no, no, no, you can't think like that. Each person must think individually."

So then he went and talked to Laurie. Laurie, thank God, backed me up and said, "Yes, I think I would like to do nine, I think we should do nine, but if anybody feels they can't do it then we shouldn't do it." Max said the same thing. After that, the Soviets saw that if the Canadians were ready to do nine, maybe they had to be ready to do nine too (otherwise they may look weak).We did nine.

MAY 3. DAY 62

Laurie

Visibility was very poor again. The wind was strong enough to give blowing snow quite a lot of the time, not heavy blowing snow, but enough to obscure the ski trails quickly, and visibility was not helped by the continuing overcast ceiling. Since leaving the North Pole, we have only seen the sun for parts of a couple of days. However, a lot of things were in our favour. For a start, the wind was not quite directly behind us today, but very much at our backs, and helped push us along, as well as helping the general drift of the ocean. The best thing of all was that we ran into no big leads. We had a few small ones, which we were able to cross fairly quickly, and while the ice was extremely rugged in the sense that it was very uneven and required a lot of attentive negotiation, in fact it was good for travel, and we were able to go in an almost straight line all day.

Richard

Today started out as a brilliant sunny day, minus 16°C, but you would never know it now. Max was skiing in only his underwear, but then after four marches it clouded over. It got more and more cloudy, until it was like yesterday. During the last march, it started to blow, the wind turned from the southeast to blowing from the northwest. So it is blowing us southeast, which is just what we want. During the last march I was leading. It was like being at the summer fair in one of those houses with crooked floors and funny mirrors.

It was not pitch black, but pitch white, all I could see was white.

I could have almost done better if I had closed my eyes. I gave up looking at the tips of my skis and just looked off into the distance. At one point, I thought there was a drift in front of me and a hole behind it. But it was the other way around. So I tripped over the drift and fell in the hole.

Christopher

I put a fair amount of thought today into figuring out how we could arrange our time to get more sleep out of the day. With our parachute tent, we can set it up, sleep, dictate, or fix stuff for about an hour before dinner. We should be able to do the same for breakfast, i.e., go back to sleep in our tent until the rest of the group is ready, instead of sitting around waiting for tea and being "sociable." The idea of getting this extra sleep is very appealing.

Laurie was complaining all day today. So I lectured to him for a while on how there is always someone who complains and is miserable. I'm not sure he understood who I was referring to, but I hope so. It's a nice sunny day, and yes we've been following leads a bit, but it's not a real problem since we have to go east a bit anyway. You have to expect these sorts of things. It's like the cold weather. Don't complain about it. Just cope and make the best of the situation. Being miserable isn't going to make it go away.

We have been tailoring our red anoraks with zippers down the front so that they could be more easily ventilated. This was something that I started on the second resupply, followed later by the Canadians as well as some of the Soviets. The last holdouts – Misha and Toli Melnikov – have said that they will follow suit during the next rest days. This has everyone satisfied with the jackets, and resolves the red coats debate.

MAY 4. DAY 63

Richard

As we were following a lead, all of a sudden up popped a seal. Right in the middle. A large seal, somewhat in the distance, and it didn't let us get very close before it disappeared. But a seal, nonetheless. It's the first living thing we've seen since we left Cape Arkticheskiy, except for the people at the North Pole.

After lunch today, Laurie slipped, fell, hit his head, and cut himself just above the eye. Max had a look at it and declared that it was nothing serious. But that was not good enough for Dmitri. We had to wait until Misha came and said that it was nothing serious. Just another example of not trusting our judgment.

MAY 5. DAY 64

Max

We scored another 15 minutes yesterday, which is quite satisfactory considering the amount of open water we met. We had to follow beside numerous leads, but fortunately most of them ran in a northeast, southwest orientation, and being forced westward was compensated for by an easterly drift. At the end of the day, our longitude was unchanged, though we had gained 15 minutes of latitude. This brings us to 88 degrees, 31 minutes. In six days of fairly pleasant travelling, we've covered a degree and a half. We're all hoping (and at least one of us is praying) that our favourable drift and wind conditions continue. There's been a brisk tail wind, which makes stopping a trifle cool, but makes travelling just exquisite in light clothes.

Some of the ice we've been cruising through recently is spectacularly beautiful. The formations are bright blue in the blazing sun and of truly impressive dimensions. The ice here on "our side" is thicker, because it forms on the Soviet side and grows as it drifts over. We took some photographs inside an ice cave complete with stalactites and stalagmites and "played" for a while – something we haven't done since the beginning of the trip.

Richard

The weather went "out" as we started the geomagnetic measurements last night, and it stayed out. This morning, it was blowing seven to nine metres per second, Vasa figured, and he is usually low. It was minus 10°C, with the same white-out visibility. Off we went anyway, as usual. It seems that when it blows, all the leads close up – that is, the ice goes into the open spaces where there is water. There were just a couple of leads we had to walk along, maybe a hundred feet one way or the other. With blowing snow, it makes it a little trickier for those in the front to cross the leads. They have to check carefully, because sometimes it looks solid and it is not, because drifts form over water.

We came to one tricky spot. There were two big blocks that touched, forming a triangle you could squeeze through, but it was very small. Yuri climbed down, and he pushed and he grunted and he pulled and, finally, managed to squeeze himself through – it was amazing.

MAY 6. DAY 65

Max

A recent addition to the equipment roster is a brown plastic Bailey's Irish Cream bottle. It was flown in full to appease the lavish tastes of our communist leader – apparently he had acquired a taste for it on his last visit to Canada. When it was finished and he was about to throw it out, I thought it might make a good water bottle (hip-contoured and all) so I asked him if I could have it.

"Dmitri, that would make a good water bottle," I said. "Do you want it?" He looked at it and he looked at me, and he said, "Yes, Max, I will keep," as though he had come up with the idea on his own. He filled it up with water, and when I saw him put it into his packsack, I said, "Dmitri, that will freeze." "Max, I will drink before water freeze." Two days after it had frozen, he was again going to throw it out, but decided to offer it back to me. I accepted and carried the frozen lump inside my shirt, next to my skin, and slept with it in my bag that night. By the next morning, it was usable again, so I filled it with tea and sugar. I brought it out after the third march, and was taking a parsimonious pull when Dmitri saw me and said, "Max, tea is very good idea – give me a drink." It was too absurd to refuse him.

This is socialism in action. Since then, various people have used it. Richard takes it into the parachute tent overnight and substitutes a cup of cold sugary tea in the morning for breakfast with the boys. After a few fillings of hot tea it's become quite deformed, being made of cheap plastic, but that makes it all the more appealing. At 500 cc, it's the perfect size and, as it's dark brown, it can now be left on top of my pack in the sun and it won't freeze.

MAY 7. DAY 66

Christopher

Tonight Volodi asked Richard and me if we would go over thin ice and fall into a lead so they could shoot it for the documentary film they're making. We couldn't believe he was serious; mostly because it wouldn't be true. In the end, Toli Fedjakov volunteered and will do it in the next rest days. We felt the same way about shots of Max gazing at a photograph of Nancy that were staged for Volodi's film.

Laurie had been complaining continually for quite some time, in spite of the good weather and ice conditions. This had been bothering me, since it put a damper on the rest breaks. I did mention something to the effect of there being nothing to complain about, but it must have been too subtle. So, about three in the afternoon Laurie came into one of the rest stops, dropped his pack, and said, "We are going to be so late into camp." And I said, "Why don't you fuck off?"

He said, "What? Why?"

I said, "Shut up and fuck off."

Then of course he got irate. I said, "You whine and whimper and complain all the time and you couldn't ask for a nicer day, or conditions, everything is wonderful, except for you. You're pissing everyone else off, because you are such a complainer."

He wasn't impressed by this. He said he'd never attacked me personally and this was uncalled for and that I had called him a liar and a fucking this and that, and why on earth was I saying this sort of thing to him? So I said it was easier than going over and kicking him in the head. And he said, "Oh yeah? Well just try it. I've never backed down in my life and you'll have more than a fight on your hands from me."

That surprised me, since I'm a fair bit bigger and stronger than Laurie, but I had no intention of fighting.

We skied along for another hour. At the next rest break Laurie was very quiet and didn't say a thing. On the march after that, I skied up to him and we talked for the rest of the march, flung various accusations back and forth. The whole thing started to revolve around attacks on me, accusing me of belittling a number of people on the expedition, primarily Yuri, whom I respect in spite of our differences. He also said that I was provoking him, and I said that he was doing the provoking because he was being so miserable. And he said yes, it was true, he had been pretty miserable all day, but it was because he was hungry, so it wasn't really his fault. We promised to continue our "discussion" tomorrow.

Laurie

It turned out to be a beautiful day, minus 16°C at the beginning, and minus 14°C at the end. The wind is still blowing from the same direction, but not nearly as hard as before, and for a lot of the day I was able to travel without the red top, although the temperature was just borderline because of the wind, and at the end of the day I had to put it on again. Because of our drift, we did head more towards the east, and by the end of the day had made up a couple of degrees, and ended at 81. And as far as our southerly travel was concerned, that also turned out to be pretty good, finishing at 87 degrees, 44.5 minutes.

I feel hungry just about all the time now. I made a few comments along those lines during our rest breaks, and at the end of the sixth, maybe it was the seventh, Chris shouted at me to fuck off, shut up, and that he would like to kick my teeth in.

We ended up having a long conversation later on, during which he gave his reasons as being fed up with my griping about the food and spoiling this beautiful day. I accept the fact that I should not have complained about the food situation, but one person's mistake does not excuse another person's disregard for common courtesy. He also said that he felt that I had no right to be on this expedition. I am not quite sure what his reasons were, but one of them that he mentioned was that I don't know how to ski and am not up to it.

As Chris was in the process of criticizing my skiing ability, suddenly the edge of one of the biggest holes I've seen gave way and Chris slid unceremoniously in a tangle of skis, poles, and pack, almost out of sight.

Richard

We are still flying south, making good time. We are down to 86 degrees and three-quarters. The wind is still blowing, not as strong. It is nice and clear and sunny, so it is beautiful travelling, but is blowing enough to keep the ice steady and together and no open water. It was minus 14°C most of the day. Our packs are getting light, so it is just beautiful. The best skiing we have had, the skis have been gliding well. Except that my skis glided so well today one of them finally broke. I was heartbroken! This was the only pair of skis that was going to make it from Cape Arkticheskiy to Ellesmere Island, the only pair of skis of the expedition. The only spare skis are Soviet. Tomorrow should be interesting.

MAY 8. DAY 67

Max

Three months since leaving Ottawa. Today started out sunny, but ended up white-out, with wind as strong as any we have experienced so far on the trip. Once again it blew over our left shoulders, though for a while we got slightly disoriented because Volodi's compass was too close to his camera. The resultant magnetic field overpowered the compass, and at times the wind blew suspiciously over our right shoulders. Nevertheless, we managed to knock down over 18 minutes, and we are now at 87 degrees, 25 minutes, with four days left to go in this stage.

Richard

Today I used Soviet skis. This was quite an experience. At first, I tried to ski normally on them, that is, do what you normally do on skis. It turned out to be very hard work, and I could not go very fast. They just wouldn't glide. I would transfer my weight onto the gliding ski and they would stop. When I put too much weight on the ski it stops. They don't have any back-slip, but they don't have any forward slip either. At first I thought maybe I am getting sick, and no, there is no reason I should be getting sick. Then what the hell is the matter? I am unchanged from yesterday, and yesterday I was much faster than any of these guys. Now, here I was, sweating away, working like a pig and dropping behind.

The next march I go in behind Toli Melnikov because he has the most obvious style of all. He doesn't move his body at all, only moves his arms from the elbows down, and moves his legs only from the hips, and he stays bolt upright. I got in behind him for a couple of marches and did exactly like he did. What I had to do is keep my weight exactly in the middle, if I shifted it over to one side or the other, the skis stopped. You don't push the skis along the snow, you have to pick them up and kick them forward. So you don't slide them along the snow, because this creates a lot of friction. A funny thing, skis that don't slide in the snow!

By the end of the day I could keep up with no problem, but I still think it is a lot more work. And it is not really skiing, it is just one step up from snowshoeing. The metal edges are terrible, they don't bite into the snow or the ice at all. On the good side, the wood sticks to the bare ice a lot better than the plastic skis. They are very stable and they track better.

Christopher

I had a short chat with Laurie. I asked him for examples of when I had belittled people. He said that it was just the general tone of my voice. I gave up in despair. It is very frustrating arguing with this guy. You don't get anywhere with him. Actually that's not true. He hasn't grumbled since yesterday.

MAY 9, DAY 68

Max

The song for today, actually the culmination of a couple of days of intense composing, goes like this:

> Where the sun goes round and around and around
> But it never goes down
> And the blue ice glows
> From the endless shifting floes
> And the burning cold
> Will cut right to your soul,
> There's a secret very few men hold
> The secret of the Pole.
>
> Some men claim they conquered her,
> But she was not impressed.

Others died along the way,
Their souls now lie at rest;
But come ye not in conquest,
Only knowledge there to find,
The answer lies waiting, already
Deep within your mind.

Richard

This afternoon we came upon a large, open lead. It was open water with waves on it because of the wind. Clean, open water, like I have never seen before, a summer lead. We followed the edge a little ways and there was a place to cross. Volodi went off in one direction, and Vasa inspected an ice bridge. He said it was okay, there was a big chunk that had come off and drifted sideways and jammed across the lead. It was like a gift from heaven. When Volodi came back, he said, "This is the way to go. The lead turns away. We don't need to cross it."

Vasa wanted to cross the lead, but Dmitri said, "No, we will go where Volodi wants to go." But the lead did not end and we skied along it for an hour, 30 to 60 degrees off course. At the next rest, there was some sort of argument. Perhaps Dmitri wanted to use the boat to cross the lead, or perhaps Vasa was upset that we had not crossed the lead at the first place. Then Vasa yelled at me, "Richard, lead on." So off I went. Later Vasa said to me, "I am sorry, I was angry at Dmitri." I am not sure what occurred, but as usual we Canadians are left in the dark.

We went on together for a while until we came upon an area where it seemed as if the lead broke up into many smaller cracks. There were little cracks everywhere, so we crossed a couple. We could see in the distance that the lead became wide again, so we wanted to cross via the system of little cracks. We climbed over a couple and then Vasa was going along one, the crack made a right angle corner, and he was on the inside corner. He was side-stepping up along the edge and crossing over at the same time. He was on top of an eight-foot snow-drift, with the crack through the middle. Suddenly, the ice started to shift, and the whole drift slipped sideways and fell into the lead with him on it. Luckily, there was enough snow underneath him to bridge the gap as he reached water level, and he didn't go into the water, he managed to scramble across.

He investigated the other side and came back to say it was no good. By that time, Volodi had joined me. As we stood watching, the whole thing pulled apart and this enormous piece of ice broke loose and floated up to the surface, like a large whale. But where we had crossed onto our little island it had also opened up several feet. So Volodi and I were on one island, and Vasa was on another island, and the rest of the group was on the main chunk of ice.

I went over to one spot where we had crossed before, and I was going to climb out onto the edge, and Dmitri said, "No, it doesn't look very good." It was overhanging; it would have dropped me straight into the water. Toli Melnikov walked along on one edge of our little island and said that there was a place to cross. It was a large piece of ice, bobbing freely in the middle of the lead. We bridged our skis across, enough so I could give the packs a shove, and they slid along the skis and Toli grabbed them on the other side. To get ourselves across, it was a matter of jumping onto the bobbing piece of ice and then jumping off again onto the other side before it sank!

So we got across, and then finally Vasa found his way onto our little island, because the ice was moving a lot, and eventually the crack closed up again, so he got back and joined the main group.

Today we managed to do 14 minutes, in a line directly towards Ward Hunt Island. This is to say we did 14 minutes south and a degree of longitude east. We are now at 80 degrees longitude, 87 degrees, 9 minutes latitude. If we keep this up we should be at about 86 degrees and a half for the airdrop. It means we will have done half the distance from the North Pole to Canada in two weeks.

Today is the ninth of May, the Soviets had a celebration, the day of their victory over the Germans in the Second World War. To celebrate, we each had half a chocolate bar, about two and a half teaspoons of senetatta, and there was a tube of honey to go around. The senetatta was also in a tube, like toothpaste, like the honey: that is the way the cosmonauts get it.

Christopher

Yesterday we had freezing rain. Just a sprinkling, but our packs and tent were covered with a light crust in the morning. It was pretty warm all night. We also had a few ski breakages – me and Mish. My duty went exceptionally well.

MAY 10. DAY 69

Laurie

I am finding that the time is beginning to drag. I have just about run out of ideas to think about; most of the time I am thinking about the family. Our rapid rate of progress certainly helps in giving encouragement as the end of the trip comes closer much faster than we expected.

We travelled well all day except for coming to a few open leads, which, fortunately, were running not too far off course, and even though we followed one for quite a long way before getting across, we felt that we were doing well and that we had covered a good distance. So it was quite a surprise to find that at the end of the day we had only done about 12 minutes. During our final march we came to open water, which we began to follow. Then, with only about fifteen minutes' time to go, we came to a vast plain of recently frozen ice, and so set across it in order to be on the right side of it for the next day. It took about twenty minutes or more to get across.

We then found ourselves beside yet another large open lead. As we had been making our crossing, some of the ice around us was crackling and groaning, forming ridges as we looked. There was no really safe place to camp, so, after a long debate, we moved farther along to the southerly edge of this plain of flat, new ice, and finally found a place to camp at 7:00 in the evening.

Richard

The sun is melting the snow on our kamiks – such a contrast to what it was only a month ago. We lie in our sleeping bags and there is no frost anywhere. They are always dry and we don't have to dry them out. They are so comfortable. It is so nice travelling now.

On the sixth march, I was leading through a really broken-up area. I climbed up high to see where to go. It was all churned up; there wasn't a pan more than a few hundred feet across. There were large, wide areas of really busted-up rubbles, fresh rubbles with no drifted snow on them, and lots of open water and big pools, little lakes everywhere. The lakes are completely in the open, with the wind rippling across, and little waves. Throughout the day we came across leads, some of them very large, and lakes that were maybe a couple of hundred yards across. The waves on them make rippling noises. But luckily there always seemed to be a "bridge" for us to cross.

I am becoming accustomed to the Soviet skis now. Because they don't glide they are quite good in the rough ice. I can really smash over the ice. I place them on a piece of ice and they don't slide around at all. Whereas on the flat they seem to be quite a lot more work. I wore a heart monitor today, and I compared the heart rates from before with the fibreglass skis and now with the wood skis, and it is hard to say. There are too many variables, such as snow conditions and terrain, that also affect the heart rate. With comparable conditions, it seems that fibreglass skis are less work.

MAY 11. DAY 70

Richard

The Canadians made a suggestion this evening: that we start off the next stage with seventeen days of food, so that if everything goes well and we don't hit any large open water, we could make Ward Hunt Island in one stage. It would be a shame to run out of food within sight of land, three or four days from land. There was much discussion, but it seems they are generally receptive to the idea. If we encountered Peary's big lead,* we would stop, have an airdrop, get our boats, and continue. If there was no lead, and we averaged 12 minutes every day, it would take sixteen days to reach Ward Hunt Island. All we are really asking is to carry three days' extra food. So that if we have no problems we could trek to Ward Hunt in one shot.

---

*On several occasions Robert Peary (who claimed to have reached the Pole in 1909) encountered a wide lead thirty to fifty miles offshore. He named it "the Big Lead." There seems to be a semi-permanent lead, or at least a very active area, where the land-fast ice meets the ocean ice. If the wind blows offshore the lead opens up.

MAY 12. DAY 71

Christopher

It is snowing now, there are drifts over the end of the tent. The visibility is terrible. This is the heaviest snow of the whole trip. I made a sunshield for my face; I'm starting to get white puffy bits. My left shoulder has an infection; it really hurts; but maybe it will clear up on rest day.

We started off in awful powder snow; great for downhill, but not for this; it's very light and fluffy. We skied until 3:00 p.m. We had just passed a possible landing strip that we've been keeping an eye out for, for our next resupply, and my second ski broke. I said I would ski on half of it. But no, no, they wanted to have Misha use a broken Soviet one and give his Karhu to me. I was incensed at this. It implied that I was not a good enough skier to ski on half a ski, and that Misha would have to do it instead. About a hundred yards later, Richard and Laurie decided that the area was good for a landing strip, and we decided to stop.

We had a discussion in the tent about our food. Dmitri said he agreed that we all want to get home as quickly as possible, and if it is possible to do it in sixteen days, then we will do it and take the necessary amount of food. If it is not possible, we should know after ten days and we can request a resupply then. It is also important that we have a good rest in this break if we are going to try for a sixteen-day march.

This sounds like a foreshadowing of another three-day rest break – although I'm getting used to it, and wouldn't mind trading off the next break for lengthening this one.

I have been collecting spare garbage bags and things that might come in useful if we have to go anywhere in a rubber raft. I'm sure that they will be greatly appreciated.

MAY 13. DAY 72

Laurie

Early in the morning we heard the aircraft. It did not seem to make any attempt to locate us. At least the plane is carrying our frequencies, and I was able to speak to the pilot on the radio as he was flying past. He said that he was icing up very badly and had about half an inch of ice already, and so just continued on to NP 28, intending to pick up all our freight there and land on the way back.

After he had landed at NP 28 I spoke to him, and he said he wasn't going to take off again to come to us, as he felt conditions were not good enough. He also didn't think our ice was thick enough for him to land on, and that he would have to have a low-level drop and just push things out the door. He was convinced we didn't know what we were doing. When I think of the many years I lived in the high Arctic, and the number of times I have landed in Twin Otters on the sea ice, this is ridiculous.

So we decided to measure the ice more accurately. Max and Richard went out just with a ski pole and painstakingly drilled down to about thirty-nine inches, and still had not come through the ice, so we know that we have a minimum of a metre.

Apparently the plane is very heavily laden. He has filled it full of everything, and was still not able to bring all our personal stuff from NP 28.

We are almost out of fuel and food, but we have all sorts of odd-ments left, and are managing to keep ourselves fed; but, for most of the day, people's single occupation was to sleep. People have not been writing, recording, sewing, doing repairs, just chatting in general. In some ways it has been a good day, in that we really have rested, whereas during our airdrops we normally don't get a really good rest.

The Twin Otter eventually arrived, made a pass over, and came in for a perfect landing, and then agreed that the ice was ideal, and prob-ably a good two metres thick. Amongst other interesting bits of infor-mation, Carl, the pilot, told us that on his way north from Alert he had clear visibility, and he saw no open water for the first hundred miles or so. In fact, the main open leads he saw are around our present posi-tion, and less to the south.

We know that we can travel in this area without boats for sure. So we decided to take extra food and try to make it all the way to shore in one push from here. We are going to try carrying sixteen days' worth of food, which is more than we have ever carried before. We have all managed to get rid of quite a bit of weight this time, mainly clothing. We have gone from minus 25°C to minus 10°C, and during our camp here it has been minus 6°C to 7°C. We are walking around with just a single layer of underwear, often with nothing else on top as we work outside. It is much warmer than the actual temperature would indicate because we are so accustomed to the cold, and also it has been calm. We are really comfortable, and when we start travelling again, it is possibly going to be too hot.

SUMMARY

The skiers had made good progress despite the bad weather. They were halfway to Canada, from the North Pole, more than three-quarters of their way through the journey. Helped considerably by drift, they had travelled 376 km from the Pole. Estimates at the end of the day showed that they had experienced drift of up to ten kilometres in a twenty-four-hour period, all in the team's favour.

By now, too, the skiers' physical condition was good, though many had irritating bacterial skin problems. Their two months of skiing had put them in better physical shape. The medical tests later would show an increase in muscular strength—but a drop in cardio-vascular conditioning. They had also grown more skilled at handling the rough ice and other conditions peculiar to the ice they were travelling over.

Twenty-four hour sun meant that the skiers always had to wear sunglasses to avoid becoming snowblind, even on cloudy days. Toli Melnikov neglected to do this and became partially snowblind. While he could still ski, his speed was reduced, and he was in considerable pain. During the last stage he was the slowest skier.

While the majority of the skiers carried all their gear in backpacks, small sleds were used occasionally, though they required more skill. Misha always towed a small child's sled attached to his pack. It usually contained about fifteen to twenty kilograms. By using this method he could transport more weight than with a pack alone. He routinely had forty kilograms in his pack and another twenty in a sled. All the Canadians experimented with a sled at some time during the expedition.

Since the Pole, the warmer weather had caused tricky ice conditions, with substantial areas of open water and fields of jumbled broken ice. Almost continuous white-out conditions with flat light made skiing difficult. Not being able to see the sun, the leaders had to navigate by compass. Because of their relative proximity to the magnetic Pole, the compass needle would take a while to stop moving and could be influenced by a nearby watch or camera. These conditions slowed the expedition and ate away at group morale.

Group relations had improved. Again the issue that continued unresolved was the number of hours they would ski in a day. In general, Richard and Christopher, with tentative support from the other Canadian team members, wished to travel nine marches, while the Soviets preferred to continue doing eight. Dmitri would not rule on it. Richard felt that Dmitri's reluctance to resolve the dispute was due to the fact that giving a ruling meant angering someone on one side or the other, and he did not wish to do that. Dmitri told Laurie that the greater age of the Soviet skiers was their reason for wanting to go more slowly. He never admitted this to Richard or Christopher, but simply said that the Soviets had greater experience and knew better than the Canadians.

These differences were to flare up into a dispute several days into the last leg, when Volodi and Richard argued over the number of marches a day. At that time, in an effort to spur on the Soviets, Richard would deliberately provoke Volodi, who was easily angered, and accuse him of laziness. Both Richard and Dmitri happened to be wearing heart monitors at the time because of medical testing, and their heart rates rose above the highest level measured at any time of physical exertion.

The argument between Christopher and Laurie was the closest the Canadians came to blows. The entire incident happened without either of them raising their voices. The result was that the Soviets never knew that anything had occurred. Similarly, the Canadians missed the essence of most of the Soviet arguments, of which there were plenty. On one occasion, Sasha attacked Toli Fedjakov with a cooking pot. At the time, all the Canadians were absent from the tent. They did not learn of the incident until eighteen months after the expedition.

Other issues had been resolved. By now almost all the skiers were carrying their own personal food. There had been many discussions about whether or not to try to cover the final distance of the journey without further resupply. Initially, some of the Soviets resisted, because it meant that they would have to carry food for sixteen days. They thought this was jeopardizing the expedition just to save money. A resupply would cost the Canadians $25,000, which was one reason they wished to finish without one. The Soviets also did not understand that the Canadians were personally responsible for the debts of the expedition, which the Soviets were not.

For the first time since leaving Sredny, the team was able to talk on the radio directly with Resolute Bay. During the time this second-last leg was completed, a Soviet radio operator had arrived in Resolute Bay. The Canadians previously had had the impression that the Soviets had control of the radio. At this fourth resupply, the Canadians received a lot of information from their manager, media reports, and letters.

Morale overall was very high. The Canadians especially felt positive, partly because they were in their own territory, and they were heading homeward – *demoy!*, as the Soviets said. But the Soviets were heading to Canada, where they would stay for two more weeks before going home to their families.

The thirteen skiers now made a more cohesive team than at any other time. People were anxious to get off the ice. In particular, the Canadian members were more of a single mind, and Max and Laurie supported Richard and Christopher in arguments about the number of hours to ski. Fear of the open water they expected to meet between this last rest stop and land led to endless discussions about how they would cope.

The Last Stage

MAY 13. DAY 72

Richard

Today we had a casual conversation in the tent. The Soviets believe that all political decisions made in Canada are directly influenced by the United States. The U.S. ambassador calls Mulroney or Clark down to his embassy and tells them what to do, and they say "Yes, sir." They tell us to do it and we do it. We explained this is really not the case. I asked if popular opinion has any influence in the Soviet Union; Yuri said no. He said we have been and we are at one with our government, whether we like it or not. "We have the tradition of following the government."

When I asked him, "Does the government pay any heed to popular opinion?" he said there is no mechanism in the Soviet Union for voicing popular opinion. One of the goals of *perestroika* is to construct this mechanism. Their newspapers and television are totally tools of the government and not the people.

MAY 14. DAY 73

Richard

My father said as usual to expect open water across the Lomonosov

Ridge area, and after that, fewer and fewer leads. That is exactly what we experienced. Looking at the map of the Arctic Ocean floor he had sent me, I could see that the Lomonosov Ridge extends from about 89 degrees; it cuts diagonally across our path to about 87 degrees, which is where we had a lot of our open water in the last stage. Lately, the last half degree or so, we have had very little open water, just a few very small cracks, because now we are back over the deep ocean. Deep being three to four thousand metres deep, even forty-five hundred metres deep, as opposed to about fifteen hundred to two thousand metres deep over the Lomonosov Ridge.

Chris and I went out and tried the new 308 rifle. It shoots to the right, and high a bit, too, and we can't adjust it here. We got it because during the day we get very spread out. We can now carry one gun at the front and one at the end of the line, in case we have bear problems.

For dinner, we started off with a duck-and-peppercorn pâté, with all kinds of biscuits, dry bread, all sorts of crackers, cheese, several sorts, Brie, Cheddar, Emmenthal, oka, lots of good stuff. Next was the soup, vegetable soup, this was one of the André Moreau meals, followed by sole "bonne femme," which is a sole coated in egg, with scalloped potatoes and carrots. For dessert: tea and a huge box of cakes from Josée and Pia, zucchini cakes, three types of zucchini cakes, really good. Ahhhhh, just wonderful.

MAY 15. DAY 74

Laurie

This morning, as I was working outside, I could hear the ice crunching and rumbling not too far away, and later, as I was taking a stroll along the "runway," following the tracks of the plane skis, I suddenly came to a ridge about five or six feet high, right in the middle of the area that the plane had landed on a couple of days ago. So here we are, not too far from the tent, with a new pressure ridge forming, reminding us that we are still living on a thin and unstable skin.

Today was not like a Sunday, of course, and that is one of the reasons I have come for a walk tonight, just to be alone, one of the few occasions I have been alone on this whole trip, to meditate, to pray, to recover my composure, so to speak. During the last few days before we came to this campsite, I had been reading through Romans and really enjoying it, especially chapters eight, nine, and ten. I was especially struck by this section: "The Scripture says, 'Whoever believes in him will not be disappointed.' This includes everyone, because there is no difference between Jews and Gentiles; God is the same Lord of all and richly blesses all who call to him. As the Scripture says, "Everyone who calls out to the Lord for help will be saved." (Romans 10:9-13) And I really believe that – Jew or Gentile, communist or capitalist, polar adventurer or armchair explorer. I guess this belief really affects my attitude towards the other men. I am not blind to their faults, or (hopefully) to my own, but I try to see the tremendous unlocked potential in others even when we have a difference of opinion.

Our camp is hidden behind huge chunks of pressure ice, but on the highest piece of ice above the tent I can see two flags side by side, the red Canadian flag with the maple leaf, and the red Soviet flag with the hammer and sickle, and it is one of those rare occasions when I feel a tremendous sense of achievement that we have combined these two nations, and come so far so successfully on this expedition. We received numerous newspaper clippings in the airdrop and found that we had made frontpage news, in full colour, in a number of newspapers. The expedition has obviously attracted a lot of attention. Chris had friends who have been visiting Australia, and they say it has even been on the news over there.

Sometimes I wonder what I have done by getting into this, and I feel that it may have changed my life forever. I think it may change my ministry and the whole direction and thrust of what I have been doing, especially if it involves me in becoming more intimately associated with the Soviet church. The number of contacts I have made with Christians and other people interested in the subject is amazing, and also the connections that some of the men on the expedition have with Christianity.

The other day, one of the Soviets asked me if I believed in the Second Coming of Christ. I said I did, and then talked about some of the prophecies and some of the reasons why I believed in it, and I also tried to explain the difference between Christians committed to Jesus Christ and people who just live by a Christian code of ethics. They seemed to understand that clearly enough.

Jokingly, I said to one of the Soviets, "Next time we come to some open water I will baptise you," and he replied, "Oh, there is no need to; I have already been christened. My mother took me to the church when

I was a baby." A number of the others likewise have had Christian mothers. It nearly always seems to be the women. Many of the fathers have not had any church contacts, but many of them have had that link through their mothers, and even though they themselves do not believe, there is that tiny touch which I believe can never be extinguished.

Again, I am overcome with a sense of wonder and awe as I walk out here, miles from anybody. Our little group is perhaps farther from other living people than anybody else in the world. We are tied together in this strange fashion by our polar passion.

Richard

Our last rest day. Today, nude, in the sauna, I weighed seventy-three kilograms. Normally, I am sixty-eight – and my skin folds are up to ten, twelve, and twenty-one, and, at the start, I believe they were eight, ten, and seventeen. Almost everybody is heavier, some more, some less. Perhaps it is a metabolic reaction to insulate yourself against living in the cold. Chris is nine kilos heavier than when he started. I am fat, too; I have nice little rolls on my stomach!

MAY 16. DAY 75

Richard

This morning we woke up all fogged in. Low-lying fog everywhere. After breakfast, we set about getting ready. My backpack weighed, with my parka on, about 47 kg, of which probably 5 kg or so was personal food.

We went off into the fog. Very humid, very foggy. Visibility was reduced to probably 300 metres or so. But overhead you could see the blue sky. It was minus 10°C this morning. We went very slowly – most people's backpacks are between 45 and 50 kg, except Misha's was 60, and Vasa, who has 55, because he has a camp cot. The Soviets ordered us a table for the tent, and they didn't have one at NP 28, so they sent one of the Soviet camp cots. Vasa used it during the rest period. He liked it so much he is carrying it with him.

I am now using Karhu Supreme skis. They are lighter, shorter, and more flexible – so far no problems. They seem to ride better, they are smoother, they don't plough as much as the stiff skis. And they are just as squirrelly as the yellow ones – which is not too much fun with a heavy pack. But as the pack gets lighter they will become easier to control – they do glide very nicely. For wax, I actually put on some green klister today as a base, covered over with hard wax and special green.

MAY 17. DAY 76

Christopher

The ice was really rough today. The biggest pressure ridges that we have seen on the whole trip. Quite incredible! Today is Max's birthday. Nancy had sent him a flask of brandy, which he had managed to save since the resupply for this occasion. After that we had some senetate. This is the closest that we have come to being blitzed for three or four months. Nancy had sent me some party favours which I had kept quiet for today's event – balloons, hats, harmonicas, and other good stuff. So we all sat around and wore silly hats and had a good time.

Laurie

We are optimistic about finishing on the first or second of June, and, if we were really pushed, we could even get there by the third without a resupply. Obviously, every day is critical. If we lose half a day, or even worse, a whole day, then it would throw the whole thing in jeopardy. But there is no point in second-guessing what's ahead of us.

Today turned out to be perhaps the toughest day of the whole expedition, in some ways. We started out in light fog, the sun slightly visible; but the travelling was still good in terms of clarity and contrast. We could differentiate between humps and bumps and hollows, although it was not perfect. In the past we have often gone through rough areas, sometimes taking up to two or three hours, and then it opens up into large plains of relatively good ice. But this day was unusual in that every single hour was the same. We'd get maybe fifty metres on a small pan and then have to work our way across little cracks and fissures, then balance through rough rubble and over big bumps and pressure ridges onto another two or three small pans, and continue to repeat the process hour after hour. At times, I am sure if we could have seen from the air it would have looked like a jigsaw puzzle, the edges of each piece being marked by lines or cracks with open water.

Sometimes the ice we crossed was rubbery. At one point we crossed a quite large lead about three metres wide, with open water a metre or more below; but in the middle was a huge chunk of floating frozen ice. As each person moved across, the whole thing began to tilt and neatly tipped him onto the other side across a final gap of more than half a metre, before rocking back into position ready for the next person.

All through the day people were falling, even the best skiers, and some of the falls were quite spectacular. Richard went into a huge hole at one point, and as he started clambering out, the edge gave way and dumped him with his backpack right back into the same place. I was going through another area of rough ice and suddenly slipped, rolled, and ended up on my back in a deep hole with jagged chunks of ice all around me, and my skis in the air. At another point, Max fell going up a small slope. His skis just slipped backwards, but of course, the problem is not only the falling. With these enormous packs that we have, once you fall your pack will continue to pull you down.

As Max slipped, somehow he ended up on his face with his wrist twisted underneath him, and he couldn't get any leverage. Gradually, his pack was pushing him deeper into the soft snow, and, while the pressure on his wrist was increasing, his ankles were all twisted up at the other end of his body. It just so happened that I was close by, and was able to take a few strides, get my pack off, get hold of his pack, and pull him upright.

That was the story of the day: falls, skiing short distances, sometimes having to go east-west, even backtracking at times in order to get around a bad area, and by the end of the day we knew that in terms of distance we had not done so well. But everybody was still in good spirits.

MAY 18. DAY 77

Richard

Today we had a lot of what Dmitri said is written in the Soviet books as "old Canadian ice." These are large pans that are kilometres across, and that are characteristically multi-year ice. That is, everything is melted either flat or there are only a few odd bumps here and there. These pans just don't exist on the Soviet side of the Arctic Ocean.

MAY 19. DAY 78

Max

I am pissed off! I had a sore back for most of the morning, took an Indocid SR at lunch time, and was high as a kite for the latter half of the day. Despite all this, I skied my buns off, as did everyone else, and we still ended up making only ten minutes. This was probably attributable to a consistent east wind which we thought was blowing south, but doesn't appear to have been. It's times like this that I wonder if I am ever going to make it back. Actually, I talked about this with Laurie tonight. Neither of us has mentioned it to anyone, but I think both of us still harbour a fear that there is a possibility of coming to no good end, as it were, as we enter the dangerous combination of water and ice to the south.

The conflict which evolved today had to do with the usual eight versus nine hours of marching. Volodi's favourite two expressions: "I am a simple man," and "We have very much experience," were not taken with great reverence by the Canadian members. In the end, we ended up marching eight hours, but it is apparent that with our poor progress we are going to have to shift into nine-hour days fairly quickly.

Christopher

The Soviets remind me of little boys on a camping trip; they eat badly, sleep badly, and speak with the most profane expressions, without necessarily intending offence. Vasa and Misha are exceptions, and I've only heard Fiodor swear once.

Richard said that once we reach land this argument about skiing the extra hour will just fall by the wayside and everyone will have forgotten it. So maybe it's not worth making a big issue out of it. And then he proceeded to make a big issue of it. Actually the extra hour is not the issue. The real issue is that we are not listened to.

Our colleagues keep coming up with this scheme of skiing less now, and then doing twenty hours on the last day. They have yet to demonstrate that they can ski ten hours in a day. In all these heated battles, Yuri seems to come out with very common-sense solutions.

MAY 20. DAY 79

Richard

When we finished the eighth march, I said, "We will keep on going."
Then a real battle ensued. I went after Volodi, because I really don't
want to pick a fight with Dmitri. Vasa is difficult to argue with because
he can't speak the language. Volodi is hot-tempered and becomes easily
riled. I never really believed that the Soviets, in particular Volodi, were
lazy, but I thought that if I picked their male egos hard enough then
perhaps I could get them moving. Though this method had worked in
the past it didn't.

I told him if he wanted a real expedition, he should try one
without an AN 74 as back-up, without new clothes, fresh food, more
gas, new skis, and more senetatta. He got upset about the senetatta. I
heard Dmitri say I was right about the senetatta. I also told him that I
had about 44 000 km of skiing under my belt during the last few years,
so I thought I had a bit of experience. I told him that all his experience
had worn him out and made him old and lazy! He didn't really take
too well to that, so we had a great argument going.

Max

This evening in the tent Dmitri called attention to the conflict which
existed between Volodi and Richard. When the men were arguing, his
pulse went up higher than it had all during the trip. He asked for an
open discussion, and asked that the two feuding parties shake hands,
and that this situation should not be repeated. This was done, and I
think everyone felt some degree of relief, though Richard is convinced
that when it comes time to ask for ten-hour days, the situation will
probably recur.

MAY 21. DAY 80

Richard

More money problems. We have just heard on the radio that we are being billed by the Soviets for $25,000. Apparently the Canadian plane going to the North Pole ceremony had been offered fuel at NP 28. This was in order to avoid a scheduled refuelling in Alert. This was accepted, and then after the fact Conexus was sent a bill for twice the going rate. I wonder if this is connected to the expenses of the extra two Soviet skiers.

We have heard that our gear, everything we left at the North Pole, our kamiks, our polar suits, two brand-new Stevenson's sleeping bags, all our personal stuff, is now floating away on a separate ice pan at NP 28, as NP28 is breaking up. Piotr Strezev says he still can see it in the distance, and they are hoping they will be able to retrieve it with a helicopter some time.

At the beginning of the expedition I thought that I would be sharing the job of leading the group on the ice with Vasa and Volodi. We are the strongest skiers. Though I have led now and then, usually the first march of the day or, for instance, when Vasa was sick, it has not been regular or "official."

I always had the feeling that the Soviets resented or at least did not approve of my leading. I never argued the point because there were more important issues of contention. If they wanted to lead that badly, then they could.

During my argument with Volodi yesterday, one of the things he said was, "You never work, you just stay in the back and take pictures." I said, "Well, that is because you always lead and you don't want me to lead." Volodi denied this, but Dmitri jumped in and backed me up by saying, "Yes, it is true." As a result, I will now lead every third march.

MAY 22. DAY 81

Richard

Apparently, our equipment that was drifting away from the drifting station has been rescued.

I had a lousy day today. I led the third, sixth, and ninth marches. The weather was cloudy all day, and it made it rather difficult to see, difficult to lead, difficult to find a good route. Tiring, and on top of it all, the klister that I put on at the beginning of this stage is beginning to wear off. These skis are a little softer, and the hard wax I am putting on is just not staying on, because now the snow is quite icy. My backpack started really hurting me. There is a little plastic knob that holds the metal part of the frame onto the cushioning. The cushioning has all flattened down with time – there's nothing left of it.

I am wearing fewer clothes, so I get this plastic knob poking into my shoulder-blade, which is quite painful. So all in all, not a very good day, but I did wax my skis this evening with a little green klister, so hopefully this will help things for tomorrow.

Today, we actually did 13 minutes, which means we must have a fairly substantial drift. We have also been angling about 20 to 25 degrees east, but we made almost no headway east. So there is still a strong drift to the west.

On the second-last march, we hit a large lead, followed it for twenty minutes, and kept going after the rest break. Eventually we camped beside it. It is definitely wider than it was before dinner, quite a lot wider. We are talking of the boat for tomorrow. It seems to go on for a long, long way, very open, no place to cross at all. Where we first hit it, it was just an average width lead, and now it is one of the biggest leads we have encountered so far.

MAY 23. DAY 82

Laurie

Most of the time we were crossing over fairly large fields of solid old ice, again bordered either by a ridge or open water. We came to one complicated place where three leads met. I took off my skis to walk across when suddenly a fairly large chunk that I stood on rolled over and dropped me down until my body got jammed between the lumps of ice. At first I didn't realize that it had dropped me to the water. I thought my leg was just down in a hole, but very quickly I felt the cold chill of the water as far up as my knee. I managed to get my backpack off, and realized that the whole area was made up of unstable, loosely packed ice boulders that could easily let me slide right through. So I called Vasili, who had crossed at a different place and was now on the other side. He came and helped me out, took my pack across, and then I scrambled over to solid ice.

But I have kept the really good news to the end. Due to our fast travelling, the wind behind us, and the good ice conditions, we did one of the longest days since the North Pole – a total of 17 minutes – bringing us just under the next degree to 84 degrees, 59 minutes; and, thinking of the 13 minutes' average which we had to do to finish in the prescribed time of sixteen days, we are now, for the first time, on the positive side, and have 1 minute in hand.

Christopher

My shoulder infections started acting up a bit more. My pack felt really heavy today, because I gave my sled to Max. His shoulders are worse than mine. I suppose it should be noted that I've been saving three kilos of chocolate truffles since the airdrop, for emergencies. Or a belated birthday present for Pia, if all goes well.

Dmitri and Max had a bet that we would not pass 85 degrees today. In fact we made it by one kilometre.

Max

New tune! (oh no . . .)
(With a western flavour, bull whips cracking between lines, etc.)

> *Out on the ice, wherever I go,*
> *I've got a good buddy that follows in tow –*
> *My sled, Big Red.*
>
> *Well he ain't fast, like his cousin bob,*
> *But he's a hell of a sled, and he does a good job –*
> *My sled, Big Red.*
>
> *Well Big Red glides over snow and ice,*
> *Then he bumps my ankles, and that ain't nice,*
> *So I kick him and bash him and call him names,*
> *Then we cruise along together . . .*
> *Buddies once again.*

Other major events of the day. Chris almost went for a swim, thereby providing the entertainment for the first march. A two-cubic-metre iceberg that was supporting his weight in the middle of a lead broke in two under his immense weight and sent him plummeting face first. Fortunately nothing got significantly wet, and nothing got lost. He claims it was intended. Dmitri also went for a swim today. He managed to immerse his foot to halfway up his leg, but claims that his sock stayed dry, thanks to the Soviet miracle fibre in the overboot which we're not sure of the name of. I noticed afterwards that there was some blood lying around the area, but I don't know where it came from.

I found Big Red the sled to be a delightful addition to my equipment repertoire, and I must say that at the end of the day everything hurt somewhat less. I'm still very tired, but I don't have the same foot pains, and obviously it was a great boon to my shoulder condition. I don't know how I will ever repay Chris for his generosity and kindness.

It looks like we are in for some boating. I think we can all accept that, but I harbour great fear about what is unknown. That is, we seem to be fairly accomplished skiers, and can deal with most things on the ice, but what if, for example, we set out in relatively calm conditions and find ourselves surrounded by white-caps not far off shore? Just the frigid water lapping over the sides would probably be enough to make most of us fairly hypothermic by the time we arrive on the opposite shore.

Another concern is what exactly awaits us on that shore. If there is a high wall of ice we may end up getting dashed against it, or be unable to disembark. Also, if there was a high wind it would be impossible to turn around and return to the opposite shore with the awkward rubber craft.

Richard

There was quite a debate as to whether we should use the boat or not. At first, I thought we should use the boat, as Dmitri said it would take an hour or so to cross. However, Toli M. said it would take several hours for all of us to cross the lead with one little boat. Volodi and Vasa didn't want to use the boat. Volodi said, "Let's continue on for fifteen minutes and find a better place to cross." So off he went. He was leading and he just kept on skiing for the whole march.

I have carried the boat for two and a half months and over fifteen hundred kilometres. If they had no intention of using the boat, why don't they say, "We don't want to use the boat, we will ski along the lead."? Eventually, on the third march, my march, the lead came to an end, and we went around. But the entire time we were travelling about

30 to 40 or more degrees off course, sometimes as much as 90 degrees off course, heading east.

Just when the sun came out today, we came to this spot where we had to ski down an eight-foot snowbank, and that was fun. Sasha Believ tried to go around and landed up on his head. Most people fell. I tried just to go straight down, and I made it, but there was a hole at the bottom that I couldn't see from the top. My ski went in and I fell. Chris was the only person who made it down. We were all at the bottom cheering the others to go straight down. Some people tried and fell. Yuri set himself up on top, poised like a ski jumper with his skis sticking out over the edge. Everyone was yelling for him to go. He almost made it down, but he leaned too far back and sat down. Everyone was in a good mood because the sun was out and the ice was beautiful, just gorgeous. We were all yelling and screaming and cheering each other on. It was fun!

MAY 24. DAY 83

Richard

Today, I asked Misha, "Why does not Fiodor or Sasha Believ lead marches?" He said that leading is a difficult job, that you can't just ski along and deal with your backpack, you have to virtually forget about the backpack and concentrate on where you are skiing, just in front of your skis, and also far off in the distance, and also check your direction continuously. He also said there is a tradition in these two leading, and he didn't think the other guys were strong enough, either, because day after day it is certainly a lot more tiring.

But if you split the workload among many people, it becomes far less work! There are enough skiers in the group that each person would only have to lead once each day. But it is traditionally Vasa's and Volodi's job. And you don't interfere in other people's domain of responsibility.

Myself, I like being out in front. I also feel that I am making more of a contribution to the expedition. It means that I am doing something substantial every day besides just carrying my weight.

Today was another grey day. Very hard leading, very hard indeed. Everything was white, white, white. At one time I went up quite a big, drifted, snow-covered pressure ridge, and normally one would expect a downhill on the other side. But I couldn't see the downhill, and I underestimated it and fell off and wiped out all over the place. Volodi was behind me and I said, "*Ya hkatchu solsna* (I want sun)," and he laughed and agreed with me – he wants sun too.

MAY 25. DAY 84

Richard

We got our co-ordinates late last night: we did almost 20 minutes, which puts us at 84 degrees, 40 minutes latitude, 75 degrees, 50 minutes longitude. It would appear that our westward drift has stopped and we drifted south only. But yesterday we did make good time. Also, today, the ice was similar, big, wide open pans separated by pressure ridges, maybe the odd lead, very similar to what we experienced on the Steger expedition near the Pole. The ice is now actually much flatter and less broken than when we were in higher latitudes. It is much smoother now. No sun again today; same cloudy skies.

Of course, needless to say, we were navigating with the compass, which we must do whenever it is cloudy. Until today, we were on the seventy-fifth degree of longitude, but were skiing parallel to 52.5 degrees. This meant that we were angling 22.5 degrees off course in order to compensate for the drift.

Today, I had a near mishap. I was first across a small lead. It wasn't frozen solid, but well drifted over, and looked safe. I was crossing when my ski tip caught in the snow. As I stopped to lift it clear, I could feel myself slowly sinking. I put my weight on my poles, but they offered no resistance as they went through into the water below. I stayed calm and climbed gingerly and quickly to the other side. I looked back and saw that my ski tracks were filled with water! These are the exciting things that happen that make the days worthwhile. My other turns at leading were just plain hard work.

It is after dinner now – we got our co-ordinates. We did 12 minutes today, putting us at 84 degrees, 28 minutes. This is a little low. What it means, I believe, is that we no longer have any drift.

It is becoming a long trip. The end is near, but there are so many questions still unanswered, things that could yet happen. I am okay,

I don't mind it, except I really don't like this weather, I prefer the sun. In this weather (white-out), you just ski along, you can't really see very much. You spend most of the time just looking at the tails of the skis of the guy ahead of you, or peering down at the snow, trying to see the tracks.

We did get information on ice from a Soviet satellite via NP 28. It seems that there is a lead ten to fifteen kilometres wide north of Ward Hunt, probably five kilometres or so north off the shelf, which is thin ice, broken ice, floating ice, but no open water. And there are ice bridges. So, there is probably a way to get across it, but it would be time-consuming. We have food until the morning of June first.

Christopher

There was an interesting incident last night. Misha suggested to Richard that instead of doing ten marches, they just extend each march from fifty minutes to fifty-five minutes and make up some time that way. An excellent suggestion. Misha then went and suggested this to Volodi and Volodi said that he had already started doing this. So it was kind of funny, as Volodi was the one who was so dead set against the nine hours to begin with. I just wish he would say what he means in arguments instead of simply referring to his great experience.

Two days ago Vasa said I would be first to see land.

MAY 27. DAY 86

Laurie

Today was one of the roughest days we have had in terms of the number and variety of ice problems that we had to deal with. There were big ridges and jumbles of huge, upturned chunks of ice. There was open water, there was thin ice, old ice, no ice, firm ice, suger ice, powdery snow, wet saline ice, and all this with miserable visibility, and people falling frequently. Many of the falls were not in the difficult ice, but often on the flat, simply due to bad visibility.

I actually felt pretty good most of the day, physically, but about the fifth and sixth hours I had an experience which is quite unusual for me. I very rarely get any sort of depression, but during the sixth hour, especially, it just seemed as if we were on some sort of global treadmill; every ridge we came to was one we had passed a hundred times before, and every scramble through rough ice was the same ice that we had fought and passed a dozen times in the last week. It seemed as if we were moving in a vacuum. We would look ahead, behind, to either side, and the view was always very limited, and always pretty much the same – a dull, grey jumble seen through half-fogged sunglasses.

The conversation has been lively in our tent tonight. One of the topics was the Soviet men's interest in the sexual activity of North Americans. How often do you have sex? Every night? Once a week? Who initiates, man or woman? I think the Soviets are fascinated by Western women. No pornography is allowed into the Soviet Union, not even a magazine considered relatively mild by Western standards, such as *Playboy*; certainly no sexually explicit movies.

The Soviets probably have a somewhat distorted view of the sexual permissiveness of North American women, and the sexual laxity of Western society. So it is time to settle in for the night, with whatever dreams this conversation conjures up.

Richard

Today was one of our worst days for distance. Not only did we do nine marches, but a lot of the marches were fifty-five minutes. We only did 12 minutes, so it means that the conditions are getting worse. When we are travelling in the white-out I think we zigzag an awful lot, because it is very easy to get off course, and you don't notice it because there is no sun or real shadow.

Some of the people, especially Chris, are more irritable, no doubt due to stress and fatigue.

Christopher

This morning we hit Canadian ice; it's three storeys high, big stuff. There are also bits of old flat ice. Once again the light is flat. It was the toughest we've come across yet. There was everything from drop-offs to little stuff to open water.

Fedjakov almost went through at one point. We were standing on a piece of big jagged stuff; it was all you could see for one to two hundred metres.

We should be doing more climbing up big bits to scout ahead. Now I'm looking back at one tough section; I can see where all the pans are that we should have used, but we didn't see them; we went through the toughest part.

I saw land; Dmitri came over and said, yes, Chris, we would all like to see land, in a patronizing tone. But I had been looking especially hard after Vasa's prediction. Twenty minutes later everyone else saw it too. Laurie is the only non-believer; he said that we will not see it until Sunday.

Dmitri was on the radio talking to Piotr Strezev at NP 28. Vasa had told Strezev that he was their number one radioman and that we really appreciated his work. When Dmitri heard this he said no, Leonid is, and should be treated as such. It turned into quite a discussion. Fiodor, Misha, and Volodi supported Vasa against Dmitri. This went on to a further discussion about choosing people for the expedition. Fiodor accused Dmitri of picking people because they were his friends, rather than for their qualifications and what they could do for the expedition.

I guess that everyone is changing a bit now that we are getting towards the end. Misha commented to Richard that I have been short-tempered. I think that hitting shore will be good for us all.

MAY 28. DAY 87

Laurie

What a day it has been! We started off on a few hundred relatively flat metres, and then we started getting into the rough stuff, and for the whole day we have been fighting through some of the roughest ice we have ever seen. At first, the lighting was tricky, but during the day it began to get slightly brighter, and at one point in the middle of the day we actually saw the sun. It wasn't shining enough to give shadows, but we could see where the sun was through the clouds. Finally, during the very last march of the day, the sun came out brightly, a beautiful dawn, because, of course, we are travelling during the night. As soon as the sun came out through the cloud and we stopped to make camp, people started stripping off to the waist because you could actually feel the heat of the sun, although the outside temperature is still minus 5 or 6°C.

Traditionally, it is known that the last fifty or sixty kilometres tend to be very rough, as the moving ice approaches land and builds up into pressure ridges, but here we are, a hundred kilometres or more out, and it is already showing that characteristic. It doesn't bode well for us.

It's hard to imagine anything worse than what we are going through just now. Some of the chunks of ice are towering away above us, five or six times the height of the people, and often, when we stop and look ahead, there seems to be no way to continue. Then, as we begin to move forward, and pick and forge and sometimes take off skis and walk, slowly the way opens out, and very, very slowly we make progress forward. On this rough ice I am not putting out the same volume of work per minute, but I am under tremendous tension. It involves actions which require a lot of muscular co-ordination and strength rather than the endurance for skiing rhythmically hour after hour. However, we know that conditions can change very rapidly, and we may find tomorrow totally different. At least in these conditions I find that my concentration is so intense step by step that I don't have so much time to think about other things, or to brood about the slowness of our finish.

Richard

Today dawned another clouded-over, white-out day and we started off into the gloom. On the very last march it got nice and bright and sunny, and really hot. An incredibly strong sun! This is between six and seven o'clock in the morning, in real time. Boy it was nice! So we stopped and all these Soviets immediately stripped down, took off their shirts. They ran around for about ten minutes before putting their shirts back on. Now we are back in the gloom again. Just the regulation hour of sun every four days!

MAY 29. DAY 88

Richard

Today dawned as usual; actually it was even worse than usual, it was blowing, snowing, and white-out conditions. Off we went, and the conditions rapidly improved, the ice got a lot better, and everyone was, for some reason, in good spirits, and we skied very quickly. The first march, the second march, the third march. When I was leading, things really started to flatten out, big pans again. During that march, I came across some fox tracks on a pan, and they disappeared into the pressure ridge, and we climbed over this pressure ridge, a great big pressure ridge with a valley separating it from the next ridge, like a small system of mountains. We reached the other side and started to cross the next pan, and there were the fox tracks again. They went across the pan, over the next pressure ridge, and into the next pan, too, before they disappeared.

We will have to keep a look-out for bears, as there are foxes around. They were old tracks, but not that old.

The ice on one particular lead on which we were skiing wasn't all that thick. We skied side by side instead of going single file, to distribute the weight. As we skied we disturbed the ice, sending out waves that rippled in front of us.

Later, I could see the sun's disc now and again, so the light wasn't too bad. All of a sudden, I was standing at the edge of about a twenty-foot cliff. If the light had been bad I would have skied right off. Max was skiing with me. We had a look at it and, oh well, I couldn't see any easy way around. So I sat sideways on the edge and jumped off. I fell a few feet, then slid down the slope. Max jumped off, and his sled stayed at the top; then he started skiing, and the sled just took off and became airborne and didn't catch up to him until he was at the bottom. His sled went from the top of the ridge to the bottom in one jump. Then he wonders why two of the Canadian stoves that were in the sled are not working any more!

At the end of the day, as we were skiing along, over towards the west there was a strip of blue sky on the horizon. All of a sudden, we could see mountains. Nice, white, snow-capped mountains seemingly sitting on a layer of clouds, just above the horizon. Just beautiful! Bathed in pink sunlight, just the best sight for a long time. And yeah, it felt good!

Christopher

Captain's log. Nine p.m. We have just finished an exciting meal of kasha with a little tea. Sasha gave me a piece of chocolate today. I don't know why. I've been talking to him quite a bit recently about photography. His wife is an engineer and works with metals that are used in electronics. He says that he doesn't think it's a good job for a woman, but it's her job and she can do whatever she wants.

Max

Yesterday, for the first time, the mountains of north Ellesmere became vividly obvious in the sunshine of the latter half of the day. This first vision of land after ninety days on the ice gave rise to intense feelings of joy blended confusingly with foreboding about what lies ahead. In Ottawa, they seem to think this is a *fait accompli*. They have made preparations to pick us up, and they are asking us for specific dates and times about which we really don't have a clue. It depends entirely on what transpires over the next two days.

Christopher

We saw a seagull today. It was kind of a fun day, doing all this technical skiing. Laurie thought it was a miserable day.

It's going to take us three days to reach land. So we had a discussion about what our strategy should be. The first plan was that we eat normally for two days and then we just go hungry. I was trying to convince them to start rationing. Laurie immediately said that we should have an extra plane. Then, seeing that no one was in favour of that suggestion, he said that what he really meant was for the possibility of the open water. After that he said that we could make it by rationing, and switched completely over to what everyone else thought.

Richard is rapidly losing his tolerance for Laurie.

Day food is going to be a problem. We won't have anything for lunch. I am afraid that the chocolate truffles that I was saving for Pia will probably not make it all the way home. Lean times I figure.

Starting this morning, we have Richard in front, and Toli Fedjakov in the back for polar bear patrol. Volodi suggested that we all carry our flares in our pockets. I carried mine until the first airdrop, when I buried it in a snowbank.

Laurie

In spite of the technically demanding nature of today's skiing we made good progress. Now we find ourselves in a predicament. If there is open water ahead as we have been led to believe, we could find ourselves stuck. However, we do have the rubber boats and provisions at Resolute Bay. I suggested that if we come to wide open water, we could call a plane to drop our boats and more food, and if it looks like we can cross the water and reach land quickly, just have the plane wait for us on the island. Most of the others reckon we can take a chance on not being held up for two or three days, and just begin rationing our food to give us more time to play with. That is probably the best way for the moment and we can still fall back on the other idea if we have to.

MAY 31. DAY 90

Max

We passed over a couple of areas that might have been the alleged open water – areas of reasonably thin new ice with some broken-up pieces showing maybe ten to fifteen centimetres' thickness on the chunks. It wasn't a big progress day, but it certainly was a bigger progress day than the previous one.

Furthermore, the weather was delightful through the latter half of the day, though fog remained on the southern horizon, making it difficult to ascertain our progress. At one point, after the first march, we climbed the most immense cliff of ice that I have seen on the Arctic Ocean so far: a huge, sheer blue bluff upon which we all stood soaking in the panorama of light and shadow all around us.

On awakening, we had five hours of riotously good skiing over undulating and varied terrain. We started on broken sea ice, then crossed a large, freshly frozen lead to old land-fast ice, and finally to huge chunks of very old ice and rubble the size of big houses. The latter was covered with deep snow, making for very interesting skiing. This was the first time that we had skied in the "daytime," and I could feel my face and lips frying from the brilliant warm sunshine.

I skied one march with Dmitri, and we discussed a variety of things. As I had suspected he would, he asked me if I would be interested in joining him in an international Antarctic expedition. Probably nothing would interest me less at this point, though I didn't say that immediately, and I certainly was flattered that he would value my presence on such an excursion.

We skied all through what had previously been called "night." Because of the necessity of making a twelve-hour time shift we will now call it "day," and we should be back in Ottawa time. It is now 7:30

a.m. Dikson time, and 7:30 p.m. Ottawa time, and we are going to bed. We will get up at six and finish the jaunt right to the mud, where I plan to have a good roll.

Laurie

After four hours of skiing, we came to the last really spectacular section of huge blocks of ice as big as apartment buildings in quite a jumble at the edge of the permanent ice shelf. It was a struggle to make those last few hundred metres through deep trenches and over ice falls. At any other time it would have been incredibly daunting and would have seemed almost impossible. But we were inspired with the beautiful day, and the knowledge that this was the last obstacle, and the relief that there was no massive area of open water barring our way.

Once we had overcome the ice fall we would be on a safe and secure surface for the first time in three months. Those last few hundred metres took a long time and a lot of hard work, but finally we clambered up a high wall of ice and we were there!

We moved up the slope above, and were able to look back over the jumble of frozen ocean, and realized that we were now on safe, permanent ice attached to the land. There are still maybe eight to ten kilometres to go to the landing strip, but they will be easy, safe skiing. So we moved into the shade of a rolling ridge and set up camp. We had hot milk and tea for "supper."

Richard

Ninety days on the ice. Tomorrow makes it thirteen weeks! A long, long time. Last night was nice and sunny and really warm in our tent – had my sleeping bag peeled halfway back, just lying there. The day was not bright sunshine, but there was usually sun through the mist, and we had fog that rolled in and out, lots of "tuman" and a bit of "belli meglaw" (fog and white-out).

After lunch, things changed again. It got a bit rougher, and we climbed down onto the shear zone. About three kilometres of brand-new ice. Still quite moist, same as when we crossed with Steger. Very flat, no old ice, nothing, just new ice. That must have been the shear zone which is between the fast, ocean, moving ice and the land-fast ice that is attached to the shore.

This morning we could see land again, but after about an hour, it all disappeared. And there was just mist in the direction that we were heading. After we crossed the shear zone, there were lots of raised broken-up areas. At one place, we actually had to make a little bridge with the skis, by throwing in lumps of ice and then tying the skis together and laying them across. We inched our way across on the skis. We used the sleds to pull the backpacks across.

I am lying here in my sleeping bag – we didn't bother to put up the tent. Chris and I just made a wind-block and did the theodolite. I can look along the whole panorama of northern Ellesmere. What a great sight! We will have to come back here in the summer with our wives some time for some skiing and hiking, because those mountains have "climbing" written all over them.

Today I had four and a half of the best marches of the expedition. As the mountains came closer, it was almost unreal – that we had actually skied all this way. The last land we had seen was northern Soviet Siberia. Here we were, about to crawl onto land in Canada. To be met by such beautiful landscape as the mountains of northern Ellesmere was a gift. It is why I did it.

I walked the last bit with Max. We shook hands and congratulated each other, and then Chris came along and we did similarly, and afterwards Laurie and Dmitri. Even though we have still to get to land, it is now *fait accompli*. We have about ten to twenty kilometres to ski along the ice shelf and up onto the island. But the open water is over. The hard work is done.

It is 4:30. Misha has got up to start breakfast. All we have left to eat now is one meal of muesli, and after that we are on the reserve food, which is, I believe, some "*tvwark*" (cheese curds), sugar, tea, and coffee.

So we just made it with our sixteen days' food. I think the fact that we travelled from the North Pole to Canada in just over a month is really a remarkable feat. Most expeditions take fifty plus days to go to the Pole from Canada.

I think there is a tendency, when someone does something long and difficult, too often, once it is accomplished, to think that it wasn't that bad because you managed to do it. If you can do it, anybody can do it, so it wasn't that bad. Ours wasn't really that bad a trip. This is speaking personally, of course. It was long, but it wasn't particularly hard.

Before the expedition started, Arcadi Cherkasov had stressed to me how important he thought it was that a Soviet be the first person to step onto land. I wondered how these Soviets felt. Certainly, none of them could outrace me. Today Dmitri asked me where I thought was the official end of the expedition, the ice shelf or land itself. I said I thought that it would be when we actually touch land. The rocks and earth are definitely the end. Then he said, "I think we should all do it together. Right? Right Richard?" I said, "Well, okay." So I promised that we wouldn't rush on ahead.

JUNE 1. DAY 91

Richard

This morning we got up at about 5:00 and had breakfast, and then we found out that the plane is stuck in Resolute, can't come and get us, that we were to have a radio communication five hours later. So we decided to ski on up to the hut at Ward Hunt. We skied for one march, and then we stopped and took many photographs. In front of the big hill on Ward Hunt we made our final pictures of the group, individual shots, the group skiing, and everything everybody wanted with flags, etcetera. Then we skied on to the hut and, at 12:35, we all lined up in front of the first patch of gravel that we came to, and all jumped on it together, and yelled and screamed – and that was the end of the expedition.

Christopher

Twelve-thirty, Ottawa time. Our pick-up is weathered in. Exactly the same thing happened at the North Pole. We had great weather and they were stuck in a snowstorm in Resolute. Yesterday when we were skiing towards our ice shelf, we had a rainbow the whole way. Today the sky is blue. Not one cloud. Since we left the North Pole we have not had a day like this.

Ranulph Fiennes has a hut here. I am now lying on my sleeping bag on a sheet of four-by-eight plywood at this base camp, eating "pan-coated chocolate discs," best before August 1953. (In the free world, known as Smarties.) They are rations left by the military. This food is older than I am. I filled up on fruitcake, then I started to feel a bit ill.

It is so quiet here. There is absolutely no sound at all. The wind is the only thing that makes any sound. Vegetation is limited to some lichen and thin moss. It is nice to sit and soak it in for a while, because

I know that as soon as the plane lands we will be plunged into action.

In our own individual ways we like to be out here. When I was taking pictures Dmitri would pop up behind me sometimes and say, "You know that's a really beautiful piece of ice." We are all like that — we enjoy the beauty.

Laurie

Having come to the end of this expedition, I am very impressed by the route-finding and navigational skills of the two who have been leading most of the way, Volodi and Vasili. It is no small feat to travel over seventeen hundred kilometres across an ocean with no marks, no distinguishing features, to hit the mathematical point of the North Pole, and to continue unerringly to this site on this tiny island in the North of Canada. But that is what we have done.

I come here and I stand and walk in awe at the magnificence of the North, the land and people to which I have given my life. Here I am on one of those days which may never be repeated, the absolute awesome stillness of an Arctic summer's day, where I can look around me now and see thousands of square miles of magnificent mountains. Yet, it is a desolate area in which no other living being exists, except for a few people at Alert, the military watching station along the coast, and the few people who have come across the Arctic wastes from the Soviet Union. But, as I walk, I am out of sight of everybody, and seem like the last person on earth. I can look away from the mountains to the other direction from the rise on which I am walking, and I see in the foreground a flat greyness, and away beyond that, catching the sunlight, a thin, white, broken line — pressure ice! From here, even from this distance, knowing the scale, it looks formidable and impossible. I look in awe and amazement as I realize that we have come through that, and seventeen hundred kilometres away is the other land from which we set out.

Three months it has taken, three long months, many days during which I could have wished to have been anywhere but where I was. Yet given the opportunity to escape I would not have taken it. The expedition, as far as the travelling is concerned, has come to an end. Now, somehow, we have to change personalities, change clocks, and enter a new and foreign world. This was the forbidding foreign territory three months ago, but it has become our life, our existence, and now we have to enter what some people would call the "real world."

Appendix A: Glossary

kamik A traditional Inuit footwear made of sealskin. They are sewn with tiny stitches and are consequently waterproof. The sealskin also breathes somewhat, making it the first natural "Goretex."

klister A type of ski wax.

lead Crack in the ice. These can be anywhere from a few inches wide to kilometres wide. When frozen, they form a nice flat highway-like surface for travelling upon.

multi-year (old) ice Ice that is more than one year old. It generally becomes rounded from melting in the summer.

NP 28, NP 29 Since the 1930s the Soviets have had a string of drifting research stations set up on the ice of the Arctic Ocean, and named North Pole 1, North Pole 2, etc. They are manned year round, whenever possible. They are set up usually on pack ice or on an ice island, if one is available. Once established they remain in operation, as long as they are within Soviet territory, until either the ice breaks up or the station drifts out into the Atlantic. The expedition had their radio base on the station called N(orth) P(ole) 28. The skiers skied close to the station NP 29. The stations from numbers 1 through 27 no longer exist.

pan or ice pan Large flat section of ice. Generally made up of older ice. Pans can be anywhere from a few tens of metres wide to kilometres wide. Pressure ridges are located at the edges of pans.

senetate A sweet-tasting Soviet liquor made from herbs. It is not available to the general public. It is reserved for Soviet cosmonauts, submarine crews, and, presumably, polar explorers.

theodolite A surveying instrument for measuring horizontal and vertical angles. We used it to measure the height of the sun above the horizon (angle between flat ocean and a line between the observer and the sun) in order to find true north.

Our theodolite was also equipped with a magnetometer in order for us to measure the direction of the earth's magnetic field in both the horizontaland vertical planes.

Appendix B: Diet

As jointly established on December 15, 1987. All quantities are per man per day.

ITEM	DETAIL/ MANUFACTURER	COUNTRY OF ORIGIN	WEIGHT (gm)
Breakfast			
muesli	Shaklee	Canada	100
butter	dehydrated	U.S.S.R.	25
powdered milk	whole milk	U.S.S.R.	50
dehydrated meat	hamburger	U.S.S.R.	50
sugar	white cubes	U.S.S.R.	60
biscuit	plain/pilot	U.S.S.R.	25
coffee	instant decaffeinated	U.S.S.R.	5
multi-vitamins	Shaklee	Canada	
salt	personal taste only		2
			317
Day Food			
salt pork fat		U.S.S.R.	50
food/energy bar	Shaklee Vitabar (2)	Canada	160 (2 x 80)
peanut butter	commercial/natural	Canada	50
chocolate/halva/			
dry fruit/nuts	apricots/hazelnuts	U.S.S.R.	50
biscuit	plain/pilot	U.S.S.R.	45
sausage	salami type	U.S.S.R.	50
coffee	instant decaffeinated	U.S.S.R.	5
			455
Supper			
kasha	buckwheat groats	U.S.S.R.	100
pemmican	dry meat/dry liver		
	suet/spices	Canada	150
powdered milk	whole milk	U.S.S.R.	50
butter	dehydrated	U.S.S.R.	25
sugar	white cubes	U.S.S.R.	45
dry bread	black rye	U.S.S.R.	100
salt	personal taste		2
spices	garlic/basil/thyme/		
	pepper	Canada	
tea	black/herb	U.S.S.R./Canada	
			472

Total per man day: 1.244 kg

Emergency food: *tvork*, a Soviet dried yogurt/butter, milk-like substance.

Small changes to the diet were made during the expedition in order to adjust to the team's needs.

Special notes
At the start all the peanut butter and most of the Vitabars were forgotten for the first section of two weeks.

Most of the Soviets eventually substituted their ration of Vitabars for an equivalent weight of biscuit and white sugar, which was their traditional day food.

On the second section, half the pemmican was forgotten. One kilogram of dry meat, to be shared among the team, was added in the evening. The additional dry meat continued for the remainder of the expedition, even when the pemmican was reinstated. By the third section everyone started carrying extra, "personal" food.

Appendix C: Summary of Physiologic Observations

By the Canadian Scientific group

The three-month U.S.S.R.-Canada Polar Bridge Expedition from Cape Ark-ticheskiy to Ward Hunt Island, a distance of some 1730 km, was conducted between March 3 and June 1, 1988. The thirteen members (nine Soviets and four Canadians) of the expedition were measured prior to, during, and following the expedition on selected anthropometric and fitness measurements. The mean age of the Soviets was 40.9 ± 7.2 yrs. (range 29 to 51 yrs.), mean height 177.1 ± 5.8 cm, mean weight, 80.6 ± 8.4 kg (range 75 to 91.5 kg), body mass index (BMI), 25.7 ± 2. The Canadians had a mean age of 33 ± 6.8 yrs. (range 28 to 43 yrs.), mean height of 178.1 ± 8.2, mean weight of 74.8 ± 5.6 kg (range 70.6 to 85.7 kg), and a BMI of 23.6 ± 1.1 kg/m2.

During the first month of the expedition the weights of the Soviets decreased by 4 to 5 kg. They then increased by 3 to 4 kg, so that by the end of the expedition their mean weight was 2.2 kg less (2.7 per cent) than at the onset. This reduction in weight was accompanied by a 21 per cent reduction in body fat (24.5 to 19.4).

For the Canadians, weight dropped slightly during the first two weeks of the expedition, and then increased as the expedition progressed, reaching 78.4 ± 7.3 kg in mid-May and ending with a slight increase of 1.6 per cent over their pre-departure weight, with little change in per cent body fat (1.9 per cent). Upper body strength, as measured by the shoulder-arm push dynamometer, increased in both the Soviets (79.1 to 81.6 mm) and the Canadians (78.0 to 81.5 mm). Mean maximal oxygen consumption measured on a bicycle ergometer averaged 60.5 ± 5.1 ml/min. kg prior to the expedition in the Canadians. This value decreased to a mean of 48.7 ml/min. kg (20 per cent) following the expedition and was similar to the post $VO2$ max. of the Soviets (46.2 ± 5.5 ml/min. kg. PWC170 decreased from 1812 to 1500 kpm/min. following the trek for the Canadians and from 1539 to 1308 kpm/min. for the Soviets.

The thirteen Soviet and Canadian members of the expedition were examined within twenty-four hours of their arrival in Ottawa. Generally, all members were in good health. No significant medical problems were identified, and there was no evidence of physical or mental fatigue. Injuries were primarily related to environmental factors. Each member of the expedition suffered some degree of cold injury to the extremities and face. Most of the injuries ranged from frost-nip to superficial frost-bite that had resolved by the time of the examination. Two cases of severe frost-bite occurred: one involving the tip of the nose with resulting ulcer formation and loss of tissue and the other involving the great toe and resulting in some tissue and sensory loss. All members suffered some degree of sun and wind damage to the facial skin. Seven showed mild to moderate trauma to the feet and toes; eight, rash on their knees; and seven, eye irritation from the strong polar sunlight. Seven reported having had short episodes of abdominal cramps and diarrhoea thought to be related to the high fat content of their diet. Muscular pain and aches were common during the expedition. Blood tests, urinalysis, and ECGs showed no significant abnormalities. Evaluation of lung function revealed three individuals with mild degrees of restrictive lung disease. Three members had evidence of mild hypertension. The results of this examination indicate that the members were primarily affected by environmental factors (sun, wind, and cold) rather than the cardiorespiratory demands of the expedition.

Counter-balancing Effects of Changes in Aerobic Fitness and Skiing Economy on the Relative Stress of Trekking

By M.A. Booth, J.S. Thoden, F.D. Reardon, M. Jette, and A. Rodes, School of Human Kinetics, Faculty of Health Sciences, University of Ottawa, Ottawa, Ontario; supported by the Development Fund of the Faculty of Health Sciences and the School of Graduate Studies of the University of Ottawa

Three of the four Canadian members of the three-month, 1730 km expedition were tested on a motorized ski-treadmill (TM) just before and after the trek to determine the oxygen cost of sub-maximal ski-trekking, both with and without a 37.5 kg backpack, over a range of speeds and heart rates. Heart rates (HR) were also recorded at 15-minute intervals during portions of the trek itself, using battery-operated Sports Testers. Maximal aerobic power (VO2 max.) was determined with a bicycle ergometer protocol.

Over the range of TM speeds tested (2.5–5.0 kph at 1- slope), HR and VO2 per minute increased progressively, whereas VO2 per km was relatively constant. The effect of the backpack load, which increased total weight carried by an average of 50 per cent, was to increase VO2 per km by about 30 per cent in two subjects and 49 per cent in the third.

Post-trek VO2 max. decreased by 15-20 per cent in all three subjects, from an average pre-trek "trained" level of 62.2 ml kgIE minIE, while the oxygen economy of loaded skiing improved by 6, 8, and 14 per cent in the three subjects. These two long-term adaptations appeared to have counter-balancing effects on the relative physical "stress" of skiing, such that HR following the trek was essentially unchanged from pre-trek at any given TM speed in two subjects and even decreased by an average 8 per cent in the subject with the 14 per cent improvement in economy.

The HRs recorded during the trek suggest that the majority of the distance was covered at a speed equivalent to about 3.5 kph on the TM. This speed equates to a mean oxygen cost of 370 ml kgIE kmIE (21.6 ml, kgIE minIE) for the post-trek loaded condition and a relative stress level of 39–46 per cent of VO2 max. Oxygen cost at 3.5 kph was 29 per cent greater in the least efficient compared to the most efficient trekker.

Effect of a 91-Day Polar Ski Expedition on Cold Acclimatization

By S.D. Livingstone, R.W. Nolan, and A.A. Keefe, Defence Research Establishment Ottawa, Ottawa, Ontario, Canada

In the spring of 1988 a group of four Canadians and nine Soviets took 91 days to ski across the North Pole from northern Siberia to northern Canada. The physiological effects of this cold exposure were determined in the four Canadian members of this group. Local acclimatization was determined by examining cold-induced vasodilation (CIVD), which was observed by measuring temperature changes in the mid-finger when immersed in ice water. General cold-acclimatization changes were examined by exposing each skier, wearing only shorts and reclining on a rope-mesh cot, to an ambient temperature of 10°C. Skin and rectal temperatures, electromyographs, and metabolic rates were measured. These tests were done approximately one month prior to departure and within five days after the skiers' arrival in Canada. The results showed that each skier had a greater CIVD response as a result of the exposure, indicating a local acclimatization to cold. The general cold stress test indicated no clear differences in skin or rectal temperature changes; however, onset of shivering was delayed and metabolic rate was lower in the tests after the ski-trek. This would indicate that there was an insulative-hypothermic response to a general cold stress.

Appendix D:
Communications

By Laurie Dexter, with thanks to Tom Atkins and David Adams, who supplied much of the information.

PEOPLE AND STATIONS

The Polar Bridge Expedition relied on an unprecedented international network of amateur radio operators for all its communication needs. The system was pioneered by Leonid Labutin, a well-known Soviet operator who had organized the radio communications for most of the previous polar region expeditions led by Dmitri Shparo. In March 1987, Leonid contacted the president of the Canadian Radio Relay League, Tom Atkins, to ask for the support of Canadian amateurs. The basis for co-operation would be a unique reciprocal operating and third-party traffic agreement between the two countries, the first such agreement ever for the U.S.S.R., allowing Soviet and Canadian amateurs to operate from each other's countries, and to handle messages between them, without restrictions, through base stations in the Arctic. The expedition was to have three principal radio bases: one at Sredny Island, some 200 km south of Cape Arkticheskiy; the second at the drifting ice station NP 28; and the third at Resolute Bay in the Northwest Territories.

For Tom and Leonid the task of co-ordinating the communications system became a full-time business. Leonid had lived with this sort of situation for years, but Tom was plunged into it abruptly. Living in Toronto, Tom was besieged with phone calls and visits from the media as he effectively dealt with problems of logistics, movement of equipment and operators, and a score of other matters as new situations arose. The communications work also dominated the lives of many other operators for much of the time the expedition was in progress.

Barry Garratt, a well-known Canadian amateur operator, was recruited as chief operator. During a visit to Moscow he and Tom became the first Canadian amateurs to operate from the U.S.S.R. under the newly signed reciprocal agreement.

Soon after the start of the expedition, Canadian amateur Rick Burke joined Leonid at the main Soviet base station on Sredny Island. Overall he probably had the most English-language air time with the Moving Group, and he possessed an uncanny ability to understand and make himself understood even when transmission and reception conditions were poor. For a time Sredny was a very busy station, as three other Soviets were also there: Piotr Strezev,

Victor Redkin, and Alexander Shatokhin. As the Moving Group travelled farther away, only these last two remained at Sredny.

On the Siberian mainland south of Sredny there was a radio base at Dikson. Vasily Zaushitsin commanded this base and relayed messages to Moscow, a vital link during the first half of the expedition. He was ably assisted by Valera Kondratko, a member of the Soviet cosmonaut program.

One of the most essential links was Piotr Strezev who started out at Sredny. He spoke excellent English and acted as the main interpreter between the Soviet and Canadian team members during the earlier training expeditions in the Tien Shan mountains and Baffin Island, as well as during the final preparation period.

His main area of responsibility moved to NP 28. As the expedition approached the North Pole, NP 28 became the focus of attention, as it was drifting to within 30 km of the Pole, and became the staging area for the dignitaries and media people coming from both the U.S.S.R. and Canada. At this point Barry Garratt joined Piotr Strezev on NP 28 and continued there until forced to evacuate when the pack ice began to break up – and after Barry lost some of his personal possessions and radio equipment through the ice into the Arctic Ocean! Barry then returned to Canada and joined the radio team at Resolute Bay, which became the "mission control" for the last few weeks.

Garth Hamilton operated the high Arctic station at Resolute Bay during the critical first two weeks of the expedition, and later he became the principal back-up for Tom. Later, Leonid Labutin, with his compatriot Alexander Tenyakshev, also came over to Canada and joined the base at Resolute Bay. They both speak a little English and were good choices for this position. Resolute had been a key station all the way through in terms of keeping in touch with the other base stations and the world at large, as well as with the Moving Group, especially after they had passed the North Pole and were on the last leg of their journey to Canada.

In Ottawa, Ron Belleville was the expedition's tireless anchorman, passing messages to and from expedition manager Peter Baird, and between the skiers and their families, and dealing with the government and the media. The Moscow radio headquarters was in the offices of the main sponsoring newspaper, *Komsomolskaya Pravda*, and was manned by Yuri Zolotov, assisted by Kirill Tchachin and a number of other enthusiastic operators.

In the Moving Group, the chief operator was Anatoli Melnikov, and working with him for the English side of the operation was Laurie Dexter. Laurie is not normally an amateur radio operator, but was given a special licence for the duration of the expedition. While Melnikov and Dexter handled most of the radio communications, every member of the expedition used the radio on occasion. In particular, most of the Soviet members had contracts with different Soviet publications and prepared fairly regular reports to send out. Some phone-patch communications between the Moving Group and Resolute enabled the Canadian skiers to talk directly to their families on two or three occasions.

An extra international flavour was added by Olle Ekblom and his Swedish colleagues, who maintained a constant watch throughout the expedition, recording daily satellite position reports, checking in daily with the Resolute Bay station, and keeping an eye on Soviet radio and television coverage.

EQUIPMENT

On the Soviet side there were well-established radio stations already in place, especially at Moscow headquarters; but for the Canadian base station in Resolute Bay, as well as the other temporary stations that had to be established, such as that on the drifting ice floe of NP 28, ICOM provided a full range of HF and VHF transceivers and amplifiers. ICOM also provided two-metre FM hand-held transceivers and a VHF-AM transceiver to enable the Moving Group to communicate with the aircraft bringing resupplies. The generous support of ICOM, in the person of Mrs. Evelyn Garrison, is gratefully acknowledged.

The radio used by the Moving Group was a second-generation miniature transceiver designed by Leonid Labutin. It operated on six crystal controlled frequencies, although only two, on the 20.40- and 80-metre amateur bands, were used consistently. The full range of possibilities was: 3633 LSB; 3750 USB; 7043 LSB; 7007 LSB ; 14182 USB; 14290 USB. This unit was powered by a lithium battery back giving ten watts' peak envelope power, phone only, and used a dipole antenna raised on a mast of four or five ski poles that slotted into each other.

A key element in the expedition's success was the use of the facilities of SARSAT/COSPAS. This is the joint Soviet-French-American-Canadian search-and-rescue satellite system. The Moving Group carried a beacon operating on 145.825 MHZ, which was switched on every day when the team made camp. Within a couple of hours they received a report from the base radio station giving their location. If necessary, it was also possible for them to hear their position read out by "talking computer" from the amateur radio satellite UOSAT OSCAR 11, on the ICOM Micro2AT, about every one hundred minutes. The amateur satellite control station is located at the university of Surrey, Guildford, England, while the SARSAT/COSPAS ground stations are at Trenton and Ottawa, Ontario, and at air bases in the U.S. and in the Soviet Union.

Amateur radio operators collect contacts from around the world and exchange cards to confirm those contacts. These are known as QSL cards. Special commemorative QSL cards were provided courtesy of the Hammond Manufacturing Co. of Guelph, Ontario, for the station at Resolute Bay, and David Adams, as QSL manager of the contact system, sent many thousands of these to amateurs all over the world to confirm their contact with the base station.

The amateur radio network supporting the Polar Bridge Expedition, composed entirely of volunteers, was just phenomenal. It received much acclaim throughout the world of amateur radio, but was not given as much publicity or appreciation as it deserved by the general media. The words "amateur radio operator" are so deceptive. In all but name, this was a professional operation at the highest level.

The main Canadian members of the team with their call signs are listed below.

Canadian Communications Co-ordinator: Tom Atkins, VE3CDM/ VE8UA
Expedition Moving Group Operator: Laurie Dexter, VE8LD
Chief Operator: Barry Garratt, VE3CDX, VE8CDX, 4K0DX
Ottawa Communications: Ron Belleville, VE3AUM
Publicity and Information: Al d'Éon, VE3AND
AMSAT Liaison: John Henry, VE2VQ
Packet Radio: Tony Fegan, VE3QF
Resolute Bay QSL Manager: David Adams, VE3HBF
The Operating Team: Joe Adams, VE3CPU; Alan Boyce; Rick Burke, VO1SA; Garth Hamilton, VE3H0; Garry Hammond, VE3XN; Bill Hardie, VE3EFX; Larry Horlick, VE8HL; John Hutchinson, VE3CKF; Terry Keim, VE8TF; Dennis Laliberty, VE3MFP; Garry Letford, VE3COP; Andy McLellan, VE1ASJ; Wally Mansz, VE7HQ; Dale Sackfie, VE3LVW; Stanley White, VE3FKD; Don Whitty, VO1QF; Glen Wyant, VE3lCR; Rolf Ziemann, VE8RZ

Call signs used at the base stations

Dikson – EXODR, EXOPM;
SREDNY ISLAND – EXOKP, EXOCR, EXOGZ, EXOAU, EXOQCG, VO1SA/UA0
Drifting Station NP 28 – 4K0DC, 4K0DX, 4K0DX, 4K0DR
Resolute Bay – CI8C (*Note:* the Resolute facilities were made available courtesy of Transport Canada and the local operator, Ron Lupack, VE8M).
Moving Group – EXOVE from the Soviet Union to the North Pole, and C18UA from them North Pole to Canada.

Call signs for some of the Soviet radio operators

George Inanov, Valera Kondratko, EXOPM; Leonid Labutin, UA3CR, Victor Redkin, UA0RCB; Alexander Shatokhin, EXOKP; Piotr Strezev, 4K0DC, Alexander Tenjakshev, UW3G2; Kiril Tchachin, operator of UK KP in Moscow; Vasily Zaushitsin, RW3DR; Yuri Zolotov, UA3HR; Alla Zolotova.

Appendix E:
Snow Chemistry Report

By R.M. Koerner, Terrain Sciences Division, Geological Survey of Canada

Since the Second World War, pilots flying small aircraft in the Arctic have become increasingly aware of poorer visibility conditions in an area that is supposed to be one of the cleanest areas of the world. The poor visibility was termed "Arctic haze." Research in Barrow, Alaska, showed that the haze was predominantly composed of microscopic drops of acid. These small drops (or aerosols) were not of natural origin and were in fact the product of industrial pollution.

It was determined that the source of the polluting aerosols was the industrial centres of northwest Europe and the Arctic areas of the Soviet Union. One of the reasons the pollutants travel so far is that the Arctic is a very dry area in winter with only about 20 cm of snow falling over the Arctic Ocean between August and April/May. As a result there is nothing to wash out (scavenge) the aerosols from the atmosphere. There is also ample evidence that, during the winter, air mass trajectories are often directed from Eurasia over the North Pole, and then on to the North American Arctic.

By studying ice cores taken from ice-caps where snow has accumulated for thousands of years, scientists have been able to determine that acid levels, particularly oxides of nitrogen (nitrate, NO_3^-) and sulphur (sulphates, SO_4^-) have been increasing since late in the last century.

Snow-sample collection by the Polar Bridge Expedition, therefore, formed an ideal opportunity to add more to our knowledge of the source, trajectories, and type of these pollutants. Samples were collected in clean 30 cc cuvettes. The pollutants that form Arctic haze are found only in low concentrations in the snow, usually less than one part per million. The most difficult part is the sample collection. Each cuvette must be pushed into a vertical snow wall of a carefully dug snowpit.

In order to avoid contaminating the samples, thin plastic gloves are worn, and no part of the inside of the cuvette or its cover or the snow must be touched.

The samples were always taken so as to cover the entire vertical increment of the 20-30 cm-deep snow pack that had accumulated on top of the sea ice over the winter. Six cuvettes would do this. Because of circumstances beyond our control no samples were collected on the Soviet side of the Pole. After that, one set of six snow-filled cuvettes was collected each degree of latitude until the expedition reached the Ward Hunt ice shelf.

As well, the expedition's samples that were collected from snow that had been deposited on the floating ice of the Arctic Ocean were compared with those from similar latitudes collected from snow falling inland. Average values measured on over 100 samples from five years of snow accumulation on the nearby Agassiz ice-cap on northern Ellesmere Island at an elevation of 1700 m above sea level were included.

It is the levels of sulphates and nitrates that were the *raison d'être* of sampling. Pollution in remote regions is often assessed by calculating a value known as "excess sulphate." This is essentially non-marine sulphate. By accurately measuring the concentrations of the Na^+ and Cl^- ions and assuming that they are entirely of marine origin, the amount of marine sulphate is calculated from the known $Na/SO_4^=$ or Cl/So_4 ratios in sea water. Any $SO_4^=$ left over is "excess" and, in the absence of the other natural source – i.e., a volcanic eruption – is considered to be of industrial origin.

The expedition results show a much more complicated picture. Using the marine ratios, we calculate strong sulphate "deficits." This had been found before, but only once have sulphate "deficits" been the subject of a specific study. In this case a Norwegian scientist working in Antarctica found sulphate "deficits" in snow close to the sea ice. The deficits changed to "excesses" farther inland. If we use the same $SO_4^=/Cl^-$ ratio as that found in sea water we can make little sense of the results in terms of pollution (non-marine sulphates).

Clearly the marine ratio must change during the transfer process of sea spray to snow. Nitrates are also indicative of pollution, as they have a negligible marine source. Yet the Nitrates show very low concentrations compared to the snows on the ice-cap. This is due to the fact that Nitrates appear mainly in summer snow, and there is no summer snow in the Arctic Ocean snow samples. Even then, there is a weak trend, if we exclude site F, of decreasing Nitrates from site A (near the North Pole) to site G (near the Canadian coast). This is a trend we do not find in any of the cations or the chloride.

There is still a lot of work to be done on these results, but the first thing we have done is to change the $SO_4^=/Cl^-$ ratio to make the biggest "deficit" equal zero. Using this new ration we *begin* to make sense of the results with respect to $SO_4^=$. This time, we find a general decrease in the $SO_4^=$ concentrations similar to those of NO_3^-. Again site F is the exception. We have not yet run significance tests on these trends or investigated the changes at each site within the snowpack. However, there does seem to be a trend emerging of pollutants decreasing from the North Pole towards the northern Ellesmere coast. If correct, it will be concrete evidence for the trends inferred from the early work based on various metal ratios from air samples. The minimum may not indeed be at the Canadian coast. Weather systems often track round the Arctic Ocean coastline, and they would tend to wash out some of the pollutants preferentially along their tracks. Earlier work by one of us has found that snow accumulation is higher close to the coast, which agrees with this hypothesis.

Perhaps what is most remarkable is that one can indeed make any sense out of samples collected under the extremely arduous conditions met on this expedition. Many scientists turn down the offer of travellers of this kind to collect samples. They consider that the samples will be hopelessly contaminated. This does not seem to be the case, and the crossing may prove to be not only a heroic venture but a scientific achievement as well.

Appendix F:
The Magnetic Program

By L.R. Newitt, Geological Survey of Canada

There have been very few observations of the vector magnetic field over the Arctic Ocean. Vector aeromagnetic observations were made by the Canadian Department of Energy, Mines and Resources in 1970 on the Canadian side of the North Pole. Additional vector aeromagnetic observations have been made in the Arctic by the U.S. Geological Survey and by Project Magnetic, but no observations have been made on the Siberian side of the pole. Dr. V.V. Kuznetsov of the Institute of Geology and Geophysics (IGG) of the U.S.S.R. Academy of Sciences in Novosibirsk suggested that magnetic observations be made in this area by the Polar Bridge Expedition. The observations would contribute a small but useful amount of badly needed data to existing data files. These observations could be compared to current charts and models of the magnetic field as a test of their validity in the polar regions. Observations on the Canadian side of the Pole could be compared to the aeromagnetic observations of the EMR 1970 aeromagnetic survey to give some indication of the secular variation of the magnetic field over the eighteen-year interval. In addition, Kuznetsov hoped that the data would help him to test theories he had developed concerning the non-dipole nature of the earth's magnetic field in the Arctic regions.

Expedition members agreed to carry, on the trek, a magnetometer-theodolite for measuring the declination (D) and inclination (I) of the magnetic field, and a proton-precession magnetometer for measuring the field intensity (F). A complete vector observation of the magnetic field would thus be made.

During the trek, observations of inclination were made almost every day except when temperatures dipped below minus 45°C. Less frequent observations of declination were made, since it was not always possible to sight the sun to determine true north. Only a few observations of total intensity could be made because of equipment problems. In all, 57 observations of I, 46 of D, and 9 of F were made.

Observations can be seriously contaminated by solar magnetic disturbances. An examination of magnetograms from the magnetic observatory at Alert on Ellesmere Island showed that twenty-four days were subject to magnetic disturbances. Observations made on those days should therefore be interpreted with caution and should not be considered in isolation.

Due to the lack of F observations it was not possible to calculate the north, east, and vertical components of the magnetic field, which are the preferred components for analysis in high Arctic regions. However, an examination of the angular data is still useful. The observed values of inclination were compared with values computed from the IGRF for the same dates. In all, 40 differences between observations and the model are positive and 17 are negative, with the mean differences being $0.053° \pm 0.131°$. Although this is significantly different from zero in a statistical sense, it indicates only a slight negative bias ($.053° = 50$ nT) in the IGRF over the Arctic Ocean. Such a small bias could easily result from the normal secular change errors inherent in any model of the magnetic field.

A similar analysis of the declination data shows that 32 out of 46 differences were negative, with a mean difference between observed and model values of $-1.068° \pm 3.524°$. This value seems large when compared to the mean difference in I, but it must be remembered that, in the polar regions, the horizontal component of the magnetic field is very small, and that this amplifies all variations in magnetic declination. In terms of a force, the difference is approximately -50 nT, the same as the I difference. Therefore the IGRF fits both the declination and inclination data obtained during the expedition extremely well.

There are eight locations at which the Polar Bridge observations are approximately coincident with the aeromagnetic observations made in 1970. Differences between the inclination observations made during the two surveys are all positive and ranged from 0.5' to 19.4' of arc. Since the points are not exactly coincident, and since transient disturbances have not been accounted for in either survey, values of secular variation cannot be calculated with any accuracy. However, the observations demonstrate an increase in secular variation as one moves from Ellesmere Island towards the North Pole, with an average rate near the Pole of roughly 1.0' per year. A positive secular variation in inclination is consistent with the observed northward motion of the North Magnetic Pole.

The observations taken by the team indicate that there is no second magnetic pole in the Soviet sector of the Arctic Ocean.

Appendix G:
Clothing and Equipment

By Christopher Holloway

The clothing used was specialized. The selection was influenced by the experience of the Inuit of both countries and of other expeditions that had travelled in the far north. The polar suits and socks had been tested, developed, and used on the Steger expedition.

The Soviet clothing had evolved continually since Dmitri began with the Pravda expedition. The Soviet team had a great deal of experience with their clothing and knew its capabilities and limitations. They also did not have access to the synthetic fabrics of the West.

The major difference between the clothing provided by the two sides was that the Canadian equipment was primarily synthetic, while the Soviets used natural fibres. When dry, there is not much difference in warmth between the two. When damp, the natural fibres within the material (wool, cotton) absorb water and consequently take longer to dry. Individual fibres in synthetic material are waterproof plastic, consequently polypropylene or nylon fabrics dry quicker. As body warmth was the main source of heat to dry clothing, this was an important advantage.

It had been agreed that each person would have the option of choosing what clothes to use for the expedition, and each was provided with a complete set of both Canadian and Soviet equipment. This was a strain on the Canadian team when much of their equipment was left untested.

Canadian Clothing

Goretex windbreaker and pants
Thermax double layered one-piece
    suit with a trap-door in the back,
    and zipper/Velcro in the front
Polar Plus jackets
Thermax long underwear
various wool and synthetic hats
beaver fur hat
Paris gloves and mittens
Thermax socks (this material we
    found to be extremely durable
kamicks (sealskin mukluks made in
    Broughton Island, N.W.T.

Soviet Clothing

fine wool long underwear
brown wool shirts (the same brown
    shirts Stalin had used)
wool turtleneck sweaters
high-topped close-weave wool pants
    with button fly
canvas windbreaker and pants
wolf fur hat
wool Balaclava
wool mittens, canvas wind overmitts
fur mittens with knitted wristlets
fur socks for sleeping
wolverine ruffs for hoods

sheepskin overboots for walking
around the camp
Neoprene face masks
Carrera sunglasses

wool socks
leather ski boots
leather and nylon overboots with
felt soles

The problems of clothing for this expedition were not simple. Various elements had to be contended with, chief among them body moisture that caused condensation in clothes. The rule of winter travel is not to sweat. Layers of clothing are removed or vents opened to prevent perspiration. This is vital, as sweat will condense in clothing, reducing insulation and increasing weight. Some people naturally sweat less than others. It was rare to see any frost on Vasa's wool sweaters or canvas windbreaker. In contrast, Max and Toli Melnikov were generally covered in a layer of ice. It may be of interest to note that Toli had lost toes to frost-bite in 1986, and Max had a frozen toe on this expedition. Their damp clothing may have been a factor.

Each night in our snow house, I would take off my three layers of polar socks, which were damp from skiing, and fold them against my chest inside my polar suit. Through the night the heat from my body would drive the moisture through the socks into the suit. In the morning I would have dry socks, and a damp suit. During the course of the day the moisture from my suit would form as frost on the inside of my windbreaker or the outside of the polar suit, where it could be brushed off. Each person carried a toilet brush specifically for this purpose.

OTHER EQUIPMENT

Stoves
The Soviet word for stove is *primus*, which is hardly surprising, as it looks very similar to the Swedish stove of the same name. It has a fuel tank on the bottom with an air pump, and a pressure release valve. The burner is directly on top of this. In order to light the stove, two tablespoons of alcohol are poured on the burner and then collect in a cup above the tank. The alcohol is lit. When it burns off, the tank is warmed enough so that the fuel will vaporize and burn. If it has been heated enough by the burning alcohol, the stove will produce a welcome blue flame; otherwise it will flare up in a large yellow flame. The valve must then be shut off quickly and the process repeated.

From the beginning of the expedition the cold weather compounded the regular problems. The person "on duty" was given Toli Fedjakov's watch, which was the only one that had an alarm. This had to be tucked under the duty person's hat, as it could not be heard when on the wrist. Unless he was very tired, it would also wake him up with its hourly beep that could not be shut off. After getting dressed (in the dark) the duty person had to use about three matches to warm up the wax of the candle enough so that it would melt once the wick was lit. Lighters do not work at this temperature. Though everyone was still trying to sleep, six stoves had to be pumped and primed to get them fired into action.

One morning, when in a particularly generous mood, I applied more than the recommended two tablespoons of alcohol to the Soviet stoves to ensure that I would not have to prime them a second time. Naturally, some of the alcohol spilt on the floor, but I didn't worry about it much, thinking that it would soak into the snow. I had all the stoves going, the snow was starting to melt nicely, and the stalactites of frost were melting into the morning showers on the sleeping bags. In the meantime the alcohol that had been spilt on the floor had not soaked into the cold snow and had now warmed up enough to vaporize. At about 5:15, it reached the flash point. The entire cooking area ignited into flames. I started hopping about smothering the flames with Yuri's assistance each time they resurfaced between pots, food, or equipment. In a minute things were back to "normal," and everyone went back in search of their final forty minutes of sleep. The Canadian stoves were made by MSR in the U.S.A. While more efficient for their weight, they were also more fragile. Both Soviet and Canadian stoves could be rebuilt in the field, and spare parts were carried for this purpose.

Tent

The Soviet tent had been specifically designed for Arctic conditions. It had a titanium frame for the roof, into which ski tips fit. With the tails of the skis in the snow they completed the frame for the walls. The erected tent was about fifteen feet in diameter with walls sloping inwards at a fort-five-degree angle. The centre of the tent was about five and a half feet high, so it was always necessary to stoop when moving around inside. The covering was made of two layers of porous parachute-type material. It also had a skirt along its bottom edge, which would have snow piled on it to anchor it. There were four guy ropes for high winds. The lack of the coating that most tents have made the fabric more forgiving, and thus stronger, as well as enabling some moisture and vapour to pass through the tent. The door had a drawstring closing, as did the vent in the roof. As we passed through the door its layer of frost was invariably wiped off onto our backs as we entered.

Because of the number of people in the tent, there was quite an accumulation of frost on the walls and roof by morning. When the person on duty lit the stoves, this frost melted and rained on the team members. I left the tent after one night because of this moisture/rain problem, Richard after two. Within two weeks, we were joined by Misha, Fiodor, and occasionally Vasa and Max. We started building snow houses that evolved from wind breaks to 'A'-frames to igloos. We were teaching ourselves, and so our structures were not very good, but they were adequate. They did not have the moisture or noise problems of the main tent and, in the long run, they were warmer. After about four weeks we started using a parachute for the roof of our shelter. We slept under a frame of six or eight skis stuck in the snow with a parachute stretched over the top and weighed down with snow around the edges. This took us five or ten minutes to set up, slept four or five comfortably, and weighed 1 kg.

Packs

The Canadian packs were Karrimor Condor. At 100 L in volume, they were the largest we could find. They had internal frames and weighed about 2.5 kg empty. They were used by all the Canadians and two of the Soviet members.

The Soviets had two types of packs. The older type was essentially a bag with two unpadded shoulder straps. It had a thin pocket, inside which the sleeping pads could be folded, providing some stiffness to the pack and some padding for the packer. These packs were light (1 kg), but did not have a waist belt, so all the weight was on the shoulders. This type was used by five of the Soviet members. Their other pack had an external frame pack with padded shoulder straps and waist belt. This was used by two Soviet members, and was about the same weight as the Karrimor pack.

Sleds

Most Arctic expeditions use sleds to some extent, as it takes less energy to pull equipment on a sled than to backpack it. On the rough ice of the Arctic Ocean, however, it is also slower, as it is necessary to negotiate the sled as well as yourself through the pressure ice. Two sleds are attached together, one upside down on top of the other, so that it can roll over. All the Canadians tried sleds for various amounts of time, but Misha Malakov was the only one to use them for the whole trip. The Canadian sleds were made by Norca in Montreal, and are sold as child's sleds for about ten dollars. They are fast, light, and available in any colour so long as it is red. Misha's Soviet sled was slightly shorter and not available in red. With either sled it was possible to carry an extra 10 kg by splitting the weight between one's pack and sled.

Skis

The Soviet skis were made from simple laminations of wood with steel edges. The skis were about 207 cm long and about 8 cm wide. The wooden bases were well suited to getting over pressure ridges, as they stuck to the cold ice. However, when they crossed newly frozen ice, the brine would soak into the wooden bases, and slow them down considerably. There were unpredictable breakages early in the trek, but this was probably due to flaws in the wood as there were fewer later on.

Three Canadians used Karhu skis (made in Canada). These were designed for telemark skiing, and it took some skill to keep them in a straight line. These skis were the strongest that we could find. These broke at predictable intervals, depending on the weight of the skier. This was due to the foam core, which became fatigued and snapped, much as a piece of metal does if bent too often. My skis, for example, broke every thirty days, with one ski breaking within days of the other. Richard's skis lasted twice as long as mine, because he was lighter. These skis worked well on salty ice, and were very fast, especially in warmer weather. They were slippery on pressure ridges. If these skis had a wooden core, and a groove in the base, they would have been better suited to our particular needs.

Bindings

These cannot be discussed without also talking about boots. The Soviet system relied on a stiff boot used in combination with a loose metal binding. The Canadian system used kamiks (a sealskin mukluk) in a plastic "Berwin" binding that offered some lateral control. Binding breakage was not a problem for either type. The kamiks never iced up inside as badly as the Soviet boots – their thinner leather meant that the ice would crack and peel off. Scraping the Soviet boots became a necessary evening chore, and it was common for skiers to chip the ice out of their boots with the same spoon that they had just finished dinner with.

Cooking and eating utensils

The pots were of thin stainless steel. The eating bowls were 1.5 L stainless-steel mixing bowls. Each person was issued with a Victornox Swiss army knife (salesman's model, of course). This contained two blades, scissors, can and bottle openers, screw drivers, awl, tweezers, and toothpick. These knives were terrific. Spoons were made from Lexan (polycarbonate plastic). Mugs were plastic souvenir coffee mugs from First Air, but they did not handle the continuous temperature contrast between minus 40°C and scalding coffee well, and did not last beyond three weeks. Enamelled Soviet steel mugs were then imported, and behaved in a utilitarian manner until the end of the expedition.

Camera Equipment

The threats to camera equipment were the cold temperatures and the condensation problems in the warm tent. To solve this, there were two approaches. Outside shots were taken with totally manual cameras: Nikon FM2s. The only electronics in this camera were the light meters, which would not work below minus 35°C. Our FM2s were never brought into the tent or put under clothing to warm them, to avoid the risk of condensation. To take photos in the tent, we had a Nikon L35AWAF. This is an auto focus, auto exposure camera with a built-in flash, and is waterproof. With this camera, the care was totally opposite. Because of its electronic features, this camera had to be kept warm; therefore it was carried inside clothing. Each of the photographers had the experience of winding the film too quickly and snapping the cold film inside the camera. In order to preserve the frames already exposed, the film had to be removed by hand inside Volodi's dark bag brought for this purpose. This was a painful exercise, and taught the virtues of patience.

The film used was from Black's Cameras in Canada. Their house brand 100 ASA film was used almost exclusively.

We never had one mechanical failure with any of our Nikon cameras. Even Dmitri's L35AWAF continued to work in manual mode after he fell on it and shattered the auto-exposure mechanism.

Appendix H: Daily Log

DATE	NO. OF MARCHES	DISTANCE MADE GOOD	LATITUDE	LONGITUDE	TEMPERATURE
3 Mar.	3	11 km	81°17.0'	95°45.0'	-35°C
4	7	24.3	81 21.2	96 12.8	-31
5	8	6.8	81 35.8	96 52.4	-28
6	7	22.2	81 46.4	97 30.7	-30
7	8	8.8	81 50.6	97 15.1	-40
8	8	17.8	----------	----------	-41
9	7	17.8	82 09.3	97 47.0	-47
10	8	15.2	82 16.9	97 24.6	-47
11	9	22.2	82 28.8	97 13.0	-45
12	9	19.5	82 39.2	97 00.1	-39
13	9	24.5	82 52.2	97 19.8	-42
14	7	16.6	83 01.0	97 07.0	-38
15	0	0.0	----------	----------	-37
16	0	0.0	82 58.7	97 28.9	-37
17	4	24.1	83 11.7	97 26.6	-37
18	8	26.3	83 25.9	97 24.3	-32
19	9	22.2	83 37.9	97 21.7	-32
20	9	25.8	83 51.8	97 27.4	-35
21	8	21.8	84 03.5	97 40.4	-38
22	8	28.4	84 18.5	97 08.2	-34
23	8	21.7	84 28.9	96 12.4	-34
24	1	6.6	84 25.6	95 58.2	-37
25	9	16.3	----------	----------	-38
26	9	16.4	84 43.1	95 50.5	-43
27	8	31.6	85 00.1	93 31.5	-45
28	8	13.6	85 07.1	95 17.4	-41
29	8	22.2	85 18.9	94 55.3	-40
30	0	-0.2	85 18.8	94 40.0	-40
31	0	-1.5	85 18.0	94 03.7	-42
1 Apr.	3	10.3	85 23.2	93 40.0	-40
2	8	24.1	----------	----------	-38
3	8	25.0	85 48.8	92 20.5	-40
4	8	22.6	86 00.7	91 44.5	-36
5	9	22.0	86 12.4	92 07.2	-38
6	9	27.5	86 26.3	93 18.3	-42
7	9	32.8	86 43.0	91 49.9	-42
8	9	32.5	87 00.2	91 03.5	-32
9	10	26.6	87 14.2	91 48.4	-33
10	9	29.2	87 28.4	91 03.1	-30
11	9	26.7	87 42.4	94 55.7	-35
12	9	37.7	88 02.7	95 34.9	-35
13 April	5	17.2	88 11.5	97 07.0	-35
14	0	-18.8	88 01.4	95 09.9	-35
15	0	17.3	88 10.7	91 48.2	-32

DATE	NO. OF MARCHES	DISTANCE MADE GOOD	LATITUDE	LONGITUDE	TEMPERATURE
16	0	-3.4	88 08.9	90 44.6	-29
17	8	21.5	88 20.3	91 28.9	-32
18	8	25.2	88 33.9	91 47.9	-34
19	8	23.1	88 45.8	94 31.6	-34
20	8	26.4	89 00.0	95 42.8	-29
21	8	24.7	89 11.9	89 20.6	-24
22	8	21.2	89 21.0	80 26.2	-22
23	9	19.8	89 30.9	87 54.9	-20
24	9	33.2	89 46.4	107 25.7	-26
25	6	20.9	89 56.6	147 18.8	-24
26	2	5.0	NORTH POLE		--
27	0		90	--	--
28	0	1.7	89 51.1	109 53.9	--
29	0	3.5	89 48.2	104 35.9	--
30	7	19.8	89 37.9	94 29.8	-14
1 May	9	35.9	89 18.6	90 17.4	-13
2	9	24.8	89 05.6	86 03.0	-11
3	9	37.0	88 46.6	81 41.8	-16
4	8	27.6	88 31.7	81 07.0	-14
5	9	23.7	88 14.7	80 44.2	-17
6	9	30.0	87 58.6	83 14.5	-14
7	9	28.0	87 43.5	81 31.5	-16
8	9	33.5	87 25.4	81 13.9	-12
9	9	30.0	87 09.0	80 33.8	-10
10	9.5	24.0	86 56.6	79 20.3	-10
11	9	25.0	86 44.7	77 32.1	-12
12	5	14.0	86 38.1	75 32.1	-9
13	0	0.7	86 38.5	75 20.1	--
14	0	1.9	86 37.5	75 19.9	--
15	0	-0.9	86 36.0	75 39.2	--
16	4	9.3	86 31.3	75 48.4	-10
17	8	19.4	86 21.3	76 29.0	-12
18	8	28.7	86 06.4	77 25.1	-12
19	8	19.5	85 56.2	76 54.5	-12
20	8	26.0	85 42.4	77 20.4	-9
21	9	25.0	85 28.8	77 09.5	-11
22	9	24.0	85 15.8	77 04.9	-9
23	9	30.0	84 59.4	77 19.2	-7
24	9	39.0	84 40.2	75 47.4	-7
25	9	22.5	84 28.2	75 31.5	-9
26	9	31.5	84 11.9	74 56.6	-8
27	9	22.0	84 00.3	74 43.2	-9
28	9	23.5	83 47.8	74 40.2	-9
29	9	26.6	83 33.6	74 27.3	-14
30	9	11.0	83 28.0	74 11.1	-10
31	9	21.9	83 16.6	74 31.4	-11
1 June	7	18.8	83 06.8	74 39.2	-10

Appendix I:
Sponsors and Supporters

The idea of Polar Bridge, skiing from one continent to another across an ocean, was ambitious to say the least. Making it a joint venture compounded the problems to be overcome. A group of people who deserve special mention, provided us with the faith and support that enabled the expedition to become a success.

From the Soviet Union we must thank Vladimer Snegirov and Alexander Shumilov for their organizational skills and their patience in dealing with four persistent Canadians. We also extend our gratitude to many other supporters in the Soviet Union, too numerous to list individually.

The Canadian department of External Affairs, initially stipulated that this would be a joint expedition. Alan McLaine was instrumental in negotiating on our behalf, and was always eager to help, in spite of the occasional midnight call from Siberia.

Marcel Masse, the Minister of Energy, Mines, and Resources extended his generous support, greeting us personally at the North Pole and on our return to Ottawa. He consequently extended an invitation to the Soviets to do research on Canadian ice islands in the high Arctic, which the Soviets accepted and reciprocated.

The Government of the Northwest Territories and the community of Iqaluit opened its arms to the expedition during the November 1987 training camp, and continued to assist throughout the expedition.

Mr. Albert Reichmann of Olympia and York Developments was a valued patron, never asking for a return in publicity, while wholeheartedly supporting our goals.

George Cohon, Sam Joseph and Peter Beresford of McDonalds Restaurants were always quick to aid us in making the Soviets welcome in Canada. We would like to think that our expedition helped in paving the way to their announcing the introduction of McDonalds restaurants in Moscow, the day after we reached the Pole.

Steve Locke and Mike Rowlands of Shaklee Canada kept our diet on track, producing food tailored to our requirements.

John Rogers of The Molson Companies emphasized his commitment to the expedition by sending us beer for our North Pole sauna.

Desmond Cunningham and Brian Hedges of Gandalf Data granted Christopher leave from his regular job, and lent the financial support of the company to the trek.

Matt Houston of W.L. Gore and Associates kept us out of the wind and water.

Chlorophylle Haute Technologie custom made most of the clothing that kept us warm and in the height of fashion.

In the front line of communication, and our first allies in the event of an emergency, we owe thanks to Tom Atkins, Barry Garrett, Ron Belleville and all the volunteer operators of the Canadian Radio Relay League who kept us in contact with the "outside" world for 91 days.

Enabling images of the trek to be captured, Nikon Canada responded to our every need in terms of photographic equipment.

Shirley Smyth was instrumental in insuring that our radio messages and photographs made it to press. Without television, radio and newspapers keeping the world up to date on our progress, this expedition would have little public impact.

A group of ultra-distance runners, the Polar Bears, made a major contribution to celebration at the North Pole, bringing food and banners, and presenting every expedition member with a specially-made commemorative plaque, They were Joe Womersley, Jill Cobb, Charles Grassie, Paul Grassie, Tim Karpinnen, Jonathan Leavitt, Hans Maier, Jo Wells, Frank Wood, Sherry McLean, Paul de Biasi and Robert Fear.

In the fall of 1987, Conexus was hired as the expedition's managing company. Collecting over half million dollars worth of cash, supplies and services on short notice was a monumental task. With their tireless enthusiasm, Peter Baird and Paul Larocque ensured that the money coming in, matched what was going out, and with a few exceptions were responsible for introducing the expedition to all our sponsors. Daniele Packwood faithfully responded to our endless lists of requests, sent them to us in resupplies, kept Conexus organized, and provided vital energy at home while we were on the ice.

With our Soviet teammates we laughed, cried, fought, struggled and survived our trek across the Arctic Ocean; Dmitri, Fiodor, Misha, Sasha, Tola Fredykhov, Tola Melnikov, Vasa, Volodi, and Yuri will always be in our thoughts.

Our wives provided us with the quiet strength to persevere when things got bad, and to never give up when things got worse.

What follows is a list of the many sponsors and supporters of the expedition:

SPONSORS

Aerographics
Alay Zary (perfume company)
Andrè Morean Gastronomie
Boart Canada
Carrera

Coca-Cola Limited
Dupont Canada
Energy, Mines and Resources Canada
Environment Canada
External Affairs Canada

Sponsors *continued*

Fitness and Amateur Sport
Gandalf Data Limited
Government of the Northwest
    Territories
Hard Rock Drill
Henry Birks and Sons of Canada
    Limited
Karhu = Titan of Canada Limited
Karrimor
Komsomolskaya Pravda
Krustin Furs
McDonald's Restaurants of Canada
    Limited
Mac's Convenience Stores
Marek Pharmaceuticals
Matsushita Electronic of Canada
    Limited (Panasonic)
Minski Chasovoy Zavod (Minski
    Watch Factory)
The Molson Companies Limited
Mountain Safety Reasearch
Nikon Canada
Norca Industries Limited
Olympic and York Developments
Paris Gloves of Canada
Parke-Davis Canada
Pfizer Pharmacenticals
Rhone-Poulenc Pharmacenticals
Shaklee Canada
Soviet Institute of Biophysics
Soviet Institute of Clinical and
    Experimental Medicine
Soviet Institute of Standardization
and Control of Drugs
Sovietski Sport (newspaper)
Sputnik: Soviet Youth Travel Bureau
Strathcona Mineral Services Limited
Sure Foot Corporation
Toshiba of Canada
Trailhead

Winthrop Pharmacenticals
Transport Canada
W.L. Gore & Associates Incorporated

SUPPORTERS

Canadian Supporters

Bryan Aller
Kay Baggley
Ron Belleville
Peter Beresford
Dennis Bevington
Brent Boddy
Jacques Bouffard
John Boyd
Wolfe Brehme
Gilles Breton
Sharon Buness
Peter Burke
Andy Campbell
Jackie Charneene
George Cohon
Gilles Couet
Jim Creskey
Jim Crowell
Vicki Crowell
Louisa Dowe
Jim Ellsworth
Mark Entwhistle
Graham Farquharson
James Fermoyle
Dennis Foley
Cameron Fraser
Doug Fulford
Peter Larry Gaye
David Gilday
Jim Gleason
Alla Goldberg
Razelle Goldman
John Goodman

Canadian Supporters continued

Betty Green
Judith Grant
Michel Gratton
Stephen Handelmann
Joy Harrison
Gordon Henderson
John Henry
Anne Hillmer
Dorothea Holloway
Maurice Holloway
Len Hooper
Matt Huston
Malcolm Hunter
John Jamison
Maurice Jette
Bruce Jonasson
Sam Joseph
Rudy Keller
Fritz Koerner
Jerry Kobalenko
Jon Larson
Steve Locke
Doug Long
Lane MacAdam
Bruce Macdonald
Lorraine McKenzie
Alan McLaine
Ken MacRary
Graeme Magor
John Majors
Craig Makinson
Hon. Marcel Masse
Hon. Don Mazankowski
John Merritt
Joan Monk
Peter Monk
Barry Moore
Rt. Hon. Brian Mulroney
Larry Newitt
Steve Nielsen

Don Noble
Dave O'Malley
Dennis Patterson
Bernard Pigeon
Albert Reichmann
Philip Reichmann
Lee Richardson
Jennifer Richens
Gilbert Rioux
Irving Rivers
Bob Roddick
Andy Rode
John Rogers
Mike Rowlands
Victor Royce
St. John's Anglican Church Fort
    Smith, congregation
Roger Samson
Wally Schaber
Belle Shenkman-Smith
The Slave River *Journal*
Walter Slipshenko
Dave Smith
Dennis Stozzel
Tom Taggart
Andy Theriault
Allen Tonks
Andre Tourigny
Hans Weber
Meg Weber
Jo Wells
Steve Wolsthenholme
Joe Womersley

Air Canada
Black Photo Corporation
Bradley First Air
British Airways
Budapest Delicatessen
Canada Post Corporation

Canadian Supporters continued

Canadian Arctic Resources
  Committee
Commission for Fair Play
Cross Country Canada
Domus
Gowling and Henderson
Harkey's Garage
The Navigator Inn, Iqaluit
Nor-Tur Limited
Ontario Science Centre
Polar Pacers
Rolex Canada
Smico Incorporated
Stevenson's Warmlite Equipment
Students of Deer Park School
Students of Le Phare
  Elementary School
Students of Rockliffe Park
  Public School
Students of St. Puis XII Elementary
  School
University of Ottawa
YMCA

Soviet Supporters

Vasily Baranochnikov
Anatoly Bulanenko
Alexander Chernosvitov
Artur Chilingarov
Vlamimir Chistyakov
Sergey Gorbik
Alexi Khokhlov
Michail Komolikov
Victor Kotcheev
Igor Lobanov
Alexei Makarov
Alexander Mironov
Lev Panin
Yuri Pavlenko
Irena Polozova
Alexi Rodionov
Stanislav Rodionov
Gennady Seleznev
Alexander Shumilov
Vladimir Snegirev
Victor Sukhodrev
Ruben Tigranyn
Oleg Yershenkov